2ND EDITION

Gundogs
THEIR LEARNING CHAIN

A pointer and his handler on the moor. (Photo courtesy of Derry Argue)

2ND EDITION

Gundogs
THEIR LEARNING CHAIN

Joe Irving

SWAN·HILL
PRESS

Acknowledgement

My most grateful thanks are due to Mr Derry Argue for the use of two photographs.

British Library Cataloguing-in-Publication Data
   A catalogue record for this book
   is available from the British Library

ISBN 1 84037 033 5

Typeset by Servis Filmsetting Ltd, Manchester
Printed in England by MPG Books Ltd, Bodmin, Cornwall

Swan Hill Press

an imprint of Airlife Publishing Ltd
101 Longden Road, Shrewsbury, SY3 9EB, England

CONTENTS

F.T. Champion, Advie Smokey Jake, By Ballymac Pall of Advie X Moanruad Mourne of Advie. Bred and owned by Derry Argue (exported 1981). (Photo courtesy of Derry Argue)

INTRODUCTION

Many years ago, I remember a professor telling me that in his opinion, the secret of happiness was first of all to discover what you liked doing best, then find someone who would be willing to pay you for doing it.

A wise enough philosophy, I feel sure my reader will agree, unfortunately a goal which eludes most of us. Except for the privileged few or the more fortunate, the majority are compelled, through circumstances beyond their control, to the more mundane business of making ends meet in a highly competitive and mercenary world.

Perhaps I can count myself blessed, one of the more fortunate, in that I have been allowed to make my living from what I like doing best – training dogs.

Most of my clients are less fortunate from the standpoint that they are compelled to earn their daily bread in the hustle and bustle of the town and city. Not surprisingly, therefore, in spending the majority of their working lives in these concrete canyons, their escape is to the countryside at the weekend and I have found that they envy me my way of life.

Over the years, in my capacity of professional gundog trainer, and from my writings in the sporting press, in correspondence and conversation with a multitude of novice gundog trainers, it has become increasingly apparent that whilst the novice has an abundance of enthusiasm and a great thirst for knowledge concerning their hobby, in the main, they lack confidence.

There is evidence in plenty to suggest that whilst they may envy the professional his lifestyle, they appear to believe that it is the reward for possessing some 'divine gift' only given to a select anointed few and, furthermore, they have the impression, undoubtedly fostered by some sections of the gundog fraternity, that the training of dogs is *difficult*.

There are those already firmly established within the gundog sphere, thankfully few in number, who, for reasons best known to themselves, would have the newcomer believe that the training of dogs is beyond the average man's or woman's capabilities, that by some divine providence they are unique in some way, in that they have special skills which set them apart from the common herd.

I do not subscribe, and never have, to this particular school of thought. In my opinion, the training of dogs is most definitely not difficult; indisputably it may be made to *appear* difficult, even mystical. It is my contention, however, that this is due mainly to the preponderance of ambiguous and sometimes downright nonsensical advice given to the novice. To credit the innocent pursuit of channelling a dog's basic instincts to our own ends as skilled, demanding years of experience, is to ridicule by inference those professions more deserving that demand intelligence, dedication, education and expertise from their practitioners. By the widest stretch of the imagination I consider it generous to attribute dog-training as anything more than semi-skilled, well within the scope of any man or woman of normal intelligence in possession of reliable guidance and information.

Therefore, I have written this book in an attempt to provide the novice with the necessary guidance and information, whereby he or she may then train their dog to a credible standard, without having to seek advice, or send their dog away for a lengthy and expensive education.

Within its pages, I hope to convey to the reader an understanding of the dog's thought processes, his eye-view of his surroundings, and to illustrate that, generally speaking, the problems do not stem from the dogs themselves but, for the greater part, from our ineptitudes and pre-conceived, very often erroneous ideas. I believe that to understand the reasons for teaching the dog a particular action (that the trainer may then understand at the outset, before implementing the lessons, what the end result will be), makes the understanding for the first-time trainer that much easier, the task more interesting and success more likely.

To that end, throughout the book, I have explained at the appropriate time the reasons for which the dog is to be trained to perform what may appear to be a small and unimportant duty, before the trainer introduces it; together with the problems that may arise, how to avoid them, and the relevant remedial training should they arise. Wherever applicable, I have outlined the different approaches so that the trainer may have an alternative to suit the dog's particular temperament.

I am convinced that there is too much emphasis in gundog training placed on physical chastisement and not enough attention to the prevention of the problem arising in the first place. To my mind, this is the negative approach and cannot be termed training, for it resembles very closely the methods employed by the old-time 'breakers'. Surely it is all the more rewarding and satisfying to get compliance with our wishes by conditioning – habit-training the dog. In an effort to obviate the need for punishment, I have purposely set out the lessons in such a way that, providing the trainer conditions the dog at a leisurely pace in each progressive link in the dog's learning chain, the end result should be that the dog performs to please you, not for fear of retribution. Punishment, therefore, should not be uppermost in your mind; it should be regarded as surgery is to medicine – the last, unfortunate resort.

I am confident that, providing the novice is prepared to devote the time normally occupied in exercising his or her dog to the implementing of the successive, progressively linked 'little games' and lessons as set out in the text, at a leisurely pace, together with the enlightenment regarding his or her dog's learning chain, he will discover that not only has he found a fascinating and rewarding hobby, but that the training of dogs is, after all, only common sense.

CHAPTER ONE

THE DOG FOR THE JOB

It is my intention from the very beginning and throughout this book, to try and put my reader 'in the picture' as we go along, as to what the likely result will be to a particular course of action, before he embarks upon it. It has always been my contention that in learning anything, no matter what, it is advantageous that the student should understand from the outset why it is that he is doing it in a particular way.

In this way, the reader will not only know what to expect from a specific approach, but will be able to recognise the symptoms when things go awry and understand the predisposing cause, before they have escalated beyond the point of no return and developed into a deep-seated habit.

Therefore, you will realise that the emphasis throughout is not in the curing of problems once they have arisen, although these are dealt with also, but in their prevention in the first place.

Many times I have been struck forcibly by the fact that, as a rule, the novice trainer, on acquiring his puppy, almost immediately – certainly within the first few all-important weeks of its life – proceeds, unwittingly, to instil the embryonic stages of the problems yet to come, once proper training commences at perhaps six months of age. As a result, he has very often beaten himself from the very beginning.

I have come to the conclusion that this is primarily due to a combination of the owner's own, very often erroneous, preconceived ideas, contradictory advice and insufficient access to suitable guidance from reliable sources of information. It is hardly surprising, then, that he feels inadequate and, as a result, anxious to the task of training his pup, and starts off on the wrong foot. For, in such a frame of mind, he is unable to relax and consequently tends to inhibit the natural instincts of the puppy.

It is because of this veritable minefield of misconception that the newcomer becomes confused.

When it is considered that, in attempting to train the dog, all that you are doing is curbing his natural instinct to chase, fostering a strong, inherent desire to carry, in that he brings the game to hand,

10

There are only poorly trained or bred dogs. The 'bad' dog does not exist.

The spaniel is 'The Maid of All Work'. She has no equal.

and habit-training him so that he hunts methodically as opposed to haphazardly, then there should be no room for confusion, and certainly no need to approach the task in trepidation; for, providing that the trainer understands his task and goes about it in a methodical, progressive manner, nothing could be more simple. As you proceed through the following pages, I will endeavour to make apparent the mistaken beliefs and mystique that the humble dog is surrounded with, that they may be dispelled in order that you will not fall prey to them. For if you do, the most important facet of all suffers – the relationship between the dog and his trainer. Obviously, then, we must break down all aspects of training as we go along into simple segments, applying each in its proper place, so that we may then proceed in a methodical fashion. This, I feel, will go a long way towards building confidence in the trainer and at the same time prevent confusion arising, not only in his mind, but from the puppy's point of view as well, thus contributing toward a happier and more relaxed atmosphere when in each other's company.

The first mistake made, and probably one of the most common, certainly a major contributory factor in making life difficult for the inexperienced trainer, is that very often he will purchase a puppy which is totally unsuited to his type of shooting. I suspect that this is because, whereas the man who has trained one or two dogs in the past gradually in time comes round to the way of thinking that 'handsome is as handsome does', the newcomer tends to be influenced by his eye, for he is apt to subscribe to the maxim that 'beauty is in the eye of the beholder'.

It is of the utmost importance that you take into consideration, before procuring a puppy, for what form of shooting you are likely to require him. For instance, if your shooting consists mainly of driven game then, obviously, you will require one of the retrieving breeds. Then again, if you enjoy shooting walked-up game through cover, it will be one of the hunting variety from which you will derive most benefit – the spaniels. If, on the other hand, your shooting tends to be over wide, open spaces, such as stubble for partridge, or walked-up grouse on the moor, or anywhere that the game is scarce, requiring a dog who will quarter the ground, hunting in a wide sweep, then your choice must fall within the pointer/setter variety.

Gundogs fall mainly within these three categories: the retrievers, the hunters, and those that hunt and point. Each particular breed is bred for a particular, fundamental purpose. In other words, by breeding with a particular aim in view for generations upon generations, specific instincts have been fostered and enhanced to improve the dog's performance in relation to a duty singular to his genre, whilst the less desirable traits have been suppressed; and so it is that, within the sphere and scope of the duties and environment for which a particular breed has been nurtured, he has no equal.

Each breed has its own devotees; each and every breeder has his own first love; and, if they are honest, will admit to a certain amount of bias. Generally speaking, the more experienced a trainer is, the more likely he is to admit that there is a lot to be said for the other breeds. The raw recruit to dog training, on the other hand, is more likely to be an advocate of one breed and can see little or no good in any other – a little knowledge is usually dangerous.

In my formative years, I must admit that I was a 'dyed in the wool' spaniel man, and could see no useful purpose to which I could put a labrador, except, perhaps, as fodder for the canned dog-meat industry. Extremely bigoted of me, I know, but there you are. Nevertheless, everyone is entitled to make mistakes, a wise man learns from them, and so, although I am very much a spaniel man first, my views have changed with the passing of time. My ambition now is to have a spaniel for rough shooting and a retriever for driven shoots, duck flighting and pigeon decoying, *et cetera*. Unfortunately, it seems that every time I get a retriever trained to my satisfaction, some chap comes along with a bulging wallet; naturally, being a Scotsman, I find his entreaties to my parting with the dog irresistible and so, invariably, I am left with no other alternative but to shed many tears on my journey to the bank.

I have learned that each breed specialises in a particular sphere of shooting. The point that I am making is this: from the very outset you must realise that whilst you may utilise any breed of dog to perform in another field of shooting for which he has not been bred, *you will enhance the possibilities* of problems arising.

Please understand at this point that if your desire is ultimately to own a high-class, all-round performer, then you have no choice, for you will only achieve this happy state of affairs with one of the spaniel group, for that is their function, 'the maid of all work', in that they excel in hunting, finding and flushing the game and are more than adequate retrievers from land or water. THERE IS NO OTHER BREED IN EXISTENCE that can perform such a multitude of duties to a comparable standard. Utilise a dog from any of the other breeds, by all means, but you must, to a varying degree, make allowances for him outwith his normal sphere of duties. After all, that is primarily what this book is all about – that you may train a dog of any breed for your own particular use to a far higher standard than hitherto.

By the time that you have acquired this book, it may be that you have already embarked upon the training of a gundog puppy. Having read so far, you may also, by now, realise that perhaps he was not the ideal choice for your particular mode of shooting after all. But don't despair, for in implementing the training schedule as set down in the following chapters, and adapting the various techniques outlined to suit your individual requirements, taking into account the subtle differences appertaining to each breed, and making allowances for the varying reactions which may manifest themselves in the dog performing in a 'foreign field', you may yet achieve a very creditable standard at the end of the day.

Choice of a puppy

The basic guidelines to be followed in purchasing a puppy are the same, no matter what breed, with one proviso. In almost all the larger breed of dog, whether they belong to the gundog group or not, it is an unfortunate fact that the two conditions known as P.R.A. (Progressive Retinal Atrophy) and H.D. (Hip-Dysplasia) are, despite all efforts, becoming increasingly more prevalent.

Therefore, before purchasing a puppy from this group, you would be well advised to ascertain from the breeder as to whether or not there is a history of one or both these conditions in the ancestry. It is a wise policy at all times to buy only from (a) a reputable breeder and (b) preferably one that can furnish you with documented veterinary proof that the ancestry of both sire and dam are free from these conditions. Do not be lax in this; ask the question – you are entitled to – and if you don't get a satisfactory answer, then don't buy the puppy. This is the only way to save yourself heartbreak and at the same time discourage the unscrupulous.

I am, of course, referring to the retriever-, pointer-, setter-sized dog. These conditions are so uncommon in the smaller breeds, such as the springer or cocker spaniel, that they are hardly worth mentioning. There are, as in all things, the occasional incidences, but these are by far the exception rather than the rule. Therefore, unless you have some particular reason for suspecting a particular bloodline, then these conditions should have little or no bearing on your choice. If you deal with a reputable breeder of working stock, then you should have no trouble; you will note that I have not mentioned the show-blood breeder or, as some of them like to be called, dual-purpose breeders, which means bred for show and work; this is for a very good reason. I am firmly of the opinion that in the spaniel and retriever breeds, show-blood is positively taboo. For instance, first noted in the late seventies, RETINAL DYSPLASIA, a hitherto virtually unknown medical condition, began ever increasingly to make itself apparent in the working strains of the English Springer Spaniel, a breed which had previously manifested very few serious congenital or inherent diseases as compared to other breeds. In an effort to stem the spread of this malady and thereby prevent it from pervading the entire breeding stock, a certificate has been introduced so that those animals free from this condition can be identified and therefore be bred from with confidence. Whilst this certificate is not compulsory it is strictly recommended. It begs the question, however, where did it come from? Some one, at some time in the recent past, has introduced it; such people have a lot to answer for. Similarly, anyone who knowingly breeds from stock carrying this complaint is beneath contempt.

The cross-bred puppy

Mis-matings or accidental matings are fairly common between dogs of different breeds. Indeed, I have discovered that quite a sizeable number of once-cross pups have proved to be very efficient, providing, of course, that both parents were of the gundog genre and of good working stock.

On numerous occasions whilst training a mongrel, various advantages have become apparent. For instance, probably due to the strengthening of the two parental genetic propensities due to the intermixing of the blood, the all too-common neurotic tendencies, apparent in closely bred animals, are nullified to a great extent. Mental disorders are also minimised for the same reason, and I am of the opinion that the mongrel has greater resilience against debilitating disease and better recuperative powers both to illness and trauma. Very often I have been struck by the intelligence and natural aptitudes displayed by such dogs, both in their training and subsequent performance in their duties.

This is not to say, however, that I would advocate the deliberate cross-mating of two different breeds, for within such a policy lie many hidden hazards and you are just as likely 'to come a cropper' as you are to strike 'pay dirt'. Nevertheless, due to the numbers utilised to good effect in the shooting field, I think that they deserve their place within the pages of a comprehensive training manual.

As I have said, depending on the type of shooting you normally indulge in, will pre-determine what type of puppy you should purchase. On the other hand, if you are already the owner of a puppy, you will wish to adapt the training of it to suit your own ends. Therefore, if you are a wildfowler, or are a driven game shot, you would train him as a no-slip retriever. Whereas if you prefer rough-shooting, then you would train him to hunt.

Obviously, if your puppy is a spaniel then you would naturally expect him to face cover well and be a proficient hunter, perhaps a little weak on the retrieving aspect, but not overmuch; whereas if he were one of the retriever or pointer group, you would not be surprised if he were not too keen on entering a gorse bush or bramble patch. You would make allowances. The breed of your puppy gives you a clue as to what to expect from him. Not so the cross-bred puppy, for without a deep understanding of the capabilities, not only of the various breeds in his ancestry, if you know what they are (and you probably don't), and – even more difficult – which dogs in his ancestry exert the dominant influence, you are dealing with a potential conglomeration of surprises.

Therefore, training a mongrel puppy is pretty much a case of pinning your heart on your sleeve, offering up a prayer and proceeding with caution. In saying that, however, I must point out that on more occasions than I would care to count, I have succeeded in training a cross-bred puppy, ultimately to achieve a very creditable standard, reflecting both sire's and dam's particular breed capabilities advantageously. Usually the puppy's dam was a springer, thus providing the instinctive panache for hunting against the weaker performance of the father, from whom, if he were of the retriever variety, would come the endorsement on the fetching and carrying aspect. Whatever the mix, and the permutations are mind-boggling, *i.e.* purely for example's sake, one of either sex, thus two of each breed and, say, twenty-two breeds; the possible permutation of mixed blood examples would be a staggering 4,194,303. Therefore, all you can go by is the dam and train accordingly.

Purchasing a puppy

There is an ever-increasing tendency over the past few years to purchase a puppy by telephone or post without ever having seen it. This, in my opinion, is a bad thing – both for the vendor and the buyer. It gives rise to misunderstandings on both sides. So, whenever possible, go and see the puppies in their home environment.

Nevertheless, due to business commitments or circumstances, you may be unable to do this and therefore are left with no choice but to purchase from an advertisement in the sporting press.

Consider this: even when you can go and see the puppies, it is very much a case of 'backing your hunch', for, contrary to popular belief, the breeder does not know what is likely to turn out to be the best of the bunch at the end of the day. After all, at eight weeks of age they are just little, playful bundles of fun. How much more of a gamble must it be to buy by post? To select an advertisement out of the multitude that appear each week in the popular sporting press? Almost without exception, each and every one will proclaim: sire F.T. Champion 'so-and-so'; dam, first-class working bitch; or, the one I like best, *pedigree includes*, followed by a proliferation of some of the best known prefixes in the business, which invariably appear in most of the working pedigrees in existence anyway. What chance have you got in this lottery? And to cap it all, at the end of the day, you've paid your money and, provided that the puppy that awaits you at the pre-arranged time on the local railway station platform is healthy, then the breeder has fulfilled his part of the contract; you have no redress. The poor breeder, on the other hand, who may be genuinely offering the public top class material, has his problems too. For he would much prefer to see his clients in person, that he may judge as to what type of home his puppies are going to. He cannot make a character assessment over the 'phone or by letter. Furthermore, it is by no means unusual for someone to call him up late at night making enquiries, book a puppy, promise faithfully to send the cheque next day, or come and collect the puppy the following week-end, never to be heard of again.

So, a little honesty goes a long way at either end.

Probably the best advice I can give you is: if on seeing an advertisement you are uncertain of the veracity of the claims made, seek guidance, either from a known breeder, a gundog correspondent in the sporting press, or write directly to the Kennel Club, enclosing a stamped addressed envelope, of course, and they will put you in touch with the nearest field trial secretary concerned with that particular breed. These are a little band of hard-working men and women who, generally speaking, have only the good of the breed at heart and, providing that you are considerate and call them at a reasonable hour, will be only too pleased to put you in touch with a reputable breeder in your locality. A little effort at this stage pays dividends in the long run, for you cannot be too careful.

Let us imagine that you have succeeded in your quest and are at last examining a litter of likely-looking puppies.

The two most important things to look for are cleanliness in their surroundings and whether they look lively and alert.

This is, once again, only common sense, for if their surroundings are clean, it indicates that they are well cared for. When standards fall in a kennels, the first signs are the lack of hygiene; therefore if they are clean it's a safe bet that they are well fed and that their general wellbeing, such as worming, has been attended to. Liveliness is also indicative of being well kept and healthy, for if they are feeling 'under the weather', they are most certainly not going to be frisky.

Look for a bright eye, a shiny coat (not so apparent in the lighter coloured species), and pay special attention to the legs; these must be straight – 'Queen Anne' legs are not only unsightly, they are a sure indication of calcium deficiency or lack of light. I shall indicate in the feeding guide for puppies how to go a long way to straightening the bow legs if attended to soon enough. Nevertheless, I do not think that you should deliberately inherit this problem by buying a puppy that you have noted has this deficiency.

Whilst I am a firm advocate of 'handsome is as handsome does', I like to see a labrador or a spaniel puppy with a good broad skull, nicely spaced eyes which are of a good, dark colour, with a kindly look about them. Whilst the breeder probably doesn't know which puppy is likely to turn out to be the best, he can give you advice and, if asked, will be only too willing to give guidance and indicate which puppy he likes best.

However, you must bear in mind that the development of a puppy over the first few months of its life can vary from pup to pup quite dramatically. As a result, any advice the breeder may give you is no more or less than a 'gut-hunch'! – founded, probably, on his past experience. In other words, the pup that exhibits traits that are reminiscent to him of traits displayed as puppies, in successful dogs he has trained in the past, will be his natural choice.

That is not to say that the puppy indicated will necessarily be the one best suited to your personality, and the two personalities are very closely linked; that is, yours and the puppy's. What may suit the breeder's personality may not be compatible with yours. Say, for instance, he is a 'hard' trainer, then he will naturally do better with a hard, outgoing type of dog as opposed to a softer, introvertive one. Thus, if he has been breeding dogs for a number of years, he will have bred for generations upon generations for the harder type of temperament and consequently his bloodline, if he knows anything about breeding, and the fact that he has been breeding dogs for many years in no way is indicative that he does, will have become progressively of the type that suits his individuality best.

On average, litters tend to cover a fairly wide spectrum of temperament. A good litter of, say, eight pups would contain perhaps one very good pup, three or four potentially good and two or three not so good, even to the extent now and then of having one not quite right in the upper storey.

Mother nature has a wry sense of humour and is by no means the most obliging of mistresses; consequently, what may appear to be a bright, bold, outgoing puppy at eight weeks of age could very well be a dullard at six months old. So, by and large, you pays your money and takes your choice.

Probably the best advice anyone can give you in this respect is, providing that you are inspecting a quality litter, a litter with a good back-ground, you might as well close your eyes, reach into the box and take the first one that comes to hand.

When buying a spaniel puppy, it is important to note that the tail must not be docked too close to the body; approximately two-thirds should have been left on, for nothing looks sillier than a spaniel with a stump for a tail. In the case of the German shorthaired pointer, there should be about one-third of the tail left on.

Before selection and purchase it is important to examine the pedi-gree and if ultimately you intend to breed from the pup, or perhaps envisage the possibility of running him in a field trial, you must ascer-tain that there is no doubt as to the pup being registered at the Kennel Club. If there is a doubt, then my advice must be – don't buy. However, if you do decide to purchase the pup and he cannot be reg-istered, then it has to be said that the price must be correspondingly lower than that of a pup that can be registered. A puppy that for one reason or another cannot be registered with the Kennel Club must be regarded as practically valueless. It may be considered that it is a great pity that for the want of perhaps one ancestor unregistered, or some niggling little piece of red tape, or purely and simply an error made in the registration department at the Kennel Club, a top-quality puppy may be virtually relegated to the level not much higher than that of a mongrel. However, rules are rules and, in this instance at least, are for the ultimate good of the breeds.

For those of you unfamiliar with pedigrees, these are purely and simply a register of the puppy's ancestors.

The lay-person is easily influenced by these and impressed by a pedigree spattered with a conglomeration of names written in red ink; don't be too hasty in jumping to the conclusion that a prolifera-tion of red ink necessarily denotes good breeding. Remember that breeders are primarily concerned with selling their product and are all acutely aware of the powers of persuasion that the technicolour pedigree carries. As I have already said, there has been a terrific growth of interest in the breeding and training of gundogs over the past decade. By and large, this is a good thing, however, as with any-thing else, it carries with it the inevitable snags.

Contained within these ever-increasing newcomers to the pursuit, there are those who infiltrate wherever they think that there is the possibility of making a 'fast buck'. These fly-by-night Johnnies may not last very long and, thankfully, I believe that they are few and far between; but they are there, and they capitalise on the unwary.

Bearing in mind that the breeder is aware of the selling power of the red ink and that the pedigree is written out by hand by each suc-cessive breeder down through the generations, furthermore that the breeder only has to submit the correct details of the puppy's sire and dam, no more, to the Kennel Club, you will realise that this leaves the way open for a 'mistake' here and there further back in the pedigree. I have on quite a few occasions had a puppy brought in for training and, on examining his pedigree, noted dogs that had attained no distinctions in field trials marked in red ink as field trial winners (FTW), even as field trial champions (FTCH).

There are many breeders who are incapable of judging for themselves what is or is not a quality animal and consequently tend to employ the services of the current top dog in the country. On the face of it, such a policy would appear to be sound, for surely if a dog is successful in the competitive sphere, not only has he proved himself, but the breeder is accepting and consequently reaping the benefit of the judges' decision.

I say 'on the face of it', for things are not always what they appear to be. I would no more accept a dog's achievements in field trials these days as a guideline, than I would overtake a lorry on a blind hill crest just because the lorry driver waved me on.

Generally speaking, if a dog has gained top awards it can be safely assumed that he is a quality animal; however, as with anything else that suffers from human intervention, field trials, and the influence exerted upon the breeds concerned by the judges' 'decisions', are by no means infallible.

Suffice it to say at this juncture that just because the pedigree has a multitude of names in red ink, do not accept this as gospel that it signifies that the resultant litter is, of necessity, quality.

I do not wish to convey to the reader that the gundog breeders of the world are a shady lot, that you will be rubbing shoulders with a veritable host of 'Fagins'. I can hardly emphasise strongly enough that this is not the case. Chances are, especially if you have taken my advice and made enquiries, or are dealing with a breeder of repute recommended by the field trial secretary in your area, that the opposite will be the case and that consequently he will be only too eager to guide you through the pedigree.

Nevertheless, at this stage, I think you ought to know a little about a pedigree for your own interest, if for no other reason. First and foremost, it is the *first three generations* which exert the greatest genetic influence on your puppy's potential capabilities. True, by skilful line breeding, the propensities of dogs further back in the pedigree may bring to bear some extra influences on the puppy; however, this will be gone into in Chapter 9; also it is far too complicated an issue to be introduced at this stage of the proceedings. Secondly, the lower half of the pedigree is the dam line.

This is the line which carries the most weight, *the strongest influence on the puppy, so,* generally speaking, you would want the preponderant number of quality dogs in this side of the pedigree. What I am saying, put in simple terms, is this: the sire at all times can at best *only endorse* the quality of the puppies. He has no greater influence than that. A little thought will then tell you that a poor bitch, no matter how many top quality sires are used, will, in almost all instances, produce only poor quality puppies. Consequently you, as the possible purchaser, are only influenced by the parents, the grand-parents and, to a correspondingly lesser degree, by the great-grand-parents; anything else is of little note. If you eventually become interested in the breeding sphere yourself, you will obviously go into the question of genetics in greater depth, no doubt in time to form your own opinions and theorise on an altogether fascinating subject.

In the working sphere of gundogs, especially among the known men and women, those with a successful reputation, there are very few sub-standard dogs bred. Let me illustrate it in this way. Since 1974 I have had brought into kennels for training, dogs from every well-known bloodline in Britain, totalling approximately three hundred dogs, including those bred in my own kennels. Out of this number I have had eight failures: dogs that for one reason or another were untrainable. Two of these were my own breeding, which on the face of it looks bad for the Macsiccar dogs, but it is not as bad as it seems.

Both of these puppies developed what is known, for want of a better name, as *kennel-sickness,* the nearest equivalent in the human, I would suspect, is the neurosis known as *reactive depression.* This was due to pressures of work with my clients' dogs and, after all, my clients' dogs must get top priority; thus these poor wee mites became so depressed through lack of sufficient humanisation in their formative months, that I had to give them away. I am happy to say that in their respective homes, with much love and attention, they ultimately turned out very good shooting dogs, albeit a lot of patience and hard work was required to achieve this.

The moral of the story should be obvious. In the first place, you can take heart that if you are dealing with a reputable breeder, then chances are you will get a fair deal. Secondly, that there isn't as much rubbish going around as the normal shooting day would indicate; thirdly, that the fault in most cases originates from the wee dog's human counterpart and – most of all – you should realise that the puppy must have attention in the formative months. This also would tend to indicate that it doesn't matter all that much to the prospective one-dog owner, really what is or is not on the pedigree, for so long as it is working blood, without too much in-breeding (see Chapter 9), and the breeder is reputable, then in all probability the puppy will live up to expectations and consequently you will be satisfied. It really and truly boils down to – if you like the pup, you'll do well by it.

Diet

'if a dog is expected to work like a navvy, he should be fed like one'

This is a favourite 'gem' of mine but, as with most condensed snippets of wisdom, it is in danger of an over-simplification and, as such, to being misconstrued.

Simply, it means that a dog should be fed commensurate to his current requirements, *i.e.* if he is growing then he will require the essential extras. If he is working hard and is healthy, he will eat in relation to his energies expended. By following this doctrine, your puppy should be pleasantly plump, not a great fat tub of lard. Neither should he be a rattle of bones; remember this, a child or puppy who has been brought up in malnutrition and deprived circumstances will forevermore have a voracious, even morbid appetite. A dog that is worked regularly should be lean, muscular and fit. A good guide is, if his coat is shining and at a distance of ten paces you cannot see his ribs or hip joints poking up, then he is about right.

There is no doubt in my mind that in the one-man, one-dog situation there are more than sufficient scraps from the dinner table to provide an adequate diet rich in minerals and trace elements to satisfy a dog's daily needs. Providing that the starchy foods, such as white bread and potatoes are excluded. Starchy food of any kind can be very dangerous if given regularly in the dog's diet, for an excess of starch can produce epileptiform seizures.

I never give tinned food to a dog, for many reasons, but basically it's this – just as you like variety, so does your dog.

A well-balanced diet of protein and carbohydrates with the addition at frequent intervals of a small quantity of finely chopped raw vegetables will provide a dog with ample nutrients and variety.

FOR CARBOHYDRATE CONTENT:
Brown toasted bread
Good quality dog biscuit
Brown dog rusks
These can be soaked in gravy, milk, raw egg, or soup.

FOR PROTEINS:
Boiled or steamed fish
Egg (raw) or boiled and finely chopped
Good quality all-in-one dog meal, but not too often

Meat (lean) – Rabbit boiled in its fur and the bones removed is first-class.
Sheeps' heads or bullocks' heads are excellent, providing they are thoroughly cooked. (Your butcher will skin and split them for you.) Best of all is *raw green tripe* (unwashed), if you can get it, and if you can work with it – for it has a singularly offensive smell.

Whatever diet you choose to give, the following minerals and additives should be included regularly:

Adexoline: (5 drops per day). This is the A, D and C vitamins, invaluable if your puppy has rickety (Queen Anne) legs, for this will help to straighten them.
Vetsymes or *Canovel:* 5 tablets per day (B group vitamins).

There is a wide range of what is referred to as 'all-in-one' foods on the market today, which provide an alternative to the everyday diet. They are very convenient inasmuch as little or no preparation is required. However, contrary to some manufacturers' claims, I do not believe them to be satisfactory in that they can be fed to a dog *every day* of its life. They are, most definitely, in my view, not a complete diet. Furthermore, I have yet to see an all-in-one meal that could put flesh on an ailing or thin animal. In saying that I might add, they do fulfil a function in these days of hustle and bustle, wherein a dog owner may not always have the time to cook for the household pets. When feeding these types of food it is of paramount importance at all times to leave a suitable supply of clean drinking water.
The decision and consequent choice is yours.

To kennel or not to kennel

Where to keep a puppy is an aspect of management that is not without its contingent, very often contradictory, 'fors' and 'againsts'.
As with all other approaches to the training of dogs, I tend to adopt the method that I think will be the simplest and the safest, with the ultimate aim in view, usually derived from the most advantageous aspects gleaned by trial and error from the methods I have employed in the past. In this way I strike the middle road.
I try to achieve the best of both worlds by means of adapting the most advantageous portions of each doctrine.
It is important, before embarking on any new venture, to understand the fundamental cause and effect, if you are to hope for any degree of success.
If you keep your puppy indoors he will benefit enormously just by

23

being in constant contact with the family. However, there being no such thing as perfection, the home environment has its inevitable snags and a puppy, as is the child, is a reflection of his environment.

Not only will a puppy be the recipient of a great deal of love and attention in the home and, as a result, mature and become much more worldly-wise in a shorter time than his brother or sister left in the kennel, he will be subjected to many more tempting situations and, consequently, simply because he cannot be under surveillance all the time, he will pick up many bad habits which, unless noticed and remedial measures taken before it is too late, will form the embryo of problems to come in the future training.

Obviously, if you have young children, they will play with the puppy whilst you are at work. This is a good thing on the whole, for children can impart confidence into a puppy much more rapidly than we grown-ups; however, there are disadvantages in this as well.

If he is playing with the kids all day, why should he regard you as the fun-person to be with? After all, he very rarely sees you and when he does he is so tired he isn't going to be interested. Added to this, if the kids chase him around the garden all day, as they are wont to do – what fun, why should he come to you when called? It's much more fun if you can come to him, then he can run off again; after all, that's the game, isn't it? Always try to look at things through the dog's eyes.

Let us now take this a step further; if he develops the habit as a puppy of being dilatory in coming back to you, how are you going to get him to retrieve to you in the future?

Your wife has probably got a thousand and one chores around the house; she cannot be watching a mischievous puppy all the time and, left to his own devices even for a few minutes, a pup can get up to all sorts of devilment. A busy housewife could be excused if she didn't always exercise canine psychology on discovering the little 'fiend' for the umpteenth time in a morning, up to some fresh skulduggery and, in the heat of an exasperated moment, give him a cuff around the ear.

Therein lies the seed of distrust, however.

House training

On deciding to keep the puppy indoors, the first problem the family encounters is that he will be required to be 'house-trained'. Whilst this should be a relatively simple task, it appears to be a facet of training which many owners experience problems with. Smacking the puppy seems to be the commonest means whereby they hope to discourage the pup from making 'puddles'; then again, there is the common 'old wives' tale' that if the puppy's nose is dipped in the 'mess' this will in some way point out to the pup the error of his ways. Both regimes are wrong and illustrate clearly that, in the main, little thought or regard is ever paid to the humble dog's thinking processes. First of all, the making of 'puddles' is one of the most basic instincts a dog has. By doing so, he leaves his scent, he marks out his territory. Consequently, should he leave his 'mark' in time to return to that spot to find that his scent is diminishing, he will lift his leg and reinforce it. On first being brought into a house, he will encounter many odours, not all of them pleasant to his senses, neither will he recognise their origins. Instinctively, then, to gain security, he will deposit his. This is why a dog who has been housetrained many years before will enter a stranger's house, immediately to make a 'puddle' to his owner's surprise and horror. It is surprising that a parent would not dream of smacking the baby for soiling its 'nappy', even at a year old, yet will unhesitatingly smack an eight week *dog* for doing very much the same thing.

As with all training, housetraining entails a little forethought and consistency. First of all, resign yourself to the fact he is going to make puddles, therefore, as prevention is always better than cure, vigilance by some member of the family is required at all times over the first few days. Procure a soda-siphon. Should the pup make a puddle, immediately grasp him by the scruff of the neck. Do not smack him or shout, for you will achieve nothing other than to frighten him; drag him gently to the front door and take him outside for a few moments. Now, as he has already relieved himself, it is most unlikely that he will perform again outside; however, a few minutes are necessary, for you are trying to plant an association in his mind between making his little puddles and going out of doors. Returning indoors, give the spot he 'wet' a good squirt of soda water – this is one of the best ways of dispelling his scent, much more so than any disinfectant that I know of. By doing so, you are diminishing the likelihood of his performing on that spot because of the scent again.

If you are vigilant, very soon you will be able to recognise the telltale signs of his desire to evacuate his bladder or bowels. He will get up, wander around the room in a restless fashion, nose to the carpet. Be on the ready: as soon as you see him begin to circle a particular spot, get up, grasp him by the scruff and drag him out of doors. In this instance it is of the utmost importance that you have patience and wait until he has 'done his duty'. Furthermore, it is of prime importance that as soon as he has done so you will give him great praise, immediately to take him back indoors. Using these methods, problems with house-training are cut to the minimum.

One of the most common faults implanted in the young pups that come into the public trainer's hands for training is also directly, on most occasions, attributable to the children playing with him, and that is boredom in relation to picking up a dummy. This is due to the children, in and out of doors, throwing uninteresting objects over and over again for the puppy to rush out and carry back; sooner or later he gets so tired of this game that he just refuses to co-operate, which leaves the trainer with the choice of sending the puppy home as unsuitable, or embarking on the distasteful task of force-retrieving, a situation that in the main should never have arisen.

On the other hand, should you decide to keep him outside in the kennel, the poor wee mite may become so severely retarded, due to lack of humanisation, that he becomes thoroughly introvertive, to the point of being so depressed as to be virtually untrainable.

As I have said, this is known as 'kennel sick'. Nevertheless, the disadvantages of keeping a puppy in the kennel from the outset are far outweighed by the advantages.

My advice to you is, keep him out of doors if possible, taking him indoors each evening for periods of play with the family. In this way you have the best of both worlds inasmuch as he will not be subjected to the temptations to such a degree. Furthermore, when he is brought out of kennel by you, he will therefore be much more likely to associate you with his period of freedom, *thus in his eyes you will be the master*. Added to this, you will be able to keep a watching brief on the children whilst they are playing with him, thus avoiding the dangerous situation developing. For the greater part of his day he will have nothing to distract him, therefore he will sleep for the most part, will be much more alert and attentive to you when out and less likely to get bored and consequently play you up.

There is a wide variety of kennels available to the general public; however, timber being an extremely expensive commodity, not to mention labour costs, these kennels tend to be rather costly, albeit very well built.

A kennel must be dry, draught free, warm in winter and cool in summer. There should be a small door affording the dog access into a long run.

Should you decide to build the kennel yourself to save on costs, you should bear in mind that sub-standard materials will not only make the construction more difficult, but will in all probability result in an unsightly structure which your neighbours may, quite understandably, object to. Added to which, do-it-yourself kennels end by being very inefficient affairs, probably ones that your puppy will very quickly discover the weaknesses in – and once a puppy has found that he can escape, he will forever try.

A suitable size for one dog, from the point of view that he must have sufficient room to move about in, but that his body heat can have a significant influence on, is 1.2 metres × 1.2 metres × 1.5 metres (4 feet × 4 feet × 5 feet), of sound match-boarding, tongued and grooved, preferably insulated within an inner wall with fibreglass matting. The run should be long as opposed to square, thus encouraging him to run up and down. It should be concrete, with a run-off of perhaps 1 in 8, ideally asphalted on top, thus preventing dampness which in time tends to create rheumatism through the dog lying on the concrete which, even in the driest spells, has a certain amount of dampness about it. For your own peace of mind, the wire walls of the run should be about 2.4 metres (8 feet) high with a turned-in top, to prevent him climbing or jumping out. It is most definitely 'penny wise and pound foolish' to use chicken wire and, indeed, unless you use numerous fixing points, chain link fencing wire tends to be inadequate to the task of keeping a determined dog in as well. The best material I have ever found for this job, and one which is inexpensive, is concrete reinforcing weldmesh. This is readily available at most builders' merchants, and several coats of galvanising paint applied with a paint roller (whilst the wire is flat on the ground), will render it capable of many years' service. This wire is immensely strong and when nailed on the inward facing planes of 5 centimetres × 5 centimetres (2 inches × 2 inches) creosoted timber, will form a rigid and neat, clean looking structure, capable of keeping lions at home.

Summary to Chapter One

1   Remember, you may utilise any dog from the gundog breeds for your particular type of shooting, but if he has not been specifically bred for the duties he is called upon to perform, you will enhance the likelihood of problems arising.
2   Exercise a little circumspection when contemplating buying a puppy from a breeder reluctant to provide veterinary documentation regarding Progressive Retinal Atrophy and Hip-Displasia, especially in the retriever breeds.
3   Do not purchase show-blood for use in the working sphere.
4   Try, whenever possible, to go and see the puppies before making a purchase.
5   Gundog Correspondents and Field Trial Secretaries are excellent sources of good advice.
6   Pay special attention to the puppy's environment and only buy a puppy which indicates he is 'full of life'.
7   Kennel life, with frequent visits into the house for humanisation, is probably the most important factor in determining your future success or failure in training.

CHAPTER TWO

DEVELOPMENT

'Walking like agag'

In other words – proceed with extreme caution. Everything, no matter how insignificant, whether it be some small facet of the puppy's environment, probably unnoticed by you, a trivial incident perhaps, to which you attach little or no importance, or a major adventure from the pup's point of view; his relationships with you, your family; the people he meets; whether he is happy with the dogs he is kennelled with – all these aspects of his daily life go into the melting pot of development and, in time, go to mould his personality. Once you consider this you will realise that, just as a child's first few years are the most impressionable, it follows that the first few months of a puppy's life are the formative period and, consequently, the most important also. It is at this time that his environment has the most lasting and profound influence on his personality and as to whether his full aptitudinal capabilities are realised in the future. Therefore it is at this time, more than at any other, that you would be wise to regard yourself as 'walking on eggs', and realise that one hasty, unthinking act may destroy your chances of training him successfully in the future.

As with we humans, no two puppies are completely alike, therefore, if you are to envisage any hope of training dogs with any degree of consistent success, you must know a little about canine psychology. At the very least, before embarking upon the training of your dog, it will help enormously if you understand how he thinks.

Once again we must approach the question in a methodical fashion and, as with the training of the different breeds, we categorize, make allowances and act accordingly.

In the main, puppies can be placed within three main streams of personality and, by making allowances for the inevitable overlapping of the borderline cases, you should be able to place your puppy in one or the other. These are as follows: the sensitive – introvertive; the bold, outgoing type – extrovertive; and those that, due to inherent faults or mental imbalance, are untrainable. The latter, as I have already said, are thankfully few in number.

28

This, of course, for the purpose of training dogs is sufficient differentiation. There are, obviously, further sub-divisions and resultant complexities to the theme; however, do not embark on a full-length, in-depth study of canine psychology, which to my mind would not only be extremely complicated and as dry as dust, it would be unnecessary for the aims of the average chap who only requires sufficient insight into the thinking processes of his dog, that he might understand him and, consequently, be able to train him to a better standard. Indeed, I doubt if there would be many who would be interested enough to go into the subject in such detail.

There is no such animal as a dishonest one; he is motivated by instinct, therefore he doesn't know what deceit is. He may inherit faults or, due to the trainer's lack of knowledge, carelessness, or some environmental influence, acquire them. In the excitement of the moment he may succumb to temptation; that is not to say he is bad. As with the workman and his tools, the dog is only as good as his trainer in the majority of cases.

Allowing for progression or regression due to environmental or traumatic influences, a puppy may, at any time during his formative period, undergo a marked personality change. It is for the trainer to be prepared for these changes that he may make allowances, even to the extent of re-thinking his approach to the training and thereby making amends; for to press on regardless will only result in the exacerbation of the problems.

I am a confirmed advocate of the 'hands-off' technique and, by employing the 'play-safe' methods of training, thus avoiding the potentially dangerous situation – such as presenting game to the puppy before he is completely controllable on the stop-whistle – I have enjoyed success with it and trained a great number of dogs without ever having to chastise them physically. That is not to say, however, that if a dog blatantly disobeys a command to which until then he has responded, and consequently has illustrated that he knows what it means, that you allow him to get away with it. Nothing could be further from the truth; 'spare the rod and spoil the child' is also a good maxim for the training of a dog – it is just that I would prefer to train the dog without having to resort to corporal punishment. For, when all is said and done, the secret of success with any training regime is in the prevention of the puppy, or older dog for that matter, developing the bad habit in the first place. Therefore, I consider that if I have to employ a hard example, that for me is a bad day, for I have failed the dog in his past training in some way, because the situation should not have arisen in the first place.

Through the years it has become increasingly more apparent to me that the puppies, no matter of what temperament, that I have managed to train without having to resort to stern measures, have almost without exception ultimately attained a much higher standard of performance than their kennel companions who, for one reason or another, have not been as fortunate.

Just as important as understanding your dog is the ability to look inwardly at your own failings; goodness knows, none of us is perfect. Not only is it advisable to make allowances for our dogs, it is wise to curb our own natural reflexes if we are of the volatile type of personality. This is not as easy as it would first appear – indeed, there are many who have a total lack of insight, and no doubt it is to these that the inference applies when we hear the common saying that there are those that should not be allowed near a dog. 'Count ten' is an excellent maxim to go by when training a young dog, especially if you are of the type that tends to operate on a short fuse and, even though I am a 'soft' trainer, I know that I fall within that category and am always careful to ensure that it does not get the upper hand when I am working with the dogs. I must confess, however, that I am not so tolerant when dealing with people; perhaps my guard tends to be down a little more so, but I do not suffer fools gladly. In the 'bad old days', the technique for training a dog was to give the pup his head, to allow him to do his own thing, in many instances until he was well into the teens of months old. The 'breaker' would then take the dog in hand. He would proceed to 'knock the living daylights' out of the poor animal, every time he did 'wrong'. The idea being, of course, that sooner or later the dog would associate what his master wanted from him – that is, if he were resilient enough to survive the treatment. This was known as 'breaking' a dog and no doubt many potentially good dogs were so 'broken' in mind and spirit by these methods that they were useless, nervous wrecks.

There still are a few, the 'lunatic fringe', who indulge in this approach. However, most of us recognise these tactics as repugnant and wrong. Nevertheless, I think it worth while to examine their methods a little closer, in the belief that almost always there is good as well as bad in most things. It is for us to extract the 'wheat from the chaff', that we may learn from it.

There is little doubt that as the puppy was allowed free rein without restrictions during his formative months and, in many cases, for long after, he would have a carefree childhood in which he could develop – *thus, he would be confident.*

Secondly, as his natural instincts are to hunt and give chase, in this restriction-free environment he would develop these instincts to a very highly tuned degree.

Therefore the trainer of old had, before he ever commenced his breaking 'therapy', a bold, confident pup, keen to hunt and raring to go. It is from this happy state of affairs on, that the entire approach was wrong.

On the other hand, let us consider the modern day trainer, about to embark on the training of a dog, perhaps for the first time. He is full of good intentions and, in his eagerness to do the job properly, he will be as keen as mustard, his enthusiasm knows no bounds. In all probability he has pre-conceived ideas formed from the snippets of advice and information from all sorts of sources, much of which is coloured by the numerous 'old wives' tales that abound within the dog world. In his resolutions, he is determined that 'by hook or by crook' he will train his pup and, from the very outset, decides that *he is not going to let it get away with anything*. Hence, from the very moment that this little mite comes into his life, whilst it is still only knee-high to a grasshopper, it is subjected to a strict training routine. Day-in and day-out, through rain, hail or shine without variance, the training regime is adhered to. Simply because someone has told him to get him 'obedience trained' (a phrase, I might add, that ranks high in my list of pet hates). The poor wee puppy has it drummed into him night and day until, at the ripe old age of six months, he will sit at distance, walk to heel, come to a whistle, retrieve to hand – even, in extreme cases, drop to whistle and shot.

On seeing this, the layman might be excused for thinking that this 'trainer' is doing very well with the puppy; indeed, here is a man who has discovered a latent talent for the training of dogs. Nothing could be further from the truth, however, for invariably the trials and tribulations from such an approach are just around the corner, and they can be manifold.

There is every probability that such a puppy will be inhibited; so much so, that it could be so anxious and insecure as to be virtually useless and at the very least be a dull, lifeless potterer, with little or no initiative. Due to the trainer's anxieties in relation to allowing the puppy to have some freedom, and in his mistaken belief that the correct thing to do is to teach the pup to walk to heel, there is a very real chance that he will have grave problems in the approach to ground treatment in the future; for he has conditioned the pup to stay at his heel; in consequence, when initiating the hunting aspect of training, he is introducing a contradiction and one which the puppy that has been severely inhibited is very likely not to have the confidence to follow. On being met with this problem, such a trainer's anxieties will immediately rush to the fore and he will proceed to encourage, cajole and generally illustrate to the puppy that something very serious is wrong, thus further escalating the problem that he himself has instilled; for in such circumstances, the inhibited puppy will just lie down, thus taking one more step further from proceeding in front of his 'master'. The area of training that the novice trainer is most pre-occupied with is retrieving; he is very liable to throw dummies over and over again, until such time as the puppy gets so fed up with it that he ultimately registers his disinterest by simply refusing to pick up such uninteresting objects.

All these problems and many more are the end result of commencing training too soon, almost always because the trainer is unable to approach the idea of training in a relaxed, informal way.

On the other hand, we have the breaker; he is perfectly relaxed – indeed, he couldn't care less what the pup is up to, for he rests content in the knowledge that once the pup has reached a stage in his development whereby he has matured both physically and mentally to such a degree that the most brutal shock tactics imaginable can be employed, but *because the dog will always remember the thrill* of the free hunt and, providing he is resilient enough to withstand the 'hard trainer's' methods, he will, at the end of the day, remain as always – a keen hunter, raring to go and still retaining a fair amount of initiative. These tactics beg the question, however; what pleasure, what satisfaction could anyone derive out of such a method of training? I decided very early on in my career that if this were the only way to train a dog, I would seek an alternative and more amenable pastime.

One does not have to look far for a more sensible approach, either; it does not matter in this context what our personal view of keeping performing animals in a circus is, but the trainer's methods are an excellent guideline and, furthermore, conclusive proof – if proof be needed – that the conditioning approach to training is by far the most successful and the most satisfying. It goes without saying that these methods are purely consistency and an understanding of their animals, with no thought of punishment or cruelty involved, for I very much doubt if a lion-tamer would ever dream of belabouring a lion with a stick, boot or lead. Yet, sad to say, there are a great number of people who employ these methods with their unfortunate canine pupils, because they are either ignorant of the existence of an alternative, or are completely unable to implement them.

On the other hand, poles apart, we have the novice who, because of his built-up anxieties in relation to training, is completely unable to relax. His puppy never knows the joy of freedom. The victim of his master's insecurity, this poor wee mite is severely restricted, to the point that all his natural instincts are retarded.

It is, perhaps, significant that this overriding pre-occupation with obedience appears to have escalated over the past decade since the rise in popularity of the field test and training class. Another small, but all-important, point – and one well worth keeping uppermost in your mind whenever dealing with a dog – is this: *whenever you give a command, you must see to it that it is complied with.* Obviously, then, the trainer who is over-conscious about obedience is very likely to be forever nagging the puppy, giving endless commands; thus he requires the expertise to rectify matters, should the dog disobey. But what of the novice? He has very little expertise, yet due to misguided advice, he is intent on getting obedience far too early and with a boisterous pup who is going to 'have a go' and rebel at this nagging sooner or later, he has manufactured a confrontation, unnecessarily; *he then has to enforce his will upon the puppy,* for he cannot allow the puppy to best him; hardly a situation conducive to a good working relationship. This the obedience-orientated trainer, above all, destroys from the very outset the most important facet of training – the rapport between himself and his dog.

You would do well to consider both these approaches and compare them. For, as I have said, there is good as well as bad in all things. Therefore, if you can learn from them and capitalise on the advantages, excluding the disadvantages of both styles, you are then well on the road to the ideal approach to training. Obviously, the breaker was correct in allowing his puppies to develop for, invariably, they were bold and full of confidence, with highly developed instincts and initiative. The 'fly in the ointment' was his cruelty and highly wasteful breaking methods. The modern-day novice is equally correct in his assumption that the puppy must not be allowed to develop bad habits. The fault with his methods lies with his overdoing the control aspect due to his anxieties and lack of experience. By and large, his methods, whilst anything but cruel, are just as wasteful as the breaker's. Upon even the most cursory thought, this should indicate to you that if you can allow the puppy to develop in a *relaxed and happy atmosphere, and at the same time prevent him from acquiring bad habits,* you are then well on the road to success. Puppies develop at widely differing rates, also by fits and starts, both physically and mentally, rather like your own children growing up. Indeed, there are many parallels that can be drawn between puppies and children. Thus, I feel sure that it is a natural assumption on my part, that if you are an understanding parent and have managed so far to rear your children without any drastic problems arising, you should encounter little difficulty when armed with a little, albeit vital, information in training a dog. Just as your children, if you let them, will delight in playing you off against your wife, little puppies also show a marked talent for this. Furthermore, if you didn't allow your child to have human contact, he would eventually become introvertive and shy; so would your puppy.

A controlled environment is a 'must' for your child, for he will only grow up confident, secure in his surroundings, *if he knows his behavioural boundaries.* He will only learn this by knowing what your reaction is likely to be to a specific act, should he commit it; *i.e.* a stable, secure environment. This can only be achieved by consistency – so it is with a puppy.

Ask yourself, do you require to be constantly striking your child, or nagging him, to have his obedience? I doubt it; neither is this required in receiving the desired response to a given command in a puppy – once he understands the command, of course. For you would no more expect a puppy to obey a command until he understood what you wanted than you would expect obedience from a baby before it could talk, would you?

Your child acquires knowledge from experiences, therefore outwith the school environment you will allow him to play, investigate, explore, enquire, you will take him here and there, you will show him everything that you think may be of use to him in the future; at the same time, you don't expect too much from him, so you make allowances – after all, he's just a child – so it is with a puppy. Never pet a working dog – how often have we heard that one? A sure indication of the trainer who feels inadequate and anxious in relation to the simple task of training a dog. Would you bring up your children in an atmosphere devoid of love or approval? You wouldn't get very far, I can assure you. Yet you hope that ultimately he is going to go out into the world and work for a living, don't you? You would split your sides laughing if someone were to suggest that because you brought your child up in a happy home atmosphere, he turned out a wrong 'un. Is it not the opposite, the child who is deprived that is most likely to go off the rails? When you think about it, there isn't much mystique about the humble dog after all, is there?

Unlike the education of a child, however, we cannot explain things to a dog; we cannot tell him what we want *in so many words.* Only by repetitive, demonstrative actions, can we illustrate our wishes. He learns from *example* and *association.* Due to his very limited reasoning powers, it is certain that he will not understand a 'new' activity or sound on first being introduced to it; indeed, it would be surprisingly astute of him if he were to begin to understand even after two or three demonstrations. We can achieve success eventually only by consistent, unvarying repetition, in the hope that by gradual degrees ultimately he will 'cotton on' to what we desire from him.

It will depend on the puppy's intelligence, aptitudes, attitudes to training, his environmental pressures and sense of well-being as to how rapidly he will learn.

However strange though it may seem, reams and reams of paper have been used up by countless writers in trying to get this message across to the newcomer to gundog training. Nevertheless, for some unfathomable reason the novice trainer, who very often is a parent and in many instances well orientated as to the limitations in his children's learning capacity, expects a far greater learning capacity from his puppy.

All too often we hear the proud owner claim that his dog knows every word he says; this, of course, is utter nonsense; another example of crediting the dog with powers far beyond his capabilities. Based on my own observations, I would say that an intelligent dog may, through time, build up a memory bank of perhaps fifteen to twenty sounds.

Another aspect of canine psychology which apparently escapes the notice of most trainers, but one that illustrates very clearly just how limited the dog's reasoning powers are, is his view of the world around him. Have you ever considered what he sees? I would be very much surprised if it had ever even crossed your mind. Does he see cattle, sheep, rabbits, horses, humans? Of course he does – but does he *recognise them as such?* Just as certainly, he doesn't; for in this we are again assuming that his reasoning powers are such as ours, and they are most emphatically nothing of the kind.

As an animal has his shortcomings in the reasoning department, they are compensated for by his highly developed instincts. It is these instincts which motivate him in almost everything he does, and it is these that we mould to our advantage when training him.

In the wild state he would run with a pack; therefore, as with every other member of the pack, he would have to conform to the rule of the pack simply to survive. If male, he would challenge the pack leader annually, who would be usually the biggest and fittest, to secure his place in the mating order. In this way, Mother Nature ensures that only the best wins a mate, thus the quality of the next generation would be maintained. This behaviour pattern, as most of us know, is instinctive, part and parcel of the law of the jungle – the survival of the fittest.

It follows, then, that the challenging instinct, as a rule, is much more dominant in the male of the species; whereas, in the main, the female does not possess it to any comparable degree, as she was only called upon to be subservient to the male. Thus, her challenging instincts were confined only to warding off any unwelcome attentions from a mate-free female that might come too close to her whelps. It is a fair conclusion, therefore, to say that therein probably lies the reason as to why some trainers have much more difficulty in training a dog than they would a bitch.

His most governing instinct is – pack. In the normal domestic situation, he has no pack – or has he? Remember what I said earlier about his view of the world. What does he see when he looks at other animals, including you? Why, strange dogs, of course; he cannot possibly reason otherwise. It is the same with any animal. When you consider this, you will no doubt realise that the fact that you stand on your hind legs, tall above the dog, and that your eyes are the only eyes in the animal kingdom which show such an area of white, you will begin to understand the tremendous psychological advantage that you have over him.

So, as he looks around him in the home, at the family, instinct tells him that this is his pack. His instinct also tells him that he must conform to this pack, he must fit in, he must also recognise the leader, for without the stabling influence of a strong pack leader, he feels insecure. A leaderless pack instinctively spells danger to him – mob rule – unrest, until a new pack leader is found to restore order. Thus, we recognise the psychology of the dog.

We return now to what I have already said: the person who takes him out, gives him his freedom, that is his master – the trainer – it is to that person he will give the first challenge for the leadership of the pack. For his respect for the pack leader is very much akin to hero-worship. As his master, *whilst he is still a puppy*, he will give you his hero-worship; as far as he is concerned you are the 'pack' leader. In the fullness of time – sooner or later, depending on his personality and yours – he will offer you his challenge. Woe betide you if you do not recognise it for what it is when it comes along. For from then on, by degrees, he will take over; you will experience more and more difficulty in getting him to comply with your wishes; in short, he will train you.

However, there are exceptions to every theme, and in this respect there are the exceptions also.

You will note that I made the reservation 'depending on his personality and yours'. I purposely included this because the gundog has benefited by the intervention of man in almost every respect of genetic development. Due to man's intervention the law of the jungle no longer applies. Consequently, far from only the strongest surviving to ensure the continuation of their ilk, many who would have perished in the pack environment through being too 'soft', now survive and in many instances go on, ultimately to become top performers in the shooting sphere.

Without a shadow of a doubt, from the trainability standpoint this is advantageous, especially for the trainer of limited experience. For invariably this type of dog hasn't got the guts to test you out; they will respond to tender, loving care and encouragement, are usually very intelligent and are only lacking in confidence. The average newcomer to training dogs almost always wishes to be 'kind' to his dog: he wants a shooting companion who not only is obedient and efficient, but one that handles easily, one that he does not need to chastise physically and therefore, in this type of temperament, he is most likely to find his ideal.

The dog that possesses this temperament could be termed as of a 'bitchy' temperament, *i.e.* the challenging instinct is, for all practical purposes, almost non-existent. As I have said, he has benefited genetically in almost every respect. However, whilst very easy to train, this type of dog is virtually useless for breeding with. I will enlarge on this in Chapter 9.

In short, there are the stubborn, 'hard-headed' dogs, and the more tractable, 'softer' natured dogs, plus the full spectrum between. The same applies to bitches, although not to such a marked degree; in fact, I would say the bitch with a highly developed, challenging instinct is very much the exception to the rule.

In other words, on the degree of toughness and stubbornness will depend how persistently a dog, or for that matter, a bitch, will question your authority; and they do this by testing their behavioural boundaries, 'trying you on'. Some dogs never do – others will – *a few make a career out of it.* The trainer's 'nightmare' is not, as you might expect, the 'hard' dog, but the stubborn, pig-headed dog who is 'soft' to boot; for with this one, you are between the 'devil and the deep blue sea'. You have to be wary about physical chastisement, for in this approach you may well frighten the living daylights out of him; however, at the same time you cannot allow him to 'best' you.

Nevertheless, provided you can observe your puppy over a period of time, note his reactions to different situations, objects, people, *etc.*, you should be able to make an educated guess as to his temperament and adopt the appropriate approach to training. It is vitally important that you can get this question of temperament correct at the outset and that you are watchful at all times for a sudden change, in which case you must be prepared to make allowances and change your tactics. Remember this – not only does a puppy learn by fits and starts, but his development, both physically and mentally, progresses along the same lines as well. When it is considered that a dog cannot tell you when he is feeling off-colour, but will demonstrate it by his behaviour, then the wise trainer will be on the look-out for any dramatic change on a day-to-day basis. Obviously, if the dog is poorly, or for that matter the trainer is not feeling just right, then that is the day to have a holiday, for nothing good will come of pushing on in such circumstances.

Your finest yardstick is your puppy's tail; this is your barometer as to how he is feeling. So long as you manage to keep his tail wagging and train him at the same time then, chances are, all is well. Try not to fall into the trap of thinking that because a pup is charging around at breakneck speed he is hard or uncontrollable, for in many instances this is his way of displaying his joy of living; far from suppressing this, it should be every trainer's aim to foster and channel this energy to his own ends. If you can keep him happy and at the same time get compliance with your wishes, you will increase your chances of training him at the end of the day.

It may appear that I have laboured the point regarding temperament and personalities; then, so be it, for it is my contention that should you fail to assess your puppy's temperament and realise your own shortcomings and make the appropriate allowances, you are defeated from the very start.

Preparation for training

The more gundog puppies that I come into contact with from the general public, the more convinced I become that it is nothing short of a miracle that so many win through to become useful shooting companions at the end of the day.

Whereas the owner has the raw material to work with, the public trainer has not. For it is the exceptional puppy that comes in for training that has not in some way or another been meddled with and, consequently, at the very least has the embryo of a problem within him. Indeed, many have a deep-seated problem. There are those that will tell you that if you have started your puppy's education before taking him to a trainer, the trainer will refuse to accept him.

Whenever I hear this, I tend to feel rather left out, as though somehow, somewhere, I have 'missed the boat'. For I have never reached such dizzy heights of affluence where I could afford to turn away paying clients, neither do I know of any public trainer who is in such a fortunate position.

Most puppies that I have taken for training initially had one problem or another. All that the trainer can do is act in an advisory capacity, accept the pup for a month's trial, at the end of which time advise the client as to whether or not he thinks that the puppy will make the grade. He has no way of knowing how long it will take, and he will tell you so.

In such cases, you will realise that if the trainer decides to carry the pup on, he will have to expend probably quite a few weeks just eradicating the problem that you have instilled, before any thoughts of real training can be entertained. A costly business, and all because you didn't know.

If you follow religiously what I am about to tell you, there should be at least one puppy who will reach the age of trainability without any problems.

One of the most common questions I am asked is, 'What age do you take a puppy for training?' I usually reply at six or seven months of age. I suspect that most trainers reply to this question pretty much the same way, and so another myth is born – and that is, that come hell or high water, a puppy must start training at or before six months old. This is just not so; the reason that most trainers will want your puppy from you at that age is because they know from experience that if it is left at home for very much longer it will pick up every dirty trick in the book. It is to get the puppy *away from you* before it is too late. In this way, the trainer is trying to strike a happy medium, for he knows that to start a puppy before he is six months old is too soon, but that to leave him at home for much longer is courting disaster.

It will probably surprise you to know that most trainers would prefer to commence training a puppy at perhaps a year old, or even later; however, on average, in the home situation, he would by then have developed too many bad habits.

So the 'fly in the ointment' is obviously the problems that tend to take root, *before the puppy is old enough to commence training.* It follows, then, that if you can gear his environment and development in such a way as to avoid their arising in the first place, until such time as he is ready to commence his education in earnest, then you have started off on the right foot.

First and foremost, you require him to be attentive to your wishes; for this is essential if any thought of a successful outcome to his training is to be contemplated. You also require obedience to voice and whistle, the latter being the most important; indeed, it is quite common for a dog to ignore the vocal command and yet to be one hundred per cent obedient to the whistle command. This, I suspect, is probably because the whistle is never used unless it is to convey a command, whereas the dog is being bombarded from all sides constantly, especially the house dog, by the sound of the human voice and therefore regards it more of an accompaniment, the *status quo,* rather than 'it that must be obeyed'.

Whilst I am a firm advocate of talking to and 'petting', reassuring and generally spending time over humanising a puppy, I do not talk to them very much at all when out, whilst they are investigating their surroundings. I may sit down on a tree stump with the puppy at my feet and spend a few moments being friends, but I most definitely do not advise chattering away at him as you go along, just for the sake of it. When you speak to him out of the home or kennel environment, do so only for a good reason. In this way, when you speak it *will attract* and *command his attention;* only common sense once again, isn't it?

If you watch a real top-notch trainer at work, you will note to your surprise that he doesn't appear to be really training as you would visualise it. He appears to be just wandering along quite nonchalantly; everything seems easy, casual; he doesn't speak to the dog very much at all and when he does his voice is barely audible, *but it means something.* You will also notice that he gets, even with the youngest puppy, an immediate response. If you were to ask him how he does it, he would probably look at you in surprise; then, after a moment's thought reply, 'I don't know, it just happens'. He is not being facetious or evasive, *he is not hiding any magic formula;* what in fact he is saying is, that he really doesn't know. For as long as he can remember, this is the way that it has been. He expects and gets nothing else. I have given this matter a great deal of thought, usually after a client has asked me how this is achieved by me. I have arrived at the conclusion that through working with a succession of dogs, the trainer who, just like you or anyone else, starts out anxious, tries too hard; thus making a simple job difficult. As the number of dogs that he trains increases over a period of time he progressively, probably unnoticed by him, becomes more relaxed. Coupled with this is the knowledge that he gains from the mistakes he has made; gradually, not only his demeanour changes but his whole approach; he makes changes to the puppy's environment. To make the job easier for him, little by little, no one little facet being of any great importance by itself but collectively adding up to a completely different format from what he originally started out with. Almost invariably, this environment is one which is *risk free* to a greater or lesser extent, culminating in what appears to the layman a very relaxed, lazy walk in the countryside approach to training a dog.

On closer scrutiny, should you be privileged to encounter such a trainer and fortunate enough to be allowed to accompany him whilst he is out with his dogs, you will become aware of several interesting features singular to the successful dog man. You will notice that the whole proceedings are calm, relaxed and unhurried; indeed, to your inexperienced eye he may appear not to be training the dog so much as taking him for a walk. That, of course, is more or less what he is doing – taking a walk with the puppy. However, as he is strolling along, perhaps explaining a point to you, you may suddenly see him break off in mid-sentence, give the dog a command and proceed talking to you where he left off. In all probability, he has made use of an opportunity that has arisen – for the gundog trainer must, at all times, be aware of his dog and be an opportunist, so that he can capitalise on the situation as and when it arises. You will also notice that usually the dog man has a quiet voice on the few occasions that he speaks to his dog; very often you may think it hardly audible to the dog, yet he gets compliance with his wishes. He may appear pre-occupied, not quite with you; he is, for his first concern is with the puppy:

his eyes never leave the dog, he is attentive to the dog, what it is doing and the terrain around him. He is, in fact, one or two steps mentally in front of the dog. In this way he prevents the dangerous situation from developing, thus forestalling the bad habit. It is a habit with him and, should you be around dogs long enough, hopefully it will become a habit with you also.

Chastisement

I include this at this juncture, for it is necessary if you are to start out on the right lines that you realise the best way to treat your puppy from the very beginning. Remember that he has probably got an excellent memory, for his head is not cluttered up with a lot of useless information such as ours. Therefore you should remember that if he is treated wrongly, by and large, the damage has been done; it cannot be undone and he will probably never forget it. Coupled with this is his limited reasoning power; you cannot say, 'Sorry, my mistake,' to a dog – thus you must be doubly careful – you must make sure that you are just.

As I have already pointed out, just as there are 'hard' dogs and 'soft' dogs, there are their human counterparts, the 'hard' trainers and the 'soft'. Even the rawest recruit to gundog training will realise after only the most cursory consideration that each is more or less severely restricted to their canine equivalent. Each is convinced that his methods are the best, and has his particular type of dog, the type that he can train to his best advantage with the minimum of effort. Whilst this is perfectly understandable, I adhere to neither school, although in my formative period I had tendencies towards the 'soft' approach.

By adopting the methods contained in the following chapters, physical chastisement should be no more uppermost in your mind than it is when you are involved in some activity with your children. It's as simple as that.

Most certainly you would not contemplate chastising an immature puppy, no more than you would employ physical chastisement with a baby. Providing you and your family are orientated towards integrating the puppy into the environment by utilising the play situation and avoiding introducing him to temptation, chastisement should have little or no part in the proceedings.

It is important for you to realise that due to the dog's limited reasoning powers, he can only associate the deed and the consequent punishment with the *exact spot* in which they are committed. Therefore it should be obvious that if he commits the crime at point

(A), there is no point in reprimanding him at point (B). He has to be taken back to point (A) and rebuked *on that exact spot.* Furthermore, it is only common sense again, if you think about it, that if you should go charging up to him, he will realise that there is something wrong and associate it with the spot he is standing *on at that moment,* when he first hears your irate approach. It follows, also, that even if you walked calmly up to him, then started angry noises as you took hold of him, he would be in danger of associating it at the wrong spot also. Remember his limited resources of reasoning.

The correct procedure, of course, is to *quietly* and *calmly* walk up to him and *silently* take him by the scruff of the neck back to point (A) and administer your rebuke there, *without losing your temper;* for to chastise a dog in a fit of temper will do untold harm – in the heat of the moment your judgement will suffer and justice be abandoned and as dogs, like children, are acutely aware of what is just, you would be well advised, in such circumstances, simply to put his lead on, forego the rebuke and take him home. Consistency is all-important; however, this is one of the few instances where I would consider it

Fig. 1.   He must be taken back to point (A) and rebuked on that exact spot.

wiser to ignore the crime than, by losing your cool, sacrifice the dog's trust.

Due to the variations in temperament and personality between pups and, indeed, the different breeds, the administration of chastisement differs in form and degree and, furthermore, is closely related to the severity of the crime committed, and only when the pup has developed both mentally and physically can any thought of chastisement in the corporal sense be contemplated. This will be dealt with as we proceed with, and in relation to, the appropriate stages of training. Suffice it to say that for your purposes, until the puppy is around six months old, a rebuke, if any, should amount to no more than a firm shaking by the scruff of the neck, accompanied by growling like a dog at him, on the spot at which he committed the crime. His limited powers of reasoning are perfectly able to cope with this, as this is the form of chastisement that his mother would mete out to him in the 'nest' environment. Consequently, it is most unlikely that this form of sanction is ever likely to frighten him, yet it will get the message across to him in a way that he understands most readily.

Early days

We begin as we mean to go on, when you bring your puppy home for the first time he has just undergone a most traumatic experience; he has been wrenched away from his mother, brothers and sisters. So spare a thought for him and consider how things look to him as first one member of the family after another crowds round, each taking it in turns to hold him.

At this point, I would like to point out to you that it is perfectly possible literally to 'kill a puppy with kindness', simply by not knowing that there is a right and a wrong way to pick up and hold a puppy.

Upon my drawing your attention to it, it will be obvious that a small puppy's ribs are not much stronger than matchsticks and that very little pressure is required to break them. In the excitement of receiving a puppy into the home and, indeed, whilst they are playing with him, children are liable not only to snatch him from one to the other, but to clasp him too tightly. Furthermore, both the children, *and adults* for that matter, are very guilty of lifting him by clasping him around the rib cage; this is a very dangerous practice, for great strain is put upon the internal organs because of the insufficient support afforded by this method, resulting very often in diaphragmatic hernias developing which can be fatal. The correct method of lifting a puppy is by either grasping him firmly by the loose skin at the back of the neck, at the same time grasping the loose skin on his rump; whilst this may not appear very elegant, it does offer an even distribution of his weight, does not hurt him and places the minimum of strain on his innards. The alternative is to pass one hand between the back legs, reaching up and under the rib cage to support his entire weight and, at the same time, using your other hand to support him under the chin. In all probability, the breeder will not have fed him that morning because of the expected journey; this is a good thing, for it allows you to illustrate to him that he is amongst friends in the most positive and, to him, understandable way – by welcoming him into this strange new world with food; a tiny, milky meal is sufficient, as he will probably not be too hungry after the journey. Most puppies are born and brought up in a kennel; there are, of course, exceptions to this, but in the gundog world, by and large, it is the rule rather than the exception. Thus, he is used to a kennel; this is advantageous in that you may integrate him into the kennel with the minimum of fuss. He will be lonely – that is understandable – however, there are steps that you may, indeed are desirable that you should, take to alleviate his loneliness and help him to settle in over the first few nights. You would be wise to take the following precautions, for a puppy of even a few weeks old can kick up the most fearful din fit to awaken the dead, when left alone in his kennel.

Don't think that going out to him or bringing him indoors will help in any way, because it won't. If you go out to him, he will kick up an even bigger din once you leave him again, and should you fetch him indoors, you had better resign yourself to keeping him indoors for the rest of his life, for he has won the first round in the battle of wits – and he is going to remember how well he has manipulated you. This attention seeking, for that is what it is, can be alleviated by sewing a stone hot water bottle inside a stout sack and placing it in his bed; remember, a kennel must be dry and draught-proof if you are to be hopeful of any peace. The warmth and bulk of this bundle has a tremendous psychological advantage in that it is reminiscent of the size, shape and warmth of his mother's body and, consequently, in the dark he will cuddle up to it. A loud ticking clock placed high out of his reach in the kennel will also go a long way to helping him settle in to this strange new place. It is vital that you ignore the noise when you first put him out; once you give in, you are lost. He will get the message, even if it takes a couple of nights. This is a situation where you have to be 'cruel to be kind'.

Livestock are governed by daylight; when it gets dark they sleep; when the sun comes up, they wake. A little thought on this will show that in summer your puppy out in the kennel may not drop off until 11 p.m. and then, quite possibly, awake at 3 a.m. – not a situation conducive to good neighbour relations, should he disturb them at such an ungodly hour – so as a precaution, a suitable 'black-out' over the kennel door and window would be wise until such time as he is well and truly settled into his new environment. A little thought gets you there.

If you implement a rigid routine, for example allow him out of his kennel at the same time each morning and lock him up again at the same time each night, you will find that in a very short time he will become accustomed to this routine and control his bowel and bladder activities accordingly, thus saving you a great deal of unpleasant chores in the kennel.

Nevertheless, his kennel should be cleaned regularly and disinfected with a creosote-based free disinfectant. Unfortunately, most disinfectants are made from this material, so you would do well to ask specifically for one that does not contain it. For, by continuous use of such disinfectants over a period of time, on timber especially, a gradual build-up ensues and although not all that common, it has been known for puppies, who are habitual chewers, to succumb to creosote poisoning. Worth knowing, I'm sure you will agree.

Feeding and exercise are the two most important aspects of a dog's life: they are the high points of his day. Puppies of eight weeks to twelve weeks require at least four small meals per day and it is essential that there is variety; small meals as opposed to two large meals. You should also know that cow's milk contains too much water and can be harmful to a small pup's kidneys, if given in large quantities, because they cannot handle the volume. Goats' milk is by far the best, if you can get it. As the puppy grows, his meals may be increased in quantity and reduced in number until, at six months and thereon after, he gets two meals per day. It is positively beneficial for a pup from six months on to be fed six days out of seven, only to have a supply of drinking water on the fast day; this prevents his intestinal action from becoming sluggish.

As with feeding, the exercise initially is in small doses; he is just a baby, so don't take him for a route march, for he will tire easily. A scamper around the garden for five or ten minutes, two or three times a day, is quite sufficient; later on, when he is older and his bones and muscles are beginning to develop, the exercise can be embarked upon in a more vigorous way.

It is within the structure of the kennel routine and play situation, the exercise period, that you will achieve, over the next few months, a rapport, the beginnings of a working relationship with your puppy. By utilising the 'high points' of his day to your advantage, you will lay the foundation for the education that is yet to come. Depending on the standard of compliance that you achieve in a few simple 'little games' at this time, will determine the ultimate degree of efficiency that you and your dog will enjoy as a working team in the future.

As with anything else, the basics have to be right if any hope of success in the future is to be entertained.

Yet I feel, at this stage, that it is important to emphasise that you are not training: you must remove any thought of this from your mind. Provided that by avoiding the wrong habits from forming in the first place, and introducing little good habits in a game situation, you manage to rear your pup to an age of suitable maturity, then when he is of trainable age you will achieve a far higher degree of obedience than you will if you try to rush it. Your motives at this time should be to build up a desire in the puppy to please you, by the implementing of a few little games with a view to what you will require of him in the future. Therefore, within the 'game' situation you will build good habits as opposed to bad. One little game progresses on to the next and they are closely related to one another; if the trainer engages in this regime in a happy, relaxed frame of mind, with little thought of failure, then success is virtually assured. It is so simple that it could be termed the 'lazy-trainer's' way; certainly if embarked upon correctly, it qualifies very well for the title – Gundogs, Their Learning Chain. For it is much easier to avoid the problems cropping up in the first place than it is to embark upon an uncertain remedial course of training, in an effort to cure the problem that has probably been instilled through ignorance or neglect of the early games.

This is how to go about it.

'From little acorns great oak trees grow', and so it is with anything – there has to be a beginning. The training of dogs is no exception; you have to start somewhere and then build on it. The 'little acorn' in the training situation is, of course, the 'sit' command, for from this all else grows. This command is introduced in conjunction with a hand signal from the very first day that you acquire your puppy; however, there is no danger of alarming him, for it is introduced in a pleasurable situation, one which also is conducive to your success straight away – meal times. Taking his meal to him, preferably by yourself – don't have the family crowding around, for they will only distract him – stand upright in front of him and command in a low clear voice, 'sit', or 'hup', whichever you prefer, and at the same time raise your other hand, palm outward, towards him. He is not going to sit straight away, for he has no idea what it is that you want from him, so he will run around, jump, *etc.*, and generally display his frustration at not getting the food. However, after a few moments he will sit to con-template the situation, immediately he does this, place the dish on the floor in front of him. There are some authorities who advise making the puppy sit until told to eat; this, in my view, is just creating problems for yourself and I can see no valid reason for making the situation unnecessarily complicated. Nor, for that matter, any relevant value deriving from it in the future training or performance within the duties required of him in the shooting situation. The object, at this stage of the game, is simply to get the puppy to obey the command and finally to associate the action of sitting with the raised hand signal. In the majority of cases, an intelligent puppy 'cottons on' within the first few days, consequently becomes habit formed – in other words, 'conditioned' – in a pleasurable way, within the space of a few short weeks. On first encountering a modicum of success, it is very tempting to be continually commanding him to sit; however, you would be wise to exercise caution in this, for every time you give a command you are affording the puppy the opportunity to disobey and in overdoing any aspect of a dog's education lies the danger of boredom.

For the time being it would be prudent to be content to get compliance when you have the added inducement of food in your hand; remember, you are preparing the way for what will come in the future – at this juncture, training must be put from your mind.

Another 'pleasurable' situation, of course, is the exercise period; this also is utilised to your advantage.

As with the incorporation of the hand signal at meal times, everything that you do with a dog throughout training, you do for a reason; you envisage what will be required in the future. With the raised hand the idea is, of course, that the dog goes down when he sees the hand up; in the future this is utilised in that when the gun goes up, the dog goes down.

Likewise, in the play situation, everything that you do with him, although at this stage it is only a game, will ultimately be of use to you in the future.

When you first take this little toddler out, you will find that his every action is tentative; he will get under your feet, jump up at you, in fact – impatient as you may be to see him get about a bit – he will illustrate that he wants to be with you. This is because he has just been confronted with a great big world; he has never seen anything quite like it before. Naturally, he is instinctively wary, insecure; the only security he knows is you, so until he gains a little confidence, he is not going to stray far from you.

Some puppies take longer to gain confidence than others; nevertheless, it would be an extremely bold puppy which did not retain this 'togetherness' with you for some time and it is this desire in the early days that once again you make use of to suit your own ends, in that by the time he has become confident enough to wander off and explore, you will have instilled another good habit, and it is this.

In the future you will require him to carry the game back to you; that is probably the most important aspect of his work that you will ever demand of him. After all, I think you will agree that a shooting dog that will not retrieve to hand is not worth a NAAFI candle. On employing a little thought on this, it should be obvious that he must return to you confidently from the very outset and that this must be fostered for, obviously, if a dog is dilatory in coming back to command, or is anxious about it, and is therefore wary about approaching you *with nothing in his mouth*, there isn't a hope of him coming in to hand to give you what he might consider worth keeping for himself – is there?

As he is scampering about, it is a simple matter to attract his attention every now and again and, on receiving it, you crouch down and make encouraging noises to bring him up to you and then, on his arrival, give him exaggerated praise. Likewise, if he is intent in going in one direction, to alter his course you would attract his attention, crouch down, praise him for returning then, on straightening up, you may then proceed in the direction you wish to go – nothing difficult in that – but you are moulding another good habit. After a few outings, you could enlarge on this by attracting his attention with a small plastic whistle, incorporating two rapid, low 'peeps'. As usual, he hasn't got a clue as to what a new 'sound' means, but the strange sound will attract his attention and he will then see you crouching down; he knows what that means, consequently, after only a few days, he will come scampering back to the two rapid pips on the whistle alone. It's all a great game, for when he comes up to you he has already learned that this earns your approval.

Together with the encouragement routine, you incorporate the 'play safe' technique, in that you prevent the seeds of bad habits being sown. You must never be lazy and follow the puppy if he has refused to come back to you; in all probability, at this tender age, he is just engrossed in some interesting smell, or has been distracted by some object or other. Nevertheless, you must not show him by your actions that he can please himself. You must immediately attract his attention, even if it means introducing a noise that he has not heard before – such as a loud clap of your hands – and the instant he looks in your direction, make off in the opposite direction, simultaneously giving him the two peeps on your whistle, repeated at suitable intervals until such time as he catches up with you; then you would praise him for coming back. *At no time must anyone chase him.*

The exercise period may be further utilised with an eye to the future training intended.

Should you envisage ultimately to use him as a 'rough shooter's' dog, in that he hunts (quarters) the ground in front of you, then during his formative months it is useful to introduce the turn whistle 'sound' into the play situation.

I feel that, here again, I must draw your attention to the all important understanding that you are not trying to train a puppy at this age. Regard it more of a 'conditioning' approach in relation to a particular sound, so that by the time he is old enough to commence training for real, he will have been responding to these 'sounds' for as long as he can remember. In this way, by the time he is old enough to begin 'feeling his oats', he is not going to be so liable to question your authority in relation to the most basic, the most important, commands.

Consequently, if it is a spaniel or a pointer/setter breed that you are training, you are encouraging his natural instinct to quarter and thereby fostering it. On the other hand, if you are adapting one of the other breeds, you may find them rather lacking in this respect; however, by introducing him to the turn whistle, at the very least you will increase your chances of success when you approach the 'ground treatment' aspect of training later on, when he is more mature, and if it is not overdone at this early age, you are not going to do any harm.

If you overdo any part of these 'little games', you are encroaching on training and thereby in the future you will most assuredly reap the harvest of your impatience; play safe, take your time and all will come right in the end.

As your puppy gains confidence in being out with you he will, by degrees, begin to run in front of you; to introduce him to the 'new' sound, using the same whistle as you do for bringing him back to you, give one low but sharp peep on the whistle, at the same time extending either your right or left arm out in the direction you intend to go. Now, the moment he hears the 'peep' on the whistle, he will look at you and as you progress in a sideways, 'crab-like' walk, he will follow you and go on past you; it is then simply a matter of whenever you think you would like to turn him, you give this 'signal'. At this juncture this is as far as we go in relation to this. You should know also, before you implement this particular sound, that if you severely curb the area in which the setter/pointer puppy operates by the over-use of this, you will almost certainly damage, if not destroy completely, his style and free-flowing ground treatment in the future.

Up until the age of training, all that remains is to implant in his mind the act of associating carrying with bringing it back to you.

Once again, this is incorporated in the 'play situation' and it must be clearly understood at the beginning that you are not training him to retrieve at this time; you are fostering his natural instinct to carry and, at the same time, associating it with the praise that you display when he brings it back to you – no more than that. Therefore,

49

practice in this particular instance will most definitely not necessarily make perfect. If you overdo this, you may well finish up with a pup which will not pick up, far less deliver to hand.

All the same, this is not a difficult thing to implant, providing a little common sense is employed. The ideal object to use for this is one that he can pick up easily, an object that has both a pleasant feel to it and cannot hurt his mouth. For this I use a tightly tucked-up fisherman's sock; this makes a soft, light bundle for him to get a grip on easily, has a smell to it and, as almost invariably they are white, he can spot it on the grass without difficulty.

In first introducing this activity into the play situation, I do not advocate that you should hold the puppy still whilst you throw it for him; all that you are trying to do at this stage is to keep him keen, to foster his latent instinct to carry and to mould this in that he will return to you confidently with something in his mouth; in other words, once again we are orientating ourselves towards what we ultimately require from him: in no way are we attempting to train him, for he is too young. He is entitled, as we are, to a childhood, albeit we are channelling his childhood capers to our own ends at the end of the day; this does not, and should not, preclude him from enjoying it through making a chore of it.

Whilst he is running hither and thither, *occasionally* attract his attention and, upon his looking in your direction, cast the object out towards and to one side of him. He will almost surely rush out to it and mouth it with a view to playing with it.

Immediately he reaches it, adopt the format that you used when you first encouraged him to return to you, *i.e.* attract his attention, crouch down, peep your whistle; chances are, if you have not introduced him to this before he was one hundred per cent returning on the whistle, he will come bounding up to you with it. It is of paramount importance that you do not stare into his eyes as he returns to you and it is equally important that you stroke him and soothe him, praise him, *etc.*, *before you remove it from his mouth;* it is also a good plan to tickle him under the chin – this lays the foundation in the future for a good 'head-up' delivery. This is an exercise that should only be indulged in sparingly. You would be wise to take the added precaution of instructing the family that *under no circumstances must any of them throw objects for him.*

At all times when dealing with the puppy's mouth, great care has to be exercised so that you do not encourage him to get into the habit of gripping the object, although most puppies will initially, so removal must be done gently. Furthermore, you must not instil anxiety in the puppy by your attitude to this; keep calm, exercise patience and, as you remove the 'dummy', talk to him in a happy, soothing manner.

Should he be reluctant to let go, place your hand over his muzzle and squeeze his top gums with your thumb and forefinger. In an extreme case, firm pressure on his front paw with one hand will bring about the same result; however, I hasten to add that this is the very last resort – the thumb and forefinger job should be more than sufficient with a puppy.

It is important that at or around twelve weeks of age you have him inoculated against hardpad, leptospirosis, and canine viral hepatitis; there are vaccines now which incorporate the full spectrum of protection against these diseases – your vet will attend to this for you. You must exercise care whilst immunity to these afflictions is being built up between the two inoculations. For approximately two weeks after that, your puppy should not be subjected to any extreme change of weather and also he must not come into contact with other dogs, their droppings or the ground on which they have been. By far the safest bet is to keep him at home in his kennel and give him his daily exercise in the garden. A rather dangerous 'new' virus has swept the United Kingdom over the past decade, one that is very debilitating in an adult dog and can be fatal should an immature pup contract it: this is the condition known as Parvovirus – you would be wise to have your vet attend to your puppy's inoculation against this at the same time as he has his vaccinations. There have been wild rumours circulating concerning the inoculations against this condition, such as the suspicion that it interferes with the reproductive system. I have yet to see any evidence to support this theory.

Certainly, I have known of one or two litters lost because the bitch was inoculated *whilst she was pregnant*; I find this hardly surprising. Under no circumstances would I have a bitch vaccinated against anything whilst she was pregnant.

After the vaccination period is past, you can widen your horizons in the exercising of your puppy and as he will by now be getting past the 'toddler' stage, you can take him about with you.

It is at this time that you would be wise to introduce your puppy to the car, for I am a firm believer that the sooner the pup gets used to it as a mode of transport, the better for all concerned. Many dogs are poor travellers simply because they were not educated to the car until they were older. There are, of course, cases of inherent poor travellers, as with we humans but, by and large, you can save yourself a great deal of frustration and distasteful cleaning up jobs in the future simply by getting him used to the car at an age when he is less likely to question it. The first few journeys should be short and at a reasonable speed over good roads; a bumpy cart track and the like are positively taboo. The idea is that his first few outings are as pleasurable as possible and to that end it is helpful if you have someone in the car with

51

you who can 'nurse' him on their knee. In the case where perhaps you have bought an older dog that is not used to travelling in a car, he may be a chronic bad traveller; this is quite simple to cure, however, providing you are prepared to expend a little effort and patience. Once again, it is primarily concerned with getting him to associate the car with pleasure, and this can be achieved over a period of only a few weeks. Each day, instead of feeding him in the usual place, put his food in the car, then go and get him – he will soon go bounding in of his own accord to get his dinner; it is then time to take it a step further and that is, whilst he is engrossed in eating, close the door. It is important that you do not leave him alone in the car after he has finished his meal and, as soon as he has finished, take him out. After about a week you should be able to start the engine whilst he is eating, without his taking any notice; by the time you have reached this stage you have almost solved the problem and are well on the way to curing him of his fear of the car. It goes without saying that at no time do you take a pup or a dog for a 'run' after feeding him.

At this juncture, you come up against one of the variations in approach to the training of the different breeds; a small, but very subtle one, and a very important one.

As you are now going out into the wide world outside with him, it is mandatory that (a) he wears a collar with his name and your name and address on it – this is the law; (b) that whilst you are on a public thoroughfare in town or country, he is kept on a lead at all times – this is also the law of the land and, as such, ignorance will not be accepted as an excuse.

Now you come to the subtleties; if you are a rough-shooter, you look to the future once again and envisage what you require of your dog in the shooting field. You will want him to hunt, therefore you must not dwell too severely on teaching him to walk to heel; be content if he does not pull when on the lead, but is allowed to roam free when off it. Thus, on the roads, you have him safely tethered on his lead. On the other hand, if you are a wildfowler or a driven-game shot, you want a no-slip retriever; then at this stage you would initiate the commencement of heel keeping.

Another small but all-important point to note is that whilst a dog is working in the shooting field he is not required in law to wear a collar, and it is undesirable that you allow him to; he wouldn't be the first dog in history to go missing in the middle of a wood to be found strangled on some obstacle by his collar; a small but very important point that is often overlooked.

Nevertheless, no matter to which end you intend to use him in the shooting field, at this stage of the game he is too young to be undergoing strict heel keeping; suffice to say that if he is behaving on the lead at this stage, that is enough. To deter him from pulling on the lead, simply give him a *short, sharp* tug every time he pulls; do not let the proceedings develop into a tug-of-war. The final polish on heel keeping will be dealt with in the appropriate stages for the different types of dog.

I have purposely not mentioned shot as yet, for a very good reason; under no circumstances must you succumb to temptation and for curiosity's sake fire a shot over him to see whether or not he is gun-shy. The chances are that he is not, for judicious breeding has almost obliterated this from the good working stock over the past few decades. However, should you introduce him to the sound of the gun too soon, you will be in grave danger of inducing the condition known as gun-nervousness which, for all intents and purposes, generally has the same end result as gun-shyness if remedial action is not taken soon enough. This is because until the puppy is around six months old or, in some cases, even older, the tympanic membrane of the ear has not fully developed and quite simply cannot cope with the sudden, loud report. There is, as with any other aspect of training, a right way and a wrong way to go about it, and introduction to shot will be dealt with later in the book at the appropriate time.

Meanwhile, be careful – do not tow him around game fairs, field tests, trials, the local clay busting club, or anywhere else that you think he may be subjected to a shot at close quarters; for if, by your carelessness, you should induce gun-nervousness, you really will be on a 'sticky wicket' for, although it can be cured, it involves a lot of work and, furthermore, work that does not necessarily effect a cure.

All that is required from here on until he is old enough for you to embark on the serious training regime at, perhaps, six months of age, is for you to indulge in the play situation with him as much as possible to build his confidence and let him develop mentally as well as physically.

During his walks, or within the play situation, be attentive to him; introduce one of the little 'good habits' occasionally into his activities, but be careful not to overdo any of them. It is far more important at this stage for him not to acquire the bad habits. Keep in mind, when you are dealing with him, what your ultimate aims for him are, the purpose for which you acquired him, and act accordingly.

Relax, let him enjoy just being with you and as you explore the countryside, scramble over obstacles and encourage him over after you, repeating in an encouraging tone 'good boy – over-over'; he will soon associate this sound with his having to scramble under or over an obstacle in his path. As soon as he has gained confidence in this, it is advisable to add yet another small, but important, refinement in preparation for the future and that is, make him sit with your hand signal and verbal command before you surmount the obstacle; then, after he has been allowed to negotiate it, make him sit for about thirty seconds on the other side before you move on. Throughout his training and future life you must insist on this, for many reasons. First, if he is allowed to go bounding over obstacles without some measure of control having been instilled in him regarding these, there will come a day when he will go bounding over barbed wire; the folly of allowing a dog to do this should be obvious. On the other hand, if the dog is allowed to surmount an obstacle first, he is very likely to drop down the other side out of your sight and encounter game; once again, the dangers of allowing this situation to develop should be obvious to any enlightened dog man. Finally, if a dog has been conditioned to wait the command to get over, he is far less likely to go launching himself over walls into the path of oncoming vehicles, or to land and impale himself on some piece of rusty iron, *etc.*; if you value your dog, this is a simple habit to cultivate and the wisdom of it should make it worthwhile. Whenever the opportunity offers itself, take a walk through some light cover, avoiding, of course, any clumps of stinging nettles during the summer months; obviously, if a young puppy gets stung, this will implant an unpleasant association with cover in his juvenile mind. During these excursions, should you see game ahead of you – rabbits, pheasant, even crows or seagulls on the ground can present a problem – alter your direction before the pup catches sight of them; for, should he be allowed to go rushing after them in infancy, it will hardly be surprising if you have difficulty with the steadiness aspect of training in the future. Play safe – by using a little thought, a great deal can be done in the formative period of the pup's life, both in preparing and conditioning him for the future training and going a long way towards preventing the bad habits from forming in the first place. It's all just common sense, really.

One more very important precaution: do not introduce him to water at this stage, for if he gets chilled – and what may seem a mild spell of weather does not necessarily mean that the water temperature is suitable, for his little body affords him little warmth or protection from extremes whilst he is still a puppy – you may instil in him a long-lasting dislike of water, to the extent, in some cases, that the dog never again enters water willingly. Once again, all in good time.

There are those who will tell you to run the pup in the company of an older dog, in the belief that the old campaigner will adopt the role of 'schoolteacher'. My advice to you is, avoid this regime like the plague, for undoubtedly the old dog will teach the pup a great deal – unfortunately it is usually the bad habits that rub off and very little, if any, of the good.

Generally speaking, the novice trainer tends to have an air of urgency as well as anxiety in relation to training; he is preoccupied with progress, eager to get on, to the extent that in extreme cases only lip-service is paid to the basic training, for he cannot wait until he can get on to the more interesting aspect of dogwork. Without due attention being paid to the basic training, dog training becomes akin to a house without foundations. Depending on how you assimilate this Chapter, will determine the degree of success you enjoy with the next and their combined influence will govern the ultimate standards that both you as the handler, and your dog, will attain at the end of the day.

List of equipment required for the complete training

1 Small canvas 'puppy' dummy (For basic training)
2 Two larger canvas dummies (More advanced training)
3 Retriever ball (For more advanced training)
4 .22 Starter pistol (Useful for all aspects of training)
5 One rabbit skin dummy, skin wrapped around canvas dummy suffices (For more advanced training)
6 One feather dummy, duck and pheasant wings around canvas dummy held in place with stout rubber bands (Advanced training)
7 Two whistles on a lanyard, one small whistle without pea and one larger whistle (thunderer) with pea (All training)
8 Lead, rope choker type
9 One dummy launcher (not essential, but can be invaluable). Under no circumstances must this utensil be used for shot training or basic retrieving
10 Launcher ball (Advanced training)
11 The Check Cord
    Providing that you are hale and hearty, I would most sincerely advocate your doing without one; however, I would say that if you are unfortunate enough to be physically handicapped in some way as to impair your mobility, then these could be of some use. I will enlarge on this in the appropriate chapter.

Summary to Chapter Two

1 Be on the lookout for any marked changes in the pup's behaviour or demeanour, on a day-to-day basis – think it out and act accordingly.
2 Corporal punishment should under no circumstances be implemented with a puppy.
3 It is of the utmost importance that the trainer is aware of his own failings and not let these influence, in any way, his treatment of the dog.
4 Every time you give a command you are offering the pup the opportunity to disobey it. Therefore, only give a command when necessary

and try to give it when you are in an advantageous position to enforce it.

5 Do not expect too much too soon; never try to put an old head on young shoulders.

6 Be sure of your pup's temperament before attempting stern measures; a sensitive puppy may not take too kindly to a shaking, a gruff tone being reprimand enough. It is only too easy to fall into the common trap of mistaking natural flair and speed for hardness; this is not necessarily so.

7 Whilst a puppy is running free, never take your eyes off him; it follows, then, that under no circumstances would you allow him out of your sight. Therefore, should he disappear from your view, play safe – recall him immediately.

8 Try not to overdo the exercise periods, for he will tire easily.

9 Avoid over-indulgence in throwing dummies for him to carry.

10 Do not introduce him to gun-fire yet, nor take him anywhere where there is likely to be gun-fire.

11 Exercise caution regarding introducing him to water; there is more time than you think for this later on.

12 Never teach a 'hunter' to walk to heel before he is an efficient hunter; therefore, with these breeds, it is the last thing you teach him – if ever.

CHAPTER THREE

BASIC TRAINING

Not only do puppies in the same litter develop and mature at varying rates, but there is a wide variation between the different breeds. Generally the springers, labradors, flat and curly-coat retrievers tend to mature earlier than the cocker spaniel, setters and pointer varieties. By and large you could safely embark on training the former at a much earlier age than those of the latter group, always taking into account your individual pup's temperament, of course.

Obviously, a sensitive puppy requires encouragement, whereas a bolder, outgoing pup would not to the same degree. Furthermore, a sensitive pup will be more inhibited and, as a result, mature at a slower rate; consequently little, if any, harm would come of starting a pup a little later than his more precocious brother. The very earliest that I would commence basic training with any puppy is six months old. The most important aspect of dog training, as I have mentioned, is your understanding of him and thus your correct assessment of him; should you, upon commencing his basic education, see a marked loss of enthusiasm, you would be well advised to reconsider the wisdom of pushing on – indeed, it is remarkable just what a difference a little holiday will make to a dog when things have not been going right. It is by no means unusual for me to make several stops and starts during the course of training a 'problem' puppy. Continuity in training is certainly desirable – that is not to say that, no matter what, you must push on regardless, but that 'little and often' is much more satisfactory than a spasmodic 'once in a blue moon' approach. If you try to be aware of your dog and his moods and act accordingly, you will make progress; far more harm will be done by the strict, unrelenting regime, than the relaxed attitude to training. If things are not going right, then abandon training for a few days, or even a week or two, taking him for a walk instead until his tail starts wagging again; then you can feel confident and start where you left off.

The following basic exercises are necessary before embarking on the more advanced and specialised forms of training relating to your particular type of shooting. Apply them in small doses, but

57

make sure that each is absorbed well before commencing on the next link in his learning chain. These are your foundations – it is upon these that all later training is built; should you skimp these, your whole training programme and the final outcome will be at risk.

The training ground

If you have a fair sized garden, or access to a larger tract of land where there is little risk of there being any game in residence to disrupt the proceedings, then you can be sure that within such an area most, if not all, of the basics can be taught.

Providing that your pup has plenty of bounce and that you can maintain this boisterousness within an area where there are no distractions, such as people, dogs, livestock, then very few problems are liable to arise regarding the basic exercises. Nevertheless, these tend to be rather monotonous and, therefore, not only must you avoid overdoing them, you must make the effort to give him some variety by taking him about with you at invervals.

The golden rule in training is, *you, the dog and solitude*; if you bear this in mind and avoid distractions such as the kids as an audience, the family pets' company, or demonstrating your dog's prowess prematurely to your friends, you will not only avoid the likelihood of him playing you up, but you will command his undivided attention and thereby make progress.

Sitting at distance – obedience in this is essential as it is the 'cornerstone' of all training.

Sitting at distance

This exercise is obviously closely related to the 'little chore' of sitting to the raised hand for his meals and, whilst at your side, therefore, is just another progression in the learning chain. It is also vitally important as an integral part of his overall education. If you cannot have his obedience in this, you are most unlikely to achieve any control over him at any time when he is at distance from you. Ninety-nine per cent of a dog's duties are performed when he is out of your reach; furthermore, he will quickly realise your 'achilles heel' and take advantage of it in the not too distant future.

There is no excuse whatsoever for not achieving success in this, for, important though it may be, it is very simple to attain a high degree of efficiency from a pup over a short time.

Most dogs, especially if you have been diligent in making them sit at feeding times, will experience no difficulty in understanding what is required of them. However, a sensitive pup can be easily frightened if you are heavy-handed about it; patience and perseverance, even to the point of being pedantic, will win the day in the end. If you try two or three times and he is just going to have none of it, then forget it that particular day; you can always return to it another day. Cockers can be positively obtuse in relation to this exercise, for they are inveterate 'belly-crawlers'; indeed, they would try the patience of a saint – nevertheless, they can be both sensitive and obstinate, the worst imaginable combination of personality in a dog for training purposes, so you would do well to proceed with caution. Nevertheless, by perseverance and progressing day-by-day in easy stages, you will achieve success eventually.

Taking the puppy on the lead to your chosen training ground, let him have a scamper around for a few moments; call him up to you with your whistle, praise him, then let him scamper on again; throw a small dummy by all means. What you are doing here is preparing your approach to his being introduced to a new activity. *You are creating a happy atmosphere.* After a few moments of this, call him up to you again with your whistle, make him sit in front of you with the vocal command and the raised hand facing you, endorse the vocal and hand signal in a low tone as you take two steps back (see Fig. 2). Hesitate only for a second, then step forward to your original position immediately in front of him, bend down and give *exaggerated* praise. I do not envisage any difficulty in this for you, for it would be a pretty 'poor do' and a certain indication that at the very least you were going to have a job on in the future training if you could not step back from him and then return two steps without his remaining sitting; for it is an infinitesimal progression on what he should have

Fig. 2.   Sitting at distance – it is vitally important that you achieve success in this.

been doing for months, *i.e.*, sitting to command. I expect him to fidget once you get to the stage of five or six steps back; however, that is not to say that you skimp the initial introduction to this, for in all aspects of training, short cuts inevitably have to be paid for: play safe.

Fig. 3. Increase your backward steps by two each day until you can leave him on the 'drop' and walk back twenty paces.

As with all training, a new activity is only indulged in once in each session, never on its own and never overdo it; be content with success, no matter how small, for it is a step in the right direction. Each day within the exercise period you will incorporate this lesson and build on it by increasing your backward steps by two, until such time as you can retreat to a distance of twenty paces; pause, then return to him without his belly-crawling, fidgeting or trying to get up and come to you.

In the initial stages you must endorse your commands in a low tone, together with repetitive hand signals; do not walk backwards with your hand raised, for he will begin to regard this as the *status quo* and, consequently, you will have nothing to fall back on if you are a considerable distance away and he tries to get up. I would be very much surprised if your dog did not at some time or other decide to take the initiative and try to get up and come to you. In fact, I would consider a dog that didn't as lacking in the upper storey, at the very least, and to be so docile as to raise serious doubts in my mind as to the wisdom of bothering to train him in the first place.

So you must expect him to question you in this and, consequently, get up from his seat; in your anticipation of this, you will be quick to endorse your commands yet again – this time with a louder, more disapproving tone, together with the hand signal, at the same time taking one or two steps back towards him; this very often is sufficient with some puppies and they will slowly lower their posterior back to the seated position. Upon this happening, the best plan is to cut short your backward journey by taking two steps back, a short pause, then return to him, all the time reassuring him with your low verbal command and, on reaching him, give him his reward by exaggerated praise.

The object of this lesson is simply to implant by demonstration what is wanted from him by repeating over and over again a gradual build-up of the same exercise. You must not frighten him by losing your temper and smacking him; he is still a puppy, with an underdeveloped brain. Neither should you go running back to him, for this will have pretty much the same effect. You will achieve far more in a much shorter time if the whole thing is executed in a calm but firm manner.

It helps to fix your eye on a spot, just above and between his eyes as you retreat from him. Very often, little or no problems are encountered in this lesson with regard to the going back, away from the puppy, but the puppy will get up and come toward you as you are approaching him on your return journey. This must be dealt with just as you would if he did this at any other time, *i.e.*, you must issue a firm, disapproving, gruff command, together with the hand signal. In the early stages it may be necessary to reinforce your wishes on two or three occasions by stepping back to him and placing one hand under his chin, pressing his bottom back on-to the ground, repeating over and over again your sit command. In the latter stages, also, you must be able to illustrate to him exactly what you will settle for and demonstrate to him that you can and will enforce it.

This is related to his understanding and associating his deeds with the spot in which he committed them. Should he break from the drop and get even part way to you, or belly-crawl toward you, you must grasp him *quietly* but firmly by the scruff of the neck and drag him back to the *exact* drop spot. You would then proceed as prescribed above by pressing his bottom on the ground, *etc.* Whilst this is quite a simple exercise implemented over a period of a few weeks, if you are dealing with a half-grown labrador, golden retriever, *etc.*, it can be very heavy work; all I can say is, serves you right for buying a

Fig. 4.   Should he get up, you must quickly step toward him with raised hand, endorsing your command in a more aggressive, reproving tone.

big dog – the lesson has to be learnt by him, therefore you must not be lazy, you must stick unswervingly to your pedantic approach until such time as you can walk backwards away from him to a distance of twenty paces, be able to stand and look at him for a moment, then return to him, without his fidgeting or showing any concern whatsoever.

Once this has been achieved, it is a simple matter to take one step further in his learning chain, by introducing another link, another progression upon which all training is formed.

This is simply a case of dropping him as before, but instead of walking away from him and then returning, you may call him up to you with the aid of the return whistle. You will probably notice that the first time you do this he will hesitate; this is because he doesn't believe you and is a certain indication that you have bedded this lesson in properly. Therefore, you may have to encourage him the first few times until he gets the message. Once again, if you employ a little thought to this, you will realise that you are weakening what you have been teaching him over the last couple of weeks, for this is the first of quite a few contradictions in the training of a dog. So you play safe and take the middle road by *only calling him up to you once out of every three times that you leave him on the drop.* In this way, you are playing safe; for if you are careless with this, in no time at all he will be back to square one in that you will have great difficulty in keeping him on the drop at distance, for he will fall into the habit of anticipating, even to the extent of breaking from the drop when he sees your hand reaching for the whistle. It is better to incorporate this exercise into his daily routine as a deviation, rather than adopt the sergeant-major approach; try to keep the puppy interested and happy for as long as you possibly can. Whilst this is a simple lesson, it is also extremely important that the puppy gets it right before proceeding on to the next.

Steadiness to the thrown dummy

Once again this 'new' lesson is closely allied to the last, a progression, and so is integrated with it; but not before your pup has assimilated the sitting at distance and coming *only when called up* to the whistle.

As before, sit him down using your hand and vocal signal, back away approximately ten paces, stop, endorse your command; taking a small canvas dummy out of your pocket slowly, repeat your command for him to remain seated, then throw the dummy a short distance to your right or left; be ready to stop him charging out to it – you may even have to intercept him and drag him back to the drop-spot; once you have put him back on his spot and repeated your commands, you may then back off the ten paces, stand and look at him for a moment and be ready to discourage him from moving; *then you must walk out and pick up the dummy yourself,* keeping a weather-eye out for him moving whilst you do so.

Returning to him, praise him for remaining on the drop, then back off once again and repeat the episode; he will cotton on eventually. Once you have succeeded in getting him to remain in position until you have thrown the dummy, return to him, give him his reassurance by way of praise, pause, then send him for it with the verbal command 'dead'.

Whilst you should not experience too much difficulty with this, there are various alternative approaches to achieving the same end which you may prefer to use.

(A) You may adopt a kneeling position and, grasping him by the scruff to restrain him, throw the dummy out a short way in front of him; then, repeating the 'sit' command quietly over and over until you feel his straining diminish, release him and send him for it.

(B) You can keep him on a lead by your side, give the command to sit with your hand signal, then throw the dummy again out a short way in front, bringing him up with a sharp jerk when he gets to the end of the lead as he rushes forward.

Personally, I prefer the interception method as being a much kinder and more progressive, related approach to the overall training. I am a firm believer in utility of commands, for this prevents confusion in the dog's mind; therefore I do not like the 'fetch-it', or 'hi-lost' type of order, preferring the single syllable command as more easily recognisable to a dog; therefore I recommend you to use 'dead' as the command for the dog to retrieve at all times from now on.

Introduction to shot

This is also related to the sitting at distance lesson and is, at this juncture of the puppy's education – both from the age factor and the natural progression of one integral aspect to another – in its proper sequence.

Provided you have refrained from firing shot near him up until now, you should have no problem in introducing him to gunfire now. Woodland, steep-sided valley, quarries, buildings, *etc.*, produce echoes, and this is most undesirable in first letting a pup hear the sound of shot. Dummy-launchers are notorious for this also, so do not utilise this implement at this stage.

Bearing the echo aspect in mind, you must find a flat piece of ground away from buildings and as far away as possible from the woods, especially conifer plantations.

Your puppy should be highly efficient at remaining on the drop by now, so in the general format of your training sessions, you will drop him as usual and back off, this time thirty to forty paces; stop and, facing him, raise your hand and, using a *starter pistol* – nothing of a heavier calibre at this stage, please – fire *one* shot. At this distance there should be little or no reaction from him; nevertheless, one shot and one shot only, then return to him, great praise, then carry on with another aspect of his outing. This should be repeated within the training each day for a week and, if there are no untoward signs of anxiety on his part, you may then decrease the distance each outing by approximately four paces. You will realise that by raising your hand when you fire the pistol at this distance from the dog's eye view, the movement is identical to the hand signal for him to sit – just another related progression in the chain.

Within a couple of weeks or so, depending on the weather, *etc.*, you should have reached the stage where you can stand beside him and fire a shot without him bothering about it.

There are dogs who are gun-shy; as I have said, few in number – however, they do exist. Should you be in possession of one, you will be in no doubt once you initiate this lesson; unfortunately, there is no cure. If he is gun-shy, he will run off as soon as he hears the report, or at the very least show marked signs of distress, even to the point of showing distress on sight of your pistol. The only advice I can give you is to abandon all thought of training him, spare yourself the heartbreak by getting rid of him to a good home and start again with another puppy.

Gun-nervousness is, on the other hand, quite a different 'kettle of fish', provided you recognise the symptoms and make allowances by implementing remedial action before you have done untold damage. Practice, *i.e.*, repetitive shots, will do nothing but make it worse – to the point of making him gun-shy – so be warned.

Should you at any time note signs of marked anxiety when you fire a shot, cease this lesson immediately. Each day, if possible, get some member of the family to take his food out to him and, immediately preceding his getting it, fire a shot from some distance away. Your assistant will be able to report each day as to his reaction to it; in nine cases out of ten, within a few days, instead of displaying signs of wariness he should show signs of expectancy and pleasure, thus indicating that he has accepted the shot as the 'lunchtime hooter'; you are then well on the way to curing him of his nervousness. All that is left to do is to decrease the distance a little each day during mealtime, until you can fire the shot from about ten to fifteen paces away.

Once you have reached this stage, you may then discontinue with your assistant's services and recommence the shot lesson within the general activity of the training sessions.

Dropping to whistle

This again is just another step forward, another interrelated progression in what you have been teaching him until now and so should present no problems; for, if you have not been rushing things and thereby cramming the puppy's head full of new activities at too fast a pace for him to assimilate them and bed them in, he should take this in his stride with little difficulty. Whilst he is running around, I want you to drop him every now and again with the verbal command, accompanied by the raised hand signal; not too often, or he will get fed up with it; perhaps two or three times each session for a few days.

You may note, especially with a 'hard' going pup, that he may run on for a few feet before he drops. This is not good enough; however, you will remember that he associates his wrong-doings with the point at which he committed them – in this case the spot at which he *should have stopped* – so you will quietly walk out to him and quietly, but firmly, drag him back to point (A), push his posterior hard into the ground and repeat, over and over again, 'Hup-there', or 'Sit-there'. Never allow him to get away with it; he is growing in stature, mentally as well and, whilst he is still a puppy, he certainly doesn't look it. Who

Fig. 5.   Placing one hand under his chin, press his bottom back onto the ground, repeating 'hup THERE', or 'sit THERE'.

knows, it may be around about now that he is beginning to wonder whether it is you or he who should be pack leader.

Within only a few days he should be 'getting the picture' and so you may then introduce the stop whistle: this is the 'thunderer' whistle which resembles the old-time milkman's whistle. A point to note about whistle signals: always make them short and sharp, not necessarily loud, but short and sharp; as with the voice, we tend to reserve the volume for emergencies, so if you cultivate the habit of 'chirping' the whistle, rather like a small bird, if and when you wish to be more forceful about things in the future you can really blast off at him and he will take all the more notice.

As with anything else in the training of the dog, you use what he has already learned, that with which he has become familiar in conjunction with the 'new' sound or command; in this way he associates by example and demonstration – thus he progresses with the minimum of confusion. So, just as before, we take another step forward and forge another link in his chain of learning. As he is scampering around, you must drop him with the verbal command, hand signal and, adding *one short, sharp* signal with the thunderer, that's all there is to it. Within a week or so, you will be able to dispense with the verbal command altogether, which you will never need to use again unless the dog is by your side.

Dropping to shot

This, of course, is again just another progression and in this particular instance, at this stage, a natural and obvious one. For it is just a refinement of dropping to the whistle. Simplicity itself, providing, as always, that you have not been 'rushing your fences' and have been giving your puppy enough time over the preceding lessons to allow a natural build-up of learning to take place.

In this manner, problems in training a puppy are cut to the minimum and by now you will be getting the impression that perhaps, after all, training dogs isn't as difficult as it would first appear. Neither it is, but don't get too confident; 'there's many a slip twixt cup and the lip'.

To teach him to drop to the shot you simply let him run around as he has been doing and, as usual, dropping to the whistle two or three times each session; all that remains to be done is for you to fire off a shot, perhaps once, in conjunction with the stop whistle and he will drop. If he doesn't, it is the stop whistle that he has disobeyed – therefore you would drag him back quietly to point (A) and rebuke him as before, only this time you would add an extra deterrent, in that you will blast the thunderer whistle loud and clear in his ear; he will not like it, but it will drive the lesson home much more forcibly than, say, 'knocking the living daylights' out of him ever would.

As I have said before, 'a little thought gets you there' in every aspect of training. Now, if you think about it, you will realise that each time you have introduced him to a new signal or command, it has never been initiated by itself, but that there has always been a preceding signal or command that he has become familiar with for him to obey and associate the 'new' sound or movement with. Therefore it should be obvious that *initially* it is to the familiar signal or command that he is reacting and that it is only through *repetitive, demonstrative actions* he will, in time, associate and respond to the 'new' sound or action being taught.

If you can bear this in mind and act accordingly, you will further minimise your problems by preventing your pup becoming confused. For, in the initial stages of any new approach, should the dog disobey, you must not try to endorse the new command by remonstrating with him in relation to it, for chances are he has not as yet grasped what the 'new' command means. The 'breakdown' is in all probability in the familiar command, the one that you are trying to build up in association with the new sound in the dog's mind; it is that command that you endorse. You should now find it easy to avoid boring your pup, for he has already learned a great deal since you first set out to do his basic training. You now have a variety of activities to draw upon in the training sessions, which should enable you to 'ring the changes' and, as I have said, if you have been keeping a watchful eye on his reactions, he should be happy and confident in the learning environment.

I repeat – depending on his personality, whether he is bold and outgoing or liable to be sensitive and unsure – will depend on his rate of learning; you must let him develop at his own pace by making allowances. Whilst there is no hard and fast rule as to the length of time it takes to train a dog, for your guidance – and more as an attempt to curb your enthusiasm for rushing on with things – I would say that at this point of his education you should have been engaged in his basic training approximately three months. Do not worry if it is taking longer; however, should you have taken considerably less, I would advise you to re-examine his performance and consider carefully as to whether or not there is some area of training that requires a little more work; remember what I have said about the 'weak link'.

Summary to Chapter Three

1 The golden rule is: you, the dog and solitude.
2 Never overdo anything – short sessions curtail his chances of getting bored and disobeying you. Dwell on success.

This may not look very pleasant, but it is the correct way to pick up a puppy as its weight is evenly distributed.

3 Be attentive to him; if things are not going right, call it a day – there is always tomorrow.
4 Ration his retrieving, do not put him off.
5 Be consistent but never lose your temper.
6 Five minutes per day is far better than five hours at the weekend.
7 Make sure that he is efficient in the basics before progressing any further.
8 Dummy-launchers produce fearful echoes, so do not utilise these for introducing a young dog to gunfire.
9 Short cuts have to be paid for, so curb your impatience to get on to the more interesting aspects of training.

CHAPTER FOUR

INTRODUCTION TO THE 'HUNTERS'

For those of you intent on training your dog as a hunter, it is important at this stage to orientate the dog to habitually turning at approximately the same distance to make a cast across in front of you. At this juncture it is equally important for you to give some thought to the matter before proceeding further, especially should you be training a dog which has not been specifically bred for the job.

In training a dog to quarter his ground in a methodical manner, you are instilling rigid boundaries within which the dog must hunt. Depending on the amount of attention you devote to this will, of course, determine your ultimate success or failure. It should, there-fore, be clear to you that, once again, you are habit-training the dog. The most basic instinct in any dog is to *hunt*.

Undoubtedly you will encounter those who will be at variance with this view but it is a fact of nature that if a dog, and all dogs are descen-dant from one species, could not hunt in the wild state then it would perish. The fox survives very well, yet whilst his hunting suffices for his needs, it could hardly be called methodical – for he is a spas-modic, lazy animal in this respect. A parallel could be drawn between the vulpine and the wild dog in this respect. Nevertheless, to hunt is the most basic instinct of all, the urge to procreate ranking as a close second. In habit training the dog, we are simply moulding that instinct to hunt in a methodical manner within a box-like area, so that if and when he 'Finds' and 'Flushes' the game, it will be within shot.

At first, the dog will tend to go rushing around at great speed and, if not turned at a given spot, his pattern would be somewhat erratic, subservient to any distraction. However, as time goes on, depending on the degree of attention you devote to his control concerning this, he will, to a varying degree – according to his scenting capabilities and temperament, together with the type of terrain you have at your disposal – slow down; for, whereas initially he was uninhibited, by the time you have habit-trained him, he will be preoccupied, partly with

71

the task of hunting and partly with what you are requiring of him. If you dwell too severely on turning him and, by doing so, draw his attention to it over-much, he may 'dry-up' completely; in other words, refuse to hunt through insecurity because he is afraid to incur your displeasure. This may also be brought about by hunting a dog on barren ground or during a heat-wave, but it is closely linked to the dog's temperament and his relationship with his handler. This 'drying-up' condition is known in gundog training circles as 'stickiness' and, whilst it can be quite a set-back in training, it can be cured and I will deal with this aspect in due course. It can be seen, therefore, that all dogs have the basic instinct to hunt. Due to human intervention in breeding specific types of dog with a particular aim in view, we now have some breeds which are genetically better equipped to hunt than others which have been bred for other purposes. Consequently, if you are training a dog from one of these breeds, you will encounter fewer problems in relation to hunting than you would in adapting one not so well-endowed genetically. Therefore, if you were to opt for training a retriever to perform as a rough-shooter's dog, you would naturally expect less of him. On the other hand, if you were to use a spaniel purely as a no-slip retriever, you would be rather optimistic to envisage a performance in retrieving akin to that of a labrador used for the same purpose.

It is not so 'cut and dried' as all that, though, for there are subtle influences at play connected with the duties you train him to perform that affect his performance in other aspects of his work. We return here to the boundaries laid down in training the dog to hunt his ground in a methodical manner. By habitually instilling these boundaries, the dog becomes orientated to them. He knows when he is operating outwith that area of operation; therefore, depending greatly on his temperament, he will experience a degree of insecurity and this can be quite marked in a dog with a sensitive disposition. As a result, in asking such a dog to get out to a 'blind' retrieve, you are contradicting what he is in the habit of doing. He has not seen the bird down, therefore he has little, if any, incentive to 'break bounds'. Once a dog has learned 'gunsense' through experience in the shooting field, this may not manifest itself to a marked degree, the shot being the only excuse he needs to get out there and hunt for the retrieve. But some dogs never lose their feelings of insecurity and are very difficult in this respect. The same dog, however, asked only to perform as a no-slip retriever, will not have the same operational boundaries placed upon him and will therefore experience no insecurity in being sent great distances on a 'blind retrieve'. There are well-known handlers whose dogs are second-to-none in the hunting aspect, yet are equally renowned for being 'sticky' at getting out of

Above all other aptitudes, the spaniel has been bred for successive generations to hunt.

their boundary to a blind retrieve. I suspect that this is due to the dog expecting stern retribution whenever he transgressed by pulling out whilst hunting; consequently there is an 'overspill' of anxiety. He feels insecure, once again illustrating that a problem in one aspect of training may beg another in relation to it.

It follows, then, that should you utilise a retriever as a hunter not only must you make allowances for a diminished performance in his hunting standards, especially when facing punishing cover, but, by doing so – instilling the boundaries – you will undermine his natural aptitudes for retrieving. Then again, in utilising a hunter to perform as a no-slip retriever, you will undermine his hunting capabilities by implementing the strict heelkeeping regime and, even though he will not lose confidence in getting 'out into the country' – due to his size and body conformation, which have been bred for the purpose of hunting – he will never quite come up to the performance of a dog specifically bred to retrieve.

What we lose on the roundabouts, we tend to gain on the swings, however – and here we return yet again to the genetical inheritance – a spaniel is bred as a hunter; therefore successive breeders through countless generations have bred these dogs with specific criteria in mind. He is a hunter, therefore, above all, he must be able to find game; to do this he requires an excellent nose – consequently, the breeders would breed with breeding stock that was renowned for excellent game finding talents. Speed, style, flair, would be secondary to this. As a result, whilst the spaniel may be loath to get out there, especially when he is young and inexperienced, before he has learned game-sense – simply because he has been thoroughly indoctrinated regarding hunting within a given area – *once he has reached the 'fall' area,* he can knock spots off any other breed in following the line of a 'runner'. Because, in the main, these dogs have inherited the benefit of successive generations of breeding intentionally orientated to breeding dogs *to find game.* In the training of dogs we must put personal bias aside and view the task objectively if we are to understand and therefore consistently enjoy success.

Whilst the training of a hunter presents more of a challenge to the novice handler, there is no need to regard it as difficult. True, there is undoubtedly more to learn both for you and your dog, but that is not to say that you should approach the idea with trepidation. Indeed, I consider the hunters to be the 'fun' dogs to be with and, dare I say it, in comparison the training of a retriever bores me to tears sometimes.

There is a great deal of evidence to suggest that it is within the area of training a dog to hunt his ground in a systematic way that the newcomer experiences the most difficulty and, as a result, feels inadequate to the task.

The training of a no-slip retriever is simplified due to the extra measure of control that can be exercised by his being at your side for the greater part of his duties. This does not apply with the hunters because their prime function necessitates that they must run free.

Nevertheless, far from making life difficult, I regard this aspect of training as the most interesting and, providing, as always, that the trainer is in possession of a little foreknowledge, acts accordingly, and has the right material to work with, by far the most enjoyable.

However, it is by no means difficult to see where – if you have been lax in the preparation during his formative period or, for that matter, during the actual training – problems may arise. We return here to the fact that as each dog is an individual, just as with any other aspect of training, the aptitude varies from dog to dog. Some are natural hunters; therefore it quickly becomes apparent, when embarking upon the ground treatment exercises, that here is a dog that has a natural bent and consequently should present few, if any, problems in relation to it. At the other end of the scale, due to a multitude of governing factors, you may be unlucky and find that with your particular pup life seems to be one long headache in relation to this particular lesson. Then again, there are those who start out well, showing great promise – yet at the end of the day, in many cases due to possessing a very good nose, combined with a stubborn, bloody-minded streak, as soon as they are presented to game quickly deteriorate into wild, uncontrollable pests.

On reading this, the novice would be excused for thinking that, far from sounding easy, it tends to give the opposite impression; for it all sounds very complicated – indeed, there are those who may accuse me of confusing the issue. I feel, however, that anyone who writes a book that does not include the 'whys and wherefores' confuses by omission: furthermore, I am of the opinion that if I were to follow suit, this book would fall into the category of bordering on the arrogant because of its optimism; for, would I not be presuming that there are no dogs or trainers for that matter, with problems?

Surely it is far better for me to point out to you the dangers that lie in wait for the unwary or uninitiated before you embark upon the exercise, rather than disregard their probability. Then again, is it not better that, by enlightening the reader, he can look to the future and act accordingly? My contention is that in so doing, far from making the job complicated or difficult, it makes the task that much easier for the novice, for it helps him to understand from the very beginning what he is doing; thus he can recognise trouble looming on the horizon and take evasive action before it is too late.

So engrossed are we when out shooting that very rarely does it cross our mind as to just what the dog is thinking. Indeed, I sometimes wonder whether the average shooting man ever considers whether his dog is capable of thinking. This is just another small, but all-important point in the handling of a dog, for obviously, as they are most definitely not mindless morons, they must possess thoughts of a kind, and these 'thoughts' will have a bearing on their actions. The no-slip retriever, sitting by your side at a drive, no doubt would like to go rushing out to that tantalising, fluttering bird which has just hit the ground a few yards off. I feel sure that, on many occasions, he is deterred only by your proximity and the fact that you have your eye on him. Just as surely there are occasions when, purely by your being distracted, he seizes the opportunity and runs in. I have more than a suspicion that the hunter is aware that, whilst he is out there in front of you, hunting his ground, he can kick over the traces and that unless you can deter him he is pretty much a 'free agent'.

Whilst he has limited reasoning powers, that is not to say that he is incapable of making a decision and so, if you can school yourself in the habit of being conscious of the dog and observing his reactions to various situations, in time you will begin to know your dog and, on many occasions, be able, by noting a particular mannerism, to take the appropriate action. I have in the past had dogs who would give me a sidelong glance as they quartered their ground just before a 'find' and if I did not let them know that it was noted, would run in on the flush; yet all that was required to prevent it was a cautionary growl or stern vocal 'No'. As I have said, it is the attention to the little details that makes all the difference.

The quality of his nose will determine just how much attention he apportions to you when handling him and to what degree he will be engrossed in his work. There are dogs which, whilst quite manageable on a poor scenting day, can be quite a handful – even to the point of being whistle-deaf on a day when scenting conditions are good.

There are no hard and fast rules for training a dog, for by their very individuality they demand adaptability from their trainer. The successful trainer is the man who takes the trouble to know his individual pupil and act accordingly. It is this singularity of personality particular to each dog that makes nonsense out of the sweeping statements given in the guise of advice, that are commonplace on the gundog scene.

And so it is that, as you become progressively more aware of the various little 'tricks of the trade', your knowledge and expertise grows, the insolvable becomes solvable. Consequently you need not fall prey to the dubious advice, for you will be happy and secure, thus more relaxed, in your new-found confidence in your own ability.

As the basic instinct of the dog is to hunt, find the quarry, give chase, catch, kill and carry the game back to the den if there are whelps to be fed, it is these instincts that you channel when training him, to suit your own ends.

The rough-shooter's dog

Your puppy should be at or around six or seven months of age by the time you have reached the point where you can embark upon the basic training, depending on his individual temperament, of course. There are many puppies who, due to an over-sensitive nature or simply being retarded by some traumatic hang-up, would benefit by starting their training later, and so you would be wise to take another long, hard, contemplative look at him and decide whether another few weeks in allowing him to gain confidence may be the correct approach.

Pay no attention to what your friend may or may not be doing with his puppy of a comparable age. The chances are, as is usually the case, he is rushing it and, simply by cramming the puppy, will in due course pay the penalty. As I have said, puppies, like people, are individuals – no two are alike, what may be meat and drink for one may be poison for another, even between brothers and sisters – so make haste slowly, for very often the 'late developer' turns out to be brilliant, providing he is treated with a little patience.

Most puppies, no matter how bold, will at some stage in their development go through a shy stage. In the female of the species you can expect it at or around the time when her first season is due; it is not so easy with the dog, however, for he can manifest the symptoms at any time. It is for you, the trainer, to take note of this small but all–important point; be on your guard and act accordingly to encourage the puppy through this phase if and when it occurs, even if it means stopping training as such for a few weeks until his confidence returns.

It is also important for you to realise from the outset that to indulge in hunting a puppy, or young dog for that matter, during the heat of the day, is just begging for problems. It is only common sense, really – after all, you don't feel much like running around when the temperature is in the seventies and upwards, so why should your dog? To flog on with a pup in such temperatures will 'turn him off' quicker than anything else and if you allow this to happen, you will have a 'sticky' hunter to contend with.

At this stage of the game, your puppy is 'hunting', for want of a better word, instinctively, excited by a little scent – for until now he has never encountered game, and should not for some time to come. Scent is governed by temperature, among other things; suffice it to say at this stage that climatic extremes of any kind are generally bad for scent; therefore, in the heat-wave situation there will be very little, if any – consequently your puppy is left with no other incentive than to run around for the pure hell of it and he isn't going to do that for long in extreme heat. So he slows down; you, in turn, anxious to get on and make progress, start to cajole, wheedle, encourage and probably show your mounting anxiety.

You are then drawing the puppy's attention to the fact that something is amiss and, therefore, instead of dealing with the problem, you are in danger of exacerbating it. Far better, if there is a prolonged heat spell, to call it a day and let him lie in the shade with plenty of cool drinking-water available to him, for a fortnight or so; far from doing any harm, it may well do him a power of good to have a short holiday. If you feel that you would like to continue with his training, then you have no alternative but to get out of your bed at or around 5 a.m., before the sun has dried the morning dew, and give him his session then.

It is also most inadvisable that you engage in 'pressing on regardless' with the early ground treatment exercises during a spell of gale-force wind, for not only are such conditions virtually scentless, high winds tend to have a peculiar effect – not only on puppies or young dogs, but even on the most experienced of dogs. You may find that your dog, who normally is quite biddable, whilst 'hunting' in a strong wind becomes quite a handful, even to the extent of being unmanageable. Whilst there would appear to be no apparent reason for this, my own personal feeling is that the wind sets up a buffeting noise in the dog's ears, at the same time altering the tone and pitch of our whistles; in extreme cases, I suspect that normal sounds are so blotted out by the wind that they are relegated to the threshold sound level and therefore have little or no effect on him.

If you are to start off on the right foot, then the type of ground that you choose for the early quartering lessons will depend very much on the type of temperament of your pup and his reactions to the surroundings.

Here, again, I feel that I should enlarge upon this before you embark upon this aspect of his education, that you may be guided and adapt your approach accordingly.

As I have said, most puppies will rush around just for the pure fun of it; it is this exuberance that we utilise and channel to our own ends. But, as the training begins to bite, there will come a time when he will slow down – perhaps not all that noticeably so, and it will be an insidious process, but most puppies do and there is a very good, common sense reason for this.

When he is running around investigating this and that, he is uninhibited, he can give free rein to his feelings – however, as your training begins to take effect he will, by degrees, unavoidably so, become inhibited. This is simply because you are curbing his natural flair for rushing hither and thither into a methodical hunting pattern. Consequently, whereas before he commenced his training he was more or less engrossed in his own affairs, now he is beginning to realise that you are wanting something from him and, therefore, if you are making headway he will gradually become pre-occupied, partly with hunting and partly with his handler. As a result, he loses a little confidence; not overmuch, and what he loses at this stage is again advantageous; for not only is this a yardstick whereby you can gauge the degree that he is absorbing training, it also makes him that little bit more manageable. Furthermore, the sooner he realises what it is that is required of him, the sooner he will regain his confidence and speed up again, by which time you should have him under control and hunting his ground within shot in a workmanlike, methodical fashion.

Should you, in the initial stages, note a *marked loss of enthusiasm*, probably accompanied by hesitancy, this, of course, you would recognise as the embryonic stages of the pup becoming sticky and therefore would indicate a change of venue; for it is obvious that this type of pup requires an added incentive to ginger-up his confidence. Obviously, if a pup will not get up and go, you cannot train him to hunt. Needless to say that, generally, it is the sensitive type of puppy that will react like this, the bolder dog requiring little or no incentive to hunt.

So, once again, in order to avoid the dangerous situation developing, you would adapt according to the personality of your pupil. It is the preknowledge of these small, but important, integral parts of the training of dogs which renders the task simple; ignorance of them makes it more difficult.

Ideally the ground chosen should be devoid of distraction; this does not only mean that there should be no other people, dogs or livestock, but that it should be barren as regards game; for in this, it will assist you in implanting a little ground treatment into the dog with the minimum likelihood of problems arising as a result of the puppy becoming distracted by something else.

Nevertheless, as there are no hard and fast rules that allow for every contingency and as each dog is different, it is essential that the trainer dips deep into his 'think tank' before rushing headlong into this. I stress that, ideally, in the initial stages the ground should be

In the early hunting lessons you may detect a marked loss of enthusiasm.

bare for, by and large, a puppy will show enough enthusiasm to enable you to progress in the ground treatment aspect for some time before he begins to show that he is getting bored with it, especially if you keep the sessions short.

On the other hand, there are pups who will just have none of it from the very start and, should you persist, as I have said, you will beg the problem. So you must think it out and use your initiative. If he is not going to perform on bare ground, then you must afford him the added incentive by finding an area of rough grass, light bracken, heather or rushes, and make sure that there is no game on it, by either walking over the ground yourself beforehand, poking at every likely looking seat, or utilise an older dog to clear the ground for you. In using an older dog it is of prime importance that you position the car so that the puppy cannot view the proceedings, for if your older dog is somewhat lacking in steadiness and your puppy sees him having the time of his life coursing ground game, it is not going to give him the right impression, is it?

Neither should you be tempted to enter the pup into thick cover until such time as he is a competent hunter in the open, for you will never put a pattern into a dog in a bramble thicket. Even more important, you must not lose sight of him at any time until he is one hundred per cent steady to game. *Never trust a young dog*, for out of sight he will succumb to the tempting situation much more readily than if you are there to exercise some control. Not all the problems encountered within the hunting aspect of training and the later handling in the field stem from the dog, however. Indeed, I would go as far as to say that the greater majority originate from us, from our attitudes and personality defects.

Very often the trainer, simply by approaching the training in the wrong way, and with a pup that has acquired an ingrained bad habit, gives up as soon as he realises that there is a problem when, in point of fact, purely in giving the matter a little more thought and effort, the fault could have been 'nipped in the bud' before matters got out of control. Invariably he resigns himself to shooting over a wild dog and just as often it is not his fault, it is the dog who shoulders the guilt. Hence it is because of this that the spaniel has become a much-maligned 'wee beastie', through the novice handler's feelings of inadequacy in relation to his control.

Nevertheless, I maintain that, providing you have prepared and conditioned your pup correctly during his early months for what is to come, and that you resolve to approach his education in ground treatment with quiet insistency, together with the knowledge of what to expect from him, you may now proceed without qualms as to the ultimate outcome.

Ground treatment

Upwind beat

This is, perhaps, the only area of training where you can be sure that practice will make perfect, for there is little danger of the dog becoming bored by it.

Nevertheless, it is always a good plan to exercise a little caution and, therefore, indulge in it initially in small doses; remember what I have said – the longer he is out with you, the more likely your chances are of having a problem and it is preferable that, in the early stages of any 'new' approach, we dwell on success.

It is for this reason that we play safe and for the initial introduction to ground treatment we utilise bare ground. Similarly, it is for this purpose that you will commence by always hunting the puppy into the wind (upwind beat) and that you will continue to do so until such time as he illustrates to you that his pattern of ground treatment has become an ingrained good habit. This will not happen overnight and it is highly desirable that you make special note of this, for it is very tempting on approaching your chosen venue and finding the wind in your back to be lazy and, rather than walk him on the lead to the other end before releasing him into the wind, to hunt him with the wind behind you (downwind beat).

This is just another small, but all-important point, but if you do not pay special heed to it you are most unlikely ever to get a tight pattern into the dog; for working a dog down the wind naturally encourages him to pull out down the wind and in the early stages this is most undesirable. I will deal with the downwind aspect in due course; suffice it to say at this stage that whenever possible, even right up to the end of a young dog's first season's experience in the actual shooting field, it is advisable to try and hunt him into the wind as much as possible. Should you have to travel some distance to your chosen venue for the hunting exercises, you should know that most dogs are, to a varying degree, subdued somewhat upon alighting from a car and consequently do not give of their best straight away. This is due mainly to fumes in the car, probably undetectable to our senses, nevertheless to the dog's they are quite marked; the motion of the car also has a detrimental effect on some dogs, so it is a good plan to allow him a scamper about on arrival before commencing the lessons; five minutes should be quite sufficient, of course. Need I remind you, during this time – as always – to keep a watchful eye on him and not to allow him out of your sight?

It is quite in order for those of you training a dog for rough shooting purposes to utilise this time in giving him a couple of retrieves or indulging in a facet of hand training, for it is most important with a hunter that you give him his retrieves *before* hunting him, never, never, at the end of the hunting lesson – for, let's face it, he is probably tired by then and, after all, a dummy is rather an uninteresting object to expect him to be enthusiastic over after perhaps an exciting session among the scent; so, play safe, make use of his surplus energy in the mundane before he expends it in the more interesting aspects of training. Providing that you have prepared him as a puppy properly for this, as regards his turning to the single 'peep' on your whistle, you should not encounter much difficulty with the ground treatment exercise.

After he has had his scamper round for a few minutes, call him up to you, put his lead on and walk him on to a piece of fresh ground; remember, of course, that you must never take the risk and introduce him to game before he is efficient in hunting his ground and *steady to game*. This should have been cleared off the ground in the manner outlined earlier, before taking the pup out of the car. Taking his lead off, command him to 'Hup' both verbally and by hand signal; you may think this is unnecessary in such a situation – it is not, for if you are not consistent and instil the habits in the dog progressively by repetitive actions, you need hardly be surprised if you encounter an inconsistent performance in your dog later on; these little pedantries are *very necessary*.

Keeping the dog on the drop, slowly put the lead into your pocket and any signs of fidgeting or impatience on his part, such as squeaking, should be discouraged by a stern 'No'.

Here, I must tell you that there are many pups and dogs, even into the 'teens of months old, who will 'squeak' through sheer excitement and/or frustration when first cast off. Whilst this is most undesirable, I would not be too concerned about it; very often this is purely and simply the exuberance of youth, which diminishes with maturity. Most assuredly, you do not want a 'musical' dog out shooting with you and in the field trial scene it is virtually the 'kiss of death', for you would be disqualified. All things in their proper order, though, at this stage of the game, you are simply trying to get your pup to treat his ground in a methodical manner and, as it is bare ground, you must realise that his incentive to 'go' has been diminished, albeit by design, but you will be encouraging him to 'hunt' and therefore, at this juncture in the proceedings, you are not going to introduce any further obstacles to his progress, such as rebuking him unnecessarily as regards an excited squeak or two.

After a suitable pause of perhaps thirty seconds or so, cast him off at right angles to you with the verbal command, 'Get on' and a clear,

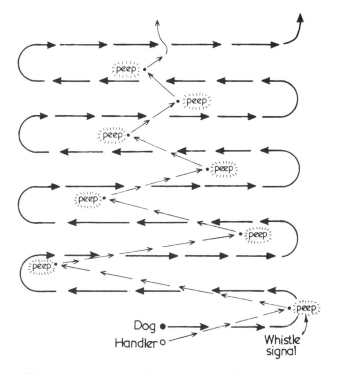

Fig. 6.   It will be quite some time before you can modify your own 'quartering'.

even exaggerated hand signal in the direction you want him to go, at the same time walking sideways yourself. When he has moved out to about three or four metres (ten or twelve feet) from you, give him the sharp, single peep on your whistle and, as soon as he turns or you have his attention, indicate the opposite direction and alter your route accordingly; once again, as he moves past you, the turn whistle is used again and you proceed as before, again in the opposite direction. In this way you will proceed slowly forward in a crab-like fashion, allowing the dog time to cover the wider 'beat'.

Apart from the multitude of reactions which may or may not manifest themselves from dog to dog, that is about all there is to fostering the dog's instincts as regards habit-training him in ground treatment. Obviously, you are not going to quarter your ground by walking from side to side in your forward progress for the rest of the dog's life, although if you attend field trials no doubt you will see some handlers who do and, indeed, I know of some who could be dubbed field trial champions themselves, for their ground treatment invariably far surpasses that of their canine companions and their game-finding capabilities are out of this world.

It will be quite some time before you can diminish your own zig-zag pattern, however, and progress forward in a straight line, for it will take many weeks before the dog's pattern becomes an ingrained good habit.

There are dogs which, from a very early age, display to their owner that they are natural hunters and so only require this aptitude embellished, which is achieved simply by consistency on the trainer's part in turning the dog at approximately the same distance each time.

You may think that three or four metres (ten or twelve feet) is working the dog extremely tight and, no doubt, would prefer your dog to cover a much wider beat. I have stipulated that you turn him close for a very good reason and that is, as time goes on, your dog of his own volition will take up ground – imperceptibly at first, but this will increase as he gains confidence; furthermore, if he tends to be rather a 'hot cookie' once he is presented to game, you will be thankful that you exercised prudence in the early stages, for he will be quite a handful; indeed, you may find that you have great difficulty in keeping him within shot; if you are rash at this stage and allow him too much leeway.

Most shooting men have a tendency to walk forward at a pace which is far too fast to allow the dog time to cover the ground thor-

Fig. 7.   You must give the dog time to quarter his beat. If you walk forward too fast, he will 'pull' out in front of you.

oughly. It is of the utmost importance, in the early stages especially, to allow the dog enough time to 'work' his ground; otherwise, not only will you fail to habit-train his pattern, but you will encourage him to pull out in front of you (see Fig. 7) and this habit will be exacerbated as time goes on as the dog learns that it is in front of you that he is most likely to find game.

You should try to cultivate the habit of making your way forward at a pace that allows the dog plenty of time to work his ground thoroughly for, in the future, once you are out shooting with him, he will be far less likely to miss game and, consequently, you will not only have a far more relaxed day's shooting but your dog will find and put up more game for your gun.

Some authorities advise you to chuck out a piece of dog biscuit or pellet to encourage your dog to hunt; I do not subscribe to this practice, for I believe that it teaches the dog to potter at the end of each cast. After all, if your dog becomes a trifle 'sticky' as regards scentless ground, common sense will tell you that he requires the added incentive of scent on the ground and so you would provide him with it, exercising caution by clearing the game off first, of course. The treatment, if he still will not hunt, is set out at the end of this Chapter.

Adapting to the prevailing situation and conditions is the secret of success with this aspect of training. Cockers are notoriously difficult as regards hunting scentless ground and will 'dry up' on you much quicker than most breeds; yet, by virtue of being rather bloody-minded little devils, should you embark on letting them have a chase, you may well find that they are most difficult to steady to game in the future. As a rule, not an easy breed to train, unless you have the facilities; yet, I must say, that if you ever see a *good* cocker at work on ground game, you will see an example of the finest gundog work that you are ever likely to see. As far as training them on a commercial basis goes, I am of the opinion that they are not a viable proposition, (a) because there are not enough devotees willing to 'pay the piper', (b) they do not command the price commensurate with the work entailed in training them when selling as fully trained dogs, as compared to the springers or labradors.

Some dogs tend to be rather 'naughty' at times regarding the turn whistle and will 'try you on'. Do not let them get away with it, or you will most surely live to regret it. Simply drop him with the stop whistle immediately you have noted that he is disobeying you, walk slowly over to him, give his ear a good sharp tug a couple of times, endorsing the rebuke with the 'turn whistle' command. Consistency will win at the end of the day.

Downwind beat

I feel at this point that I must reiterate, so that I draw your attention to its importance, before you embark upon working your dog on the downwind beat he must have attained proficiency in methodically hunting his ground in the upwind beat. Furthermore, I am reluctant to believe that we train a dog to hunt but that we do habit-train him into a pattern by giving him repetitive guidance. For, let's face it, to talk of *training* a dog in wind treatment verges on the nonsensical. When it is considered that the most influential sense the dog possesses is the sense of smell, it will be realised that it is to this sense that his instincts react. Consequently, in attempting to channel these into a methodical pattern to suit our purposes, we are there purely in the rôle of advisory assistant. True, by wrongful or insufficient attention to the guidance we give him, a dog may develop a bad habit or never reach his full potential in his ground treatment; that is not to say, however, that the dog's hunting instincts have diminished, or that his scenting talents have suffered; for we neither enhance nor diminish these by our intervention.

I believe implicitly that if a dog has reached a high standard of efficiency in ground treatment under conventional conditions, *i.e.*, the upwind beat, he will adapt quite rapidly with the minimum guidance from the trainer once he is faced with working the downwind beat.

Again, this is just another step forward in proper sequence; another link, both for you and your dog in the 'learning chain' and so nothing to worry about, providing you take note of the all–important 'little things that mean a lot'.

When it is considered that when a dog positively finds game he is invariably *downwind* of it, probably having indicated the proximity of the game by covering the last few feet by an ever-narrowing pattern, culminating in a forward thrust to flush it, you will realise that to work a beat with the wind in his rear he must be sent down the wind, turned and allowed time to work the ground back to you, *so that he is facing into the wind*, and that to allow him to do this to the best advantage you *must stand still*. Obviously, if you neglect to do this you will progress forward to meet the dog as he is working the ground back to you; nevertheless, a practice that is very common. By so doing, two glaringly obvious disadvantages make themselves apparent. In the first place, by proceeding forward you will take up possible game holding cover that the dog has not had the opportunity to investigate; consequently, game that is sitting tightly will be missed, for the dog will be reluctant to pass you to hunt the ground behind you – unless, of course, he has a super-sensitive nose and that is not a risk worth taking.

Secondly, if you persist in this, your dog will develop the habit of expecting you to be walking on and consequently, instead of covering all the ground back to your feet he will develop the habit of only making a token gesture regarding the intervening ground, resulting in his pulling out to extreme gunshot range, turning into the wind at intervals to quest a likely piece of cover, then proceeding once again to 'pull out', until eventually he is hunting out of shot. Bearing in mind that one problem usually begs another, it does not take much foresight to realise that this is the embryonic stage of the wild dog that hunts out of shot at all times, no matter what the prevailing conditions are.

Apart from standing still, there are other slight departures from the norm when working the dog on a downwind beat as opposed to working him into the wind. You will recall that as the dog is cast off into the wind, the verbal command 'get on' is accompanied by the indicative directional hand signal, followed by the hand signal as and when necessary, together with the turn whistle signal at the end of each cast.

The initial command 'Get on' is utilised in the approach to the downwind treatment also and the dog is allowed to take up ground down the wind, which he will do naturally if left to do so; standing still you then give him the single 'peep' to turn, once he has gone out in front of you to a distance of six metres (twenty feet) or so. In turning the dog at such a minimal distance you are, of course, once again, exercising caution in the early stages of a 'new' approach in the knowledge that, in time, experience will put the 'icing on the cake' and the dog will take up more ground of his own accord, by which time you will have instilled enough habitual ground treatment in him for you to be able to trust him that little bit farther out.

Once you have turned the dog you will find, providing he has a serviceable nose at all, that to a greater or lesser degree on the turn he will commence 'quartering' the ground back to you and it is, once again, this basic instinct that you take advantage of and embellish to further your own ends.

Remaining on the spot from which you cast him off, you may indicate with the appropriate hand movement, simultaneously using your turn whistle signal, in which direction you wish him to go.

Should the dog tend to hunt spasmodically and perhaps dwell overlong on one spot, clicking your tongue will help to 'gee' him up or tell him to 'leave it'. On the other hand, should he show a tendency to turn back to you, hunt a small patch, then turn once more down the wind, away from you, perhaps on some footscent or other, *stop him with the stop whistle*, then call him back to you with the two

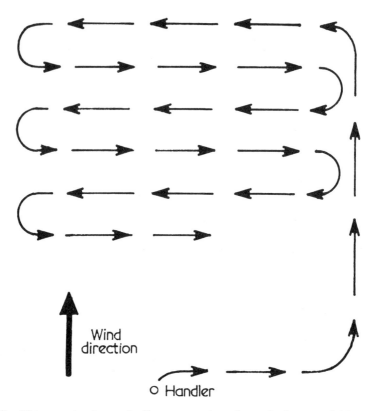

Fig. 8.   This exercise demands all your attention; do not be lax – work him – insist that he turns on the 'turn whistle'.

rapid peep-peep whistle commands and as he comes back to you, you may then swing him off to either side of you.

The average dog 'cottons on' to just what is required of him pretty rapidly regarding the downwind beat; however, that is no excuse for being careless – always work the dog, keep a watchful eye on him; what today may appear just a small instance of naughtiness is tomorrow's problem; dogs are past-masters at driving in, little by little, the thin edge of the wedge (see Fig. 8).

If you cast your mind back to when you were preparing him as a puppy for his future training, you will recall that in the initial stages when calling him back to you to encourage him, you crouched down. The following signal is a natural follow-on, or refinement and, as such, is a helpful aid when working the dog back to you on the downwind beat.

If you adopt a stooping posture and at the same time make imaginary 'patting' movements by your side (see Fig. 9), this will encour-

Fig. 9. The downwind beat.
If he tends to 'pull out' too far, recall him with the double 'peep' signal, accompanied by a 'patting motion' of the hand, indicating that you wish him to work closer on that side.

age the dog to hunt his ground right up to your feet on either side of you. Consistency in practice whenever you encounter such wind conditions will do the rest.

The cheek wind situation

Once again this is just another variation to the theme and one that, yet again, you cannot *teach* a dog to treat properly; for, providing that he has an efficient sense of smell, given a little guidance in keeping him within shot from you, the handler, he will adapt by himself accordingly.

The guidance in this instance is that on telling him to 'get on', you let him take up ground as he would on the downwind beat and once again, when you consider him at a comfortable distance, you would turn him with the whistle in conjunction with the appropriate hand signal (see Fig. 10). You will find that if you have the opportunity to compare several dogs' reactions in respect to wind treatment, that, as with any other aspect of their environment, they react in a wide variety of ways. Naturally enough, in the ground treatment in relation to the prevailing wind direction and scenting conditions, the better the nose the more marked a dog's reactions and resultant performance will be. *If he has a good nose*, obviously he will be acutely sensitive to every idiosyncrasy of air current and scent. On the other hand, a dog with poor scenting capabilities will show little or no reaction to variance of scenting conditions; it is this dog that, in all probability, will prove the biggest headache for you as the trainer when involved in the downwind or cheek wind beat. There is little that you can do when faced with such an animal for, as I have said before, you cannot give a dog talents that he does not possess; you cannot put into an animal that which is not there already.

On the upwind beat, however, a dog's capabilities in the scenting department, or lack of, whatever the case may be, make themselves apparent in several different ways also. Generally speaking the dog gifted with an acute sense of smell will display a much more irregular pattern as he quarters the ground. He will invariably turn *into the wind* at the end of each cast; furthermore, he will break off at intervals, slow down and 'feather' from side to side as he investigates little pockets of scent, nose close to the ground; then, speeding up again, proceed on his way to complete his beat. At intervals he may slow his pace, head up, with a slight prancing gait from side to side as he catches wind-borne body scent; in the majority of cases there appears to be quite a decisive link between a dog's scenting talents and body language, for very often a dog well endowed with scenting aptitudes

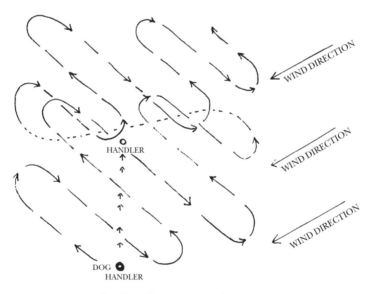

Fig. 10. The cheek wind treatment.
The dog is cast off 'downwind', turned into the wind and allowed time to work the ground in front of the handler. Once he has satisfactorily covered his ground and is then 'upwind', his handler may then proceed forward, ready to commence the next beat.

is more stylish than his counterpart less endowed. All of which tend to make such a dog exciting and aesthetically pleasing to the eye. A dog which possesses 'no nose', on the other hand, performs at a uniform speed all the time as a rule, for he has nothing to influence his speed; scenting conditions, whether good, bad or patchy, are not going to play much of an influential part in his ground treatment. Upwind, downwind, cheek wind, good scent or bad, will neither influence his speed, style – if any – nor pattern; almost invariably his pattern of ground treatment resembles that of car windscreen wipers.

Consequently, should you be fortunate enough to possess a dog with a good nose, whilst he may tend to be a bit of a handful in moulding his talents to your ultimate ends, at least he will prove in all probability to be an efficient game finder at the end of the day; whether or not he flushes it within shot will depend on the amount of application that you devote to giving him experience and guidance on ground devoid of game initially, and the gradual build-up regime you employ in introducing him to game whilst you are still gunless.

Should you be dealing with a dog somewhat lacking in 'nose', then you may console yourself in the knowledge that, generally speaking, should he be a little better endowed in the 'grey cell' store than he is in the hunting aspect, he will be very easy to control, simply because he has no incentive other than to comply with your demands. There is no doubt that as he is somewhat lacking in ability as far as game-finding is concerned, because of his 'handicap' he is going to pass over tightly tucked-in game; nevertheless, purely by instilling a tight pattern into him, game will rise to your gun purely being disturbed by the dog's proximity.

Possible problems regarding hunting

These are manifold and can be attributed to a wide spectrum of possible causes, far too many to enumerate within the confines of a training treatise.

Nevertheless, no matter how inexperienced the trainer may be, providing he has the necessary information beforehand, he should be able to recognise the problem developing and, by understanding it, may then adopt a different approach to prevent its escalation.

Stickiness is probably the most common within the training period.

Probable causes: anxiety, lack of scent, lack of confidence, sensitivity, inexperience, probably a combination of two or more.

Suggested cure: There is very little likelihood of a bold, outgoing dog becoming severely 'sticky'; however, for one reason or another, on occasions they do. The following regime with the hitherto more rumbustious type of dog must be exercised with extreme caution if the future steadiness to game is not to be undermined. On the other hand, the more sensitive type is the most likely candidate to become 'sticky'. There is little to fear with these, however, in the future steadiness – for once you have achieved the will to hunt in them, by and large they will not forget or question the drop whistle when confronted with game. To cure the reluctance to hunt, all that is required is some good groundgame holding country; let the dog hunt, encouraging him until he does; sooner or later he will encounter game which will get up and bolt. Depending on the degree of 'stickiness' will determine whether the dog will chase it or not. If he does, make no indication that you have noticed this and when he returns make a fuss of him. One or two rabbits are all that the bolder dog will require to refresh his will to hunt; the more sensitive may require a few more. Once you have achieved your aims, do not allow the dog near live game again until such times as you have reinstated the obedience to the stop-whistle and have proceeded with the hand training to its satisfactory conclusion. Needless to say, there are the exceptions to the rule; therefore it is not unknown for a dog to go through a sticky phase on more than one occasion during its training period.

Lining or pulling too far out in front.

Probable causes: very often this is a sure indication of a good nose; furthermore, if a great deal of trouble is experienced in commanding his attention and/or obedience to your commands, then almost surely he is not only headstrong but a bold, outgoing character. Then again, it may possibly indicate that you have skimped the early preparation as regards his coming back to you as a puppy, or you have introduced him to scent-holding ground too soon, before the ingrained habit regarding ground treatment has been instilled. Thus, on intercepting a footscent, he breaks off his pattern and pursues the 'line'. He may have acquired the fault by being allowed to quest under bushes and hedgerows as a pup, where game and small birds would tend to move on ahead of him. It might also suggest that a pup had been chasing game thus, due to premature experience, he has remembered the scent and its association with the game that carries it. Very often this is purely and simply a case of the dog displaying that he has no respect for his handler.

Suggested cure: obviously, as such a dog displays that he is over-scent orientated, the first thing that springs to mind is that there is little likelihood of his becoming sticky, for generally speaking this type tend to be 'hot', inasmuch as they tend to go like a bomb; thus, little harm can be done by putting the 'dampers' on him, by not allowing him on to scent, holding ground again until you are sure that you have instilled a deeply ingrained habit of pattern into him on bare ground. There are dogs which are far too intelligent to co-operate by performing on bare ground, however; should your dog display a reluctance to quarter scentless ground, yet has the tendency to hot up in relation to scent, the only course left open to you is that you re-introduce him on to open ground taking extreme care, as always, to ensure that you have cleared the resident population of game out of the immediate vicinity beforehand. Only, this time, forearmed with the knowledge that he is going to take a line at his first opportunity, you will be ready with remedial action.

Such a situation demands stern measures; however, in advising you to adopt the following regime, I have no intention of departing from the theme that I have described throughout the training. You must show a 'habitual liner' that you are just not going to accept this from him. As he breaks from his normal quartering, gets his nose down and begins to 'line out', give him the return whistle command. In all probability he will ignore it; that is your key – immediately drop him on the stop whistle. Now, if he drops, and he jolly well should – for if he doesn't, then surely that indicates that you have not instilled the drop whistle regime firmly enough – and consider this: if you cannot drop him in the mild temptation situation as regards scent, then what earthly hope have you of dropping him in the very much more tempting situation when he finds game? Refusal to drop on the stop whistle whilst lining can only indicate that before you ever present him to game you are going to have to give him a refresher concerning the stop whistle. However, usually you should have no difficulty in this particular situation. So he has dropped, *you have commanded his attention* – pause, allow him to collect his thoughts, then give him the return whistle command and, as he returns, swing him off to your right or left; consistency in this will cure the problem. Again, should he disobey the return whistle signal, there is a specific remedy for this also – drop him again as soon as you have noted that he has disobeyed. Walk slowly out to him, quietly take him by the scruff, step back, at the same time giving him a jerk toward you simultaneously, repeating each time you step back the return whistle command. Providing you treat him likewise every time he transgresses, you will soon see a marked improvement and, what is more important, you will not have cowed the dog.

Early rough-shooting days

I include this at the end of this Chapter for the sake of continuity in the text, for it will not be until you have completed the dog's training

Field tests have grown tremendously in popularity over the past two decades.

regarding the next two Chapters that he will be ready for introduction to the shooting field.

The first few days that you hunt your young dog on groundgame, it is advisable to 'load the dice' in your favour by playing safe, in that you remain gunless. Take your starter pistol with you, together with a couple of fur or feather dummies in a shoulder bag. Hunt him as you intend to on a normal shooting day but, whenever he puts up game, drop him immediately with the whistle and hand signal, exercise control over him in pattern and steadiness. Keep him on the drop until the game is out of his view, then recommence him hunting, never forgetting that you cast him off in the *opposite direction* to that which the game has taken. It is also advantageous to drop him by shot occasionally, having placed a dummy unseen by him along the route that you have just taken, so that you may send him back for it.

Providing you have satisfied yourself that he has reached a suitable standard, you may now contemplate taking him shooting. Again you would be wise to take precautions by playing safe; enlist, if you can, a friend – preferably one who is a good shot, for it is undesirable to 'miss' too often whilst hunting a youngster. It is also desirable that your friend leave his dog at home for the first few outings; the object at this stage of the game is to be able to devote all your concentration on the novice dog, therefore any unnecessary distractions are most undesirable.

Hunt the dog with your friend walking along beside you, point out to him that it is required that he remain level with you, the handler, and that he should keep noise to the minimum. For, if he is the excitable type of chap, this excitement will be sensed by the dog and affect his work. Furthermore, if a gun goes wandering on ahead of the handler, this has a detrimental effect on the dog's hunting pattern, to the extent that game-holding cover may be missed.

Heather, bracken that is dying down in the late autumn, rushes or rough grass is ideal country for initiating the dog into the shooting situation. Gorse bushes, large clumps of rhododendron, hawthorn thicket, tall root crop are not the ideal ground in which to instil a pattern. You must keep him in sight at all times for the first few days out with the gun. Hedgerows are positively taboo.

When he puts up game, drop him always with the stop whistle; do not take risks with an inexperienced dog at any time. If the game is shot, make sure that it is dead; if it isn't, ask your gun to put another shot into it. The object is to make the dog familiar with the shooting situation, the culmination of all his training, therefore we dwell on success and do not wish to manufacture problems for ourselves. If you send a young, inexperienced dog for live game, you are unnecessarily confronting him with a potentially dangerous situation. If it is a hare, it can give him the wallop of a lifetime in the face when he tries to gather it; a rabbit also, to a lesser degree; an old cock pheasant can 'spur' him rather nastily and a duck can give him a severe 'tweak' with that large, flat beak on the end of his nose. Any one of these circumstances may encourage your dog in the future to kill any game he collects, thus you are instilling the probability of his becoming 'hardmouthed'. On the other hand, a young dog may 'blink' game whilst hunting, for fear of being hurt. Should the gun miss the game, leave your dog on the drop for a few seconds then, telling him to 'leave it' – 'gone away', hunt him off in the opposite direction to that which the game has taken. Before sending him to retrieve, always, without exception, make him wait; if he tries to run into 'fall', be ready for him and spit out the 'drop whistle' command, short and sharp. Walk slowly out to him and drag him back to his original drop position and chastise him in the prescribed manner, *on that spot.*

After a few outings have been successful, your friend may like to hunt his dog in company with yours. The format is the same: take your time, give the dogs time to work their respective beats. As and when one dog finds game, drop them both, watch out and be ready to endorse your command to your young dog and be ready to nip anything untoward in the bud, for he may tend to be jealous of the other dog and run into the fall, especially after the other dog has had a retrieve or two. It is advantageous to hunt two dogs together, for it gives the pup valuable experience in working with other dogs and makes him realise that every retrieve is not for him.

Once you have successfully introduced him into the shooting field in this manner, you may take him shooting by yourself. Providing you remember, for the duration of his first season, that he is young, he can, and he may, succumb to temptation at any time, and if you accord him the necessary attention, you should have little to fear.

Sooner or later you must let him collect his first 'runner'. When you decide that he has had sufficient experience with dead game and send him for a runner, you should know that *at all times* you must allow the game down and to reach cover before sending him for it. If you send a pup for moving game whilst it is still in sight, it will not be very long before you will have a problem with his steadiness to game, because on one hand you are asking him to drop to moving game, then on the other asking him to chase it – again we must take into account his reasoning powers.

On bringing his first few head of wounded game to hand, you may find that he will release it prematurely and that it may be in danger of

A good head-up delivery into the hand is to be encouraged in the young dog.

escaping; do not get excited over this – after a bird has got away from him, he will not forget and ever after will deposit into hand before releasing it; this is just a young, inexperienced dog with an over-sensitive mouth. Again, especially in the spaniels, you may note that the pup will lay the game down and apparently 'mouth' it on is way back to you. All that he is doing is trying to get a better grip of the game; on no account must you start shouting at him – in all probability he is not biting the game, he isn't hardmouthed, but he jolly well soon will be if you start making him anxious by habitually kicking up a racket every time he lays it down.

Summary to Chapter Four

1 In habit-training the dog to quarter his ground – should you be too severe you may instil anxiety to such a degree that the dog will become 'sticky'. So make haste slowly and try to vary both the format and venue as much as possible.
2 Likewise, if you are too severe in laying down these 'boundaries', you may experience difficulty in sending him out to a blind retrieve in the future.
3 Should you instil strict heelkeeping in a dog expected to perform as a

Field Trial Winner, Macsiccar Michele, a very consistent performer in both Field Trials and the shooting sphere – a first-class brood bitch.

rough-shooter's dog, you are likely to incur problems in encouraging him to hunt out in front.

4 No two puppies are alike, they vary in rate of maturity, so pay no attention to the progress that your friend's dog is achieving. In all probability yours is just a late developer and, by and large, such dogs tend to be very intelligent.

5 If your puppy will not quarter on scent-free ground then try to provide him with ground that has had the game cleared off it beforehand.

6 Remember, any extreme in weather conditions is a bad training day – a 'lay-off' period never did a dog any harm, providing it is not for too long a period.

7 For the greater part of his first year's experience he should be hunted 'into the wind' as much as possible.

8 Always quarter him in as tight a pattern as possible; in time he will 'open out' by himself, by which time you should have him under control.

Chapter Five

Advanced Retrieving

This aspect of training encompasses the completion of the no-slip retriever's training except for his steadiness and introduction to cold and freshly-shot game before introducing him to the shooting field for further experience. It is also included as an integral part of the rough-shooter's dogs' training with the provision that too much attention is not devoted by the trainer to teaching the hunter to walk at heel off the lead; for, as I have said, this will be detrimental to the dog's hunting. Furthermore, the advanced retrieving lessons must be incorporated in his daily routine, never on its own, for he is a hunter first and a retriever second: with this in view, the trainer must adapt his approach accordingly.

In my view, I think it is fair to say that a dog of the retriever breeds, of a suitable working pedigree, trained to function only within the

Spaniel handlers at a field trial intent on the dog work in the 'line'.

sphere of duties required of a no-slip retriever, can be safely said to be one of the easiest of all the gundogs to train, presenting comparatively few problems.

No aspersions are intended: it is an indisputable fact that a no-slip retriever, as the name implies, operates at his handler's side – within reach – and, consequently, control is, or should be, easier to maintain. The only time he leaves the handler's side is to go, on command, to search for and retrieve to hand. That is his only function; consequently, not only is control easier to maintain, he has less to learn than any dog bred and used in the hunting aspect of the shooting field. He has fewer contradictions presented to him, neither is he subjected to the same amount of temptation as the hunter. Consequently, I consider the no-slip retriever as the ideal dog for the novice trainer to 'cut his teeth on'.

You will recall what I have said in relation to the hunter being orientated to working for the majority of his duties within a specified area that the game flushed will be, at all times, within shot. Thus, to a varying degree, depending on the handler's treatment of him in relation to that aspect of his training, he will experience a certain degree of insecurity and anxiety on being sent for a 'blind' retrieve at a greater distance to that in which he normally hunts. Here, I reiterate, not so the retriever; he has no boundaries placed upon him in his training for the role of a no-slip retriever; therefore he will, and does, get out to a blind as far as the handler requires to send him. It is all related to his 'learning chain' and subsequent experience in the field and, when a little thought is applied, only common sense really. It is when the labrador, golden retriever, *etc.*, are called upon to perform outwith the normal functions for which they are bred that the novice tends to encounter the majority of problems. And so, in the following retrieving exercises, I do not – apart from the exceptional case – envisage you having any problems providing, as always, you take each step in the learning chain only when the preceding link has been well and truly 'forged'.

Obedience at heel

A dog being trained as no-slip retriever should be around six or seven months of age when you first introduce him to this facet of his training; on the other hand, if you are training a dog for rough-shooting purposes he will be a little older, as you will have been involved in the ground treatment aspect of his training for some considerable time. Nor, for the reasons I have already outlined, should you be concerned in teaching the hunter to the same standards of obedience at heel that you expect from a no-slip retriever. If your puppy is reasonably obedient in that he does not pull on the lead, then that is sufficient at this stage for the rough-shooter's purposes.

From now on, whenever your retriever is on the lead, let him see that you mean it; as soon as his nose strays past your knee-cap, jerk him back good and hard, growling at him 'heel, heel'. A touch of the 'con' tricks can be of tremendous help with this also; what I mean by this is – instead of walking in a straight line, you have the dog on your *left* side, that is if you normally shoot from the right shoulder, and if you shoot off the left shoulder, then you have him on your *right* – we always look to the future and act accordingly. The 'trick' is – if you have him on the left, you walk in a straight line, but every now and again you take a *sudden* turn to your left; thus he will get a slight bump on the nose or muzzle if he has been creeping forward. After only a short time you should note a marked improvement in his performance at heel.

Another 'aid' is to carry a frond of willow herb or long piece of grass so that each time his nose creeps forward it can be tickled with the end – all very painless, but achieves the desired end result.

After a few outings, you should be able to 'snake' the lead along his back *as you walk along, so* that he is not aware of it for the first few moments. When he realises that it is loose, he may stop or try to reach round to knock it off; all attempts at this must be discouraged by slapping your thigh and the gruff verbal command – 'heel, heel' and, if all else fails, pick up the lead and continue on your way, giving him a couple of jerks accompanied by the stern command.

The natural progression is this, of course – walking at heel off the lead until released by a verbal command.

Therefore, after having walked him for some distance, first holding him strictly at heel on the lead, then letting him walk on the trailing lead, you may try him off the lead. Command him to sit, remove the lead, keep him sitting for a moment, then 'Heel', slapping your thigh and walk on, keeping a wary eye on him. Should he stray from heel, command him to sit; immediately put him back on to the lead and proceed on your way for a short distance, then repeat the lesson off the lead. Sooner or later he will learn that whenever he is disobedient when off, he will immediately lose his freedom and, consequently, will comply with your wishes. A handy tip to remember is: in the initial stages of his lead-free heel keeping, play safe as you are returning to kennels by putting the lead back on, for many dogs who have shown you that they are beginning to grasp the lesson will break from heel as they approach home base. The format is, as always, the same – if you try to take short cuts by skimping, you will pay for it in the long run; only progress on to the next

As soon as his nose strays past your kneecap, give him a short, sharp tug on the lead.

phase when he has reached a satisfactory standard in the present one.

The 'go-back' retrieve

This is closely allied to sitting at distance and is also further practice for the puppy in walking at heel; thus, once again, we are in proper sequence in his education.

Simply walk him on the lead on your chosen side and remember that once you have made your choice as to the side you want him at heel, for the rest of his life, that is the side he must walk on – not only with you, but every member of the family; never let the family undermine your training in any respect, otherwise confusion in the dog's mind will result. After you have progressed a short distance with him at your side, drop a dummy *in full view of him without stopping your forward progress*, giving the command 'No – leave it' and continuing on your way for approximately ten to fifteen yards; then stop, command him to 'sit' or 'hup', whichever is your normal command; walk on, leaving him on the drop, but remember this is a new approach – keep a wary eye on him to ensure that he doesn't break for it; be ready with the stop whistle. If he does break for it and gets it, you *must not punish him;* remember what I have said about his associating his deeds with the exact spot. If you punish a dog when he has

Fig. 11.   Retrieving problems.
To discourage a dog from rushing past on either side whilst retrieving, a stick laid on the ground to either side of the handler may be lifted to bar the dog's passage past and encourage him into hand.

Fig. 12.   If the handler stands with his back to a wall or similar structure, this will prevent a dog from rushing past on either side or circling whilst retrieving.

something in his mouth, you are in grave danger of implanting one or all of several problems. First of all, you are almost certain to make him anxious in relation to retrieving; thus, he may turn 'hard mouthed' because of his anxiety in relation to coming back to you; secondly, he will probably be wary of coming in to deliver in the future (we've all seen the classic case of this, the dog that goes out and returns at the gallop and then, in the final two or three yards, indulges in the 'catch as catch can' as he circles around his owner). You can't blame the dog, for he isn't to know whether he will be met with praise or a cuff. Thirdly, you may put him off retrieving completely, especially if he is the sensitive type.

I cannot impress upon you strongly enough – never, never must you punish a dog whilst he is in the act of retrieving nor, for that matter, when he has *anything* in his mouth.

To return to the go-back exercise: if he breaks and gets to the dummy, you have lost the initiative; all that you can do is accept the dummy, say nothing, walk him on and try again, only this time *increase* the distance between him and the dummy and *shorten* your journey on from him; thus you will have more scope in which to stop him if he breaks for the dummy. If you have too much difficulty with this, then you must be honest with yourself and consider whether you have bedded in the sitting at distance and retrieving exercises properly.

Once you find that you can drop him, walk on, then send him back with the 'Dead' command; you may increase in gradual stages the distance that you drop him in relation to the dummy, plus, by degrees, increase your distance from him, until such time as you can drop him perhaps sixty to seventy yards from the dummy then proceed on your way for another twenty yards before turning and sending him. When

A dog must only jump barbed wire, or any obstacle, on command.

you have reached a stage where he has thirty yards or more to go back, introduce an added command which is 'Dead-*Get-Out*'.

This is an excellent lesson for speeding up a dog that is slow at returning to you with the retrieve, for, when he turns around after collecting it, he sees you quite a long way away; thus it encourages him to build up a gallop, for he doesn't want to be left behind.

Of course, you have probably guessed what we are leading up to: the 'blind', or unseen retrieve. You are correct. Not only is the go-back retrieve utilised in speeding up the dog's delivery, it teaches him to get out into the country. The new sound 'Get-Out' is the fore-runner – the important link in the learning chain to going back for the 'blind' retrieve.

Whilst a simple progression, it is an all-important one from the go-back retrieve; simply drop the dummy, unseen by him, and proceed as before, remembering as always that whenever you intro-duce a variation or new activity in the initial stages you ensure success by not making it too difficult for the pup. In this case, you would start off with the dummy at ten yards behind him and, once again in each successive lesson, providing all is going well, build up the distance he has to go back.

It is helpful with both the go-back, sighted retrieve and the 'blind' retrieve to try and arrange the situation so that the dog is going back *into the wind*. Whilst this is not all that important in the early stages of either approach, it can be a great help in the final, vital few yards once the dog has to get out to a distance of fifty or more yards. Some people find it helpful to carry out these exercises along the side of a wall or fence, or to utilise a narrow lane; if you think this would be a help, then by all means go ahead; I am all for making life a little easier. As a precaution against boredom, once again may I draw your attention to the folly of embarking on any exercise on its own; *all exer-cises throughout a dog's training must be incorporated within the general context of the training regime.* In this way, you can give him a variety of pursuits and thereby keep his interest and keenness.

I must also point out before proceeding further that there are sub-tleties in the approach to retrieving appertaining to the different breeds. These are that as a retriever is bred for the job of retrieving, he will in all probability have a natural exuberance for it and, there-fore, in the main, the retriever will forever and a day go rushing out to pick up and deliver to hand with great enthusiasm; he has little else to distract him from this task. The hunter ilk, on the other hand, are a completely different kettle of fish. Think about it – if you are training a spaniel, he has been bred primarily as a hunter, therefore his strongest instinct is to hunt, whereas the retrieving instinct is prob-ably secondary; why should he remain keen on running out and picking up dull, uninteresting dummies? He would far rather be rushing hither and thither with his nose on the ground, investigating all these lovely smells. Only common sense once again, isn't it? So, with the retriever you may indulge your whims a little and give him multiple retrieves; however, with a puppy of the hunting fraternity, you would ration the retrieving aspect of training and dwell a little more on the quartering department. In this way we adapt, we make allowances.

Introduce variety as much as possible in all approaches to training a dog, no matter of what breed or for what purpose you intend using him; do not go out each day and 'drill' the dog, for in this you will most surely destroy his initiative. It doesn't matter if you don't get through his full curriculum each time you take him out; in fact, it is most desirable if you avoid this like the plague; so long as you do a little of this and a little of that as you go along your little country walk, together with the lesson that you are teaching at that particular stage of training, that is the ideal approach. A little common savvy goes a long, long way.

In other words, use the lessons that have gone before; every now and again, in conjunction with the current education as a refresher and variation. Obviously, if you are teaching your pup the go-back retrieve there is no need to include the sitting at distance routine as before, for this is an integral part of the current training.

Variety is the spice of life.

The 'three ladies'

In this exercise, once again we are just embellishing what has gone before and, consequently, are simply building up his chain of learning in proper sequence – a progression of the 'go-back' retrieving. The object is to familiarise the pup with the directional hand signals that you will use in the future handling of him at distance, whenever he is called upon to 'get-out' to a blind retrieve.

In some circles this is known as 'sheep dogging', usually by those who have never achieved a high standard in this respect.

Nevertheless, it is a great asset and a joy to watch a dog that can be handled 'out into the country' on a 'blind' retrieve. It is also mandatory from the humane point of view that a bird down and running be speedily collected, delivered and dispatched. If you think about it, providing you bed this lesson into him together with the last lesson, the more confident he will be in getting away out at speed, to be handled on to the proverbial sixpence.

This involves, yet again, a fair amount of retrieving. As a precaution

The transition from 'cold' game to warm, freshly shot game must be a gradual process.

against boredom it would be advisable to cut the retrieving aspect in the rest of his training, meantime, whilst you are indulging in this particular lesson. Furthermore, especially if you are training the hunting variety, always give this lesson at the beginning of the training sessions in an effort to keep him keen.

If you have instilled the previous training diligently, it should be child's play for you by now to throw a dummy, simultaneously dropping him by voice – hand signal, whistle – hand signal, or whistle and shot, *and he will remain on the drop until you send him for it.* Therefore, as a further precaution against him getting bored, I propose that you introduce him to the canvas dummy covered with a rabbit skin; then, once he has got over the novelty of the 'new' feel, introduce him to the feather dummy (duck, pheasant wings around the dummy).

There should be little problem to these; however, as always with any

107

'new' approach, we play safe, for it is better to be safe than sorry. So, making sure that it is a well-dried rabbit skin, that is a skin that has been 'cured' in the sun (and I emphasise this because I have known of instances where someone has skinned a rabbit and wrapped it straight away around the dummy, *then was puzzled when the puppy tried to eat it*). Consequently, you will realise that in drawing your attention to what must be obvious to most of us, I am not trying to insult your intelligence, nor am I being condescending; I am practising what I preach – playing safe.

Make sure that the skin or wings are secure around the dummy before throwing it; there is nothing more aggravating than to throw a dummy only to see the wings, *etc.*, flying off in one direction, the dummy in the other. As usual, you would take your *puppy* off the lead and let him have a scamper about, then throw a canvas dummy, dropping him at the same time – pause – make him wait, then send him for it. As soon as he has delivered to hand and you have praised him, command him to sit; then, throwing out the fur dummy, send him for it and be ready to call him back to you with your whistle. As soon as he gets his mouth over it, even if you find that he is hesitating over it and you have to crouch down and encourage him back to you by clapping your hands and calling to him, do so, for it is most important that you do not allow him time to become pre-occupied with it; given time to examine this 'new' dummy, there is a very real danger that he may refuse to pick it. Again, as a last resort, you may have to get up and run away, calling him as you go, to persuade him to pick it up and get it to you. On occasions, I have had to resort to chucking the canvas dummy, sending him immediately for it, then repeating the exercise with the rabbit skin dummy, letting him go almost before it had hit the ground. There is little danger of undermining his steadiness to the fall if you have bedded his lessons in as you have gone along. The object is, as always, to be able to adapt to the situation as and when it arises.

Should you be training one of the retriever breeds, by now he should be tall enough to put the dummy into your hand without your bending down to receive it; encourage him at all times to lift his head up, at the same time, avoid staring into his eyes; avert them as much as possible. On the other hand, if it is a spaniel, you will have to bend down to some extent. Try not to make too big a thing of retrieving with the hunters though – make allowances. From this point on you must use either or both the fur and feather dummy; do not use a canvas dummy again at any time; we must try to make retrieving as interesting as the training will allow without rushing through any aspect and, therefore, if you have implemented the retrieving exercises sufficiently in the past, we must consider the canvas dummy from now on as 'old hat', a retrograde step, and move forward to a progressive learning environment.

To implement the directional training you will require three dummies: it does not matter whether they are all fur or feather, preferably a mixture, thus increasing the variety.

However, as with every other new approach, we begin gradually and build on it, rushing nothing; we do not go on to the next phase until the present one is presenting no difficulties; that again is only common sense, for we can have no hope of success in the more difficult aspects if we are not solving the problems in relation to the simpler approach.

Sitting your pup down as you would for the 'go-back' retrieve, you must back off initially to a distance of three yards. Keeping him on the drop, throw a dummy at right angles to him, endorse your sit command, pause – keeping a wary eye on him – discourage him if he looks as though he is going to break for it; once he is settled, throw another out at right angles to him on his left. Keeping him on the drop for a further couple of seconds, send him with a step to the left and an *exaggerated hand signal,* accompanied by the verbal command 'Dead'. His natural reaction will be to go for the last dummy thrown, the one on his left (see Fig. 13); you must anticipate this and take action by first dropping him on the whistle, rebuking him with a stern 'No', then once again try to get him to go for the one on his right. A little thought will reveal to you that the further that you can place these dummies, the better; for the further he has to go, the more leeway you have to stop him before he gets to it. You should encounter little difficulty in this with the average dog. However, as with all else in the training sphere, you will no doubt realise that it is closely allied to the preceding stages and that, consequently, the stronger that you have forged the preceding links in his learning chain, the better your chances will be in arriving at a successful conclusion in relation to this one.

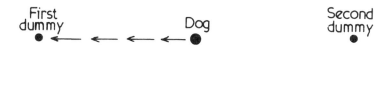

Fig. 13.   You must try to get him to go for the dummy on his right – the first dummy thrown – for he will want to go for the last dummy, the one on his left.

109

Should he get to the dummy before you can stop him, as I have previously outlined, make no noise about it; accept the dummy and return him to the drop spot. Ask yourself, did you issue the stop whistle command in time? You must be honest with yourself in this, for it is you who will pay the price in the end for the wrong decision; never blame a dog for your own shortcomings, that is a fools' paradise. If you can honestly arrive at the conclusion that he had plenty of time to drop, then you must realise that *he has ignored the stop whistle.* Therein lies the thin edge of the wedge – you cannot let him get away with that, for it will have far-reaching repercussions, not only with a no-slip retriever but even more so with a hunter, for if you cannot stop the hunter with the whistle, you may as well leave him at home, for he will be more of a hindrance on the shoot than a help.

The stop whistle must be regarded as the *ultimate deterrent* AT ALL TIMES – you must drive it home on every occasion. This is the one signal upon which all future training and work in the field pivots; without it, you cannot consider your dog as anything other than part-trained which, in the shooting field, is just about as good as useless.

If you are sure that he has ignored the whistle, take him to the exact spot where in your mind's eye he should have stopped and rebuke him there by blowing the stop whistle in his ear a couple of times. Leave him on that spot for a minute or so to let him think things out then, without further reference to it by word or deed, return him to his original drop position. Leave him there whilst you collect the other dummy, then proceed as before by throwing one dummy to either side of him. If you include this exercise within the format of each training session, you will get there in the end. Always end the training session on a happy note by giving him something that he is familiar with to do, something you are confident that he will do, so that you can praise him. Success breeds success. In this way you will maintain a happy and relaxed rapport with him.

Try to vary your routine as much as possible. Avoid calling him up to you and putting him straight on the lead to take him home, especially if he is a hunter, for he will quickly cotton on to what you are about. Indeed, it is not uncommon for the whole training session to go off without a hitch until the handler calls his dog up at the end; the dog, on seeing the lead in his master's hands, then starts playing the fool – for, obviously, he knows what is coming next. It is a good plan, on arrival back at the kennel, to allow him a few minutes' scamper about outside; this can go a long way to avoiding any reluctance on his part to returning home.

Once he has shown – over a suitable period of time – that he is one hundred per cent proficient with the two-dummy exercise, the final

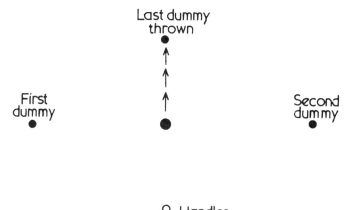

Fig. 14. The 'three ladies'.

As your daily progress continues with this exercise, you will increase your distance gradually until you are presenting the dog with the image of your hand signals at distance.

phase is simply the addition of the 'get-out' retrieve again, only this time, by introducing it in this context you can then alternate from sending him for one dummy to the other and thereby ring the changes (see Fig. 14).

To my mind, it doesn't matter all that much whether a dog sits or stands to deliver the 'retrieve', so long as he puts it into my hand. Some handlers insist that the dog should come in from the front and go round behind the handler to sit on one side before delivery. I regard such 'refinements' as bordering on the obsessional and, therefore, unnecessary; just another example of some people's eagerness to make a rod to break their backs and most certainly liable to foster problems unnecessarily. My advice to you, then, must be – if the dog comes in to hand readily, delivers with a good head-up and releases on the command 'Dead', then that should be quite sufficient; why make the job difficult when it isn't?

To return to the exercise in hand; every time he delivers the dummy, accept it gently – remember his mouth – then return him to his drop spot, throw the dummy back out to its position, return to your position, then send him for any one of the *other* dummies.

As you progress with these exercises, you will increase *your* distance from the dog until you can place the dummies, then retreat for a distance of 27.4 metres (30 yards). On consideration you will realise that this involves a fair amount of foot-slogging for you, because each time he retrieves to you, you must walk him back to his drop position, place the dummy, then walk back to your position; but it is important that you do this, for it is at this stage that the dog is being presented for the first time in his life *to the image of your signals at distance*, and when you think about this, you will realise that your hand signals *must be clearly executed.* It is most undesirable that you try to save yourself footwork by utilising the dummy-launcher for this. There is no reason to introduce multiple shots in relation to this lesson and there is a very real danger that problems could result from excessive noise.

I recommend that in relation to your hand signal to right or left, together with the verbal command 'Dead', you utilise the single 'peep' turn whistle signal, so that as he becomes proficient and unerring at responding to the hand signal, he will associate the turn whistle with it, that you may dispense with the verbal command once you are getting to a distance of 18.3 metres (20 or so yards).

You will appreciate that, if taught correctly, this phase of training, whilst anything but difficult or complicated if implemented in easy, progressive stages, will enable you ultimately to handle your dog at distance slickly and *silently.* A happy state of affairs that even some of the 'top' handlers are not very good at.

'Leave-it'

This is one of the most valuable assets that you can teach a dog for, obviously, as any experienced shooter knows, a dog that will ignore a dead bird that he has marked to the command of 'leave it' and handle out to the 'fall' of an unmarked bird which is running, is worth his weight in gold.

Yet, once again, by introducing it in its proper place in conjunction with the preceding lesson, it is the natural progression and, consequently, should present little or no difficulty whatsoever.

Once your pup has reached a high standard of proficiency with the 'three ladies', abandon that exercise; meanwhile, it can be reintroduced within the general format of training from time to time as a refresher and as a means of diversion.

Within the normal training routine, every now and again place a dummy, *unseen by the dog,* in some *light cover* such as couch grass; immediately thereafter drop your pup with the stop whistle and, once you have his attention, throw a dummy at right angles to him a fair distance out, so that it is positioned exactly opposite to the 'blind' dummy. After a suitable pause, send him with the appropriate hand and whistle signal for the 'blind' dummy, *expect* him to make an attempt for the 'marked' dummy, and take the appropriate remedial action with the stop whistle – pause, command 'no, leave it' in a stern tone, then repeat your original signals for the blind retrieve.

112

Obviously, as this is just a slight variation from the previous lesson, there should be no difficulty in getting the message across to him after only a few attempts. However, in the unlikely event that your pup begins to display anxiety in relation to this, it will do no harm if you help him a little in the first few stages if you call him up to you with the recall signal and *demonstrate* to him that *there is another dummy hidden*, by giving him repetitive hand and whistle signals, accompanied by a large dollop of encouragement; the object in all training is to succeed – it doesn't matter much how, but getting excited or losing your temper will avail nothing; neither will punishing the dog – especially in relation to any form of retrieving.

At this point in the pup's education, you are simply trying to build up in his mind the connection between 'leave it' and your desire that he should ignore the object in view and respond to your signals; you are building a trust in him, in that he has to accept your word for it at all times, so that if you indicate a direction then, no matter what he thinks, he should obey that signal. Obviously, in the future, once he is an experienced dog, there will be times when he will know better than you in certain situations just where the bird lies or has gone; but then, by that time, you also will be able to recognise the signals that *he is giving* you, and be able to *trust him.*

But at this stage of the game, if you are to hope to achieve the ultimate standard, you must have his compliance; at the end of the day, the experience in the field will only be of commensurate benefit to the degree of training he has received. Some dogs take to this type of training like the proverbial duck to water; others don't; it varies from dog to dog – you may find, in fact, that the better the nose your dog has, the less chance there is that he is going to accept your word for it straight away, for he will by now be developing his olfactory senses to a highly tuned degree and, consequently, will be severely tempted to branch off on every foot scent or pocket of smell he encounters, which will involve you in a lot of stopping him on the whistle and re-directing him. A dog of lesser capabilities in this department will quickly accept your directions unquestioningly, for he depends to a much greater degree on your telling him where it is – so that what you lose on the roundabouts you tend to gain on the swings – that's life.

Dogs who illustrate to you that they are not prepared to take your word for it and thus are probably good game finders at the end of the day, are very often rather headstrong whilst out there searching for the dummy, consequently are prone to try you on the stop whistle; remember, it is the ultimate deterrent; insist on it at all times – give this type an inch and you will undoubtedly live to regret it in another aspect of his work as well; forewarned then, you should be forearmed and act accordingly.

From now on you should be, by easy stages, building up to the more difficult as time goes on, increasingly to put out dummies into ever-more difficult cover and thus build up his retrieving experience.

The dummy launcher

This is an invaluable tool if used wisely and a tool of any description, when all is said and done, is only as good as the workman who is wielding it. Remember what I have said about the launcher in relation to echo? You would be well advised to bear it in mind and, on first using it, keep a watchful eye on his reactions to it.

Nevertheless, due to its versatility, it is a most useful implement in a wide variety of situations. As it affords the trainer the opportunity to place dummies at various distances, it obviously spares him a tremendous amount of legwork whilst, at the same time, gives a young dog a lot of experience at marking the fall at a distance.

I would like to draw your attention at this point to a little noticed aspect of a dog's work, albeit a very common problem, especially with a young, inexperienced dog; and that is, a dog's horizons are much closer than ours (see Fig. 15). On drawing your attention to this, it may appear that I am stating the obvious; that's as may be, but to watch some handlers getting uptight and puzzled when their young dog 'marks short' makes me wonder if anyone ever takes the trouble to notice at all; perhaps it's just a case of 'the wood for the trees'.

What may be in clear view to us is not necessarily so for the dog, especially on undulating or rising ground. The classic case of this is: you are standing on the side of a hill and a bird is dropped at the top; on sending your dog, you will notice that very often he will rocket out, obviously having marked the bird; however, he draws up a long way short of the actual fall and starts to quest the ground for the bird. In this instance he obviously requires help, so you would stop him on the whistle to command his attention then, with the hand signal and verbal command, you would instruct him to 'get out'.

The dummy launcher can be utilised in such terrain to give the young dog experience long before he is ready to go into the shooting situation.

Another common use for it is to simulate a toppled rabbit by launching the dummy covered with a rabbit skin (you will need strong glue for this), low across the ground in full view of the dog, accompanied simultaneously by a short, sharp blast on the drop whistle; in this way you are simulating for the dog's benefit the view he will get when a rabbit is toppled out in the open in the future, therefore you will realise that the dummy-launcher can go a long way

Fig. 15.   A young, inexperienced dog may tend to 'mark short' on rising or undulating terrain.

to steadying a dog to ground game. However, be careful that you do not inadvertently strike the dog with the dummy, for this missile has quite a velocity and could, quite possibly, inflict a mortal injury.

The manufacturers have now introduced a 'launcher ball', which is slipped onto the launcher spigot in the same way as the normal dummy; by launching, the ball will travel quite a distance and, upon striking the ground, bounce and roll for a number of yards depending on the terrain. These balls come in two colours: yellow and black; and, to my mind, are a wonderful aid in not only assisting a young dog to mark, retrieve and carry well, but – by rubbing a drop of rabbit or pheasant scent, also available from the manufacturers – teach a pup to take a line, thus simulating in one act the fall and subsequent line of a 'pricked' bird or rabbit.

A little ingenuity will open up endless possibilities in the training of dogs utilising the dummy-launcher.

The retriever ball

In my opinion, this is probably one of the best training aids to have been made available to the gundog devotee for many years. It is a rubber ball, weighing approximately 700 grams (25 oz) due to having a steel core; thus, when thrown, it will bounce and roll for a considerable distance, leaving a 'line' of sorts for the pup to work out with his nose and is, therefore, an invaluable aid in developing this aptitude also.

As a rule, I am not in favour of using heavy dummies, for the sudden introduction of a heavy dummy tends to force a young dog to grip it much more firmly than he requires to in the usual way when lifting his lighter dummy; the danger of inducing hard-mouth should be obvious. Nevertheless, in using the retriever ball, the opposite would appear to be the case and, indeed, I have noted a marked improvement both in the carrying capabilities and the delivery aspect in dogs that had hitherto had sloppy tendencies. It has proved beneficial also for dogs that tend to have an over-sensitive mouth and so you will realise and understand why I regard it so highly; it is quite inexpensive and well worth getting.

Summary to Chapter Five

1 Only progress on to the next lesson when you are satisfied that he has reached a suitable standard in the present one.
2 Never allow the family to undermine your training regime, otherwise con-

A labrador at his 'water lessons'.

fusion in the dog's mind will result. Consistency in all things.

3 Never reprimand a dog when he is retrieving, otherwise in the future he may clench his teeth as he approaches you, due to his anxiety; thus hard-mouth is instilled.

4 Adapt, make allowances; if he's a hunter, then ration retrieving; furthermore, if he shows you that he is not too happy about things, a few days' 'lay-off' from training may work wonders. When things are going wrong, do not press on regardless, for you will do more harm than good; try to think things out.

5 Never stare into a dog's eyes as he is retrieving to you; lots of dogs are 'eye-shy' and will not deliver when confronted by the human eye.

6 Exaggerated hand signals initially will help to illustrate to the dog at distance just what is required. As time goes on and he becomes efficient at distance, then you can modify them – but always make signals at distance clear.

7 The object at all times is to succeed, so getting uptight isn't going to help; if things aren't going too well, end the session on a happy note by giving him something easy to do.

8 Insist on his obedience to the stop whistle above all else; this must be regarded as the ultimate deterrent.

CHAPTER SIX

COLD GAME

It is of paramount importance that you do not jump from the fur and feather dummies straight on to freshly shot game, for therein lies the greatest danger of inducing hard-mouth.

Depending on the breed that you are involved in training will determine to a degree how likely you are to encounter a hard-mouthed dog. In the more common breeds, such as the spaniel and labrador, careful breeding has kept the incidence of *inherent* hard mouth to a minimum in the *working blood*; however, there are a multitude of dogs in the shooting field with mouths like gin-traps; by and large, this has been instilled by one means or another – one of the commonest being the owner just couldn't be bothered to make the effort in weaning the pup off the dummy on to the real thing by gradual degrees.

As with any other pursuit, you will only get out of gundog training what you put into it and, whilst I maintain that training gundogs is easy – *when you know how* – it does entail a fair bit of effort, patience and common sense.

The transition from the fur and feather dummy to the cold rabbit or bird is a fairly simple, albeit gradual one. Most shooters indulge in their sport in the winter months, the minority throughout the year, and so procuring suitable 'retrieves' during the summer months on more occasions than not, tends to pose a problem.

There are also many men and women who train gundogs purely as a hobby, who never shoot; bridging the experience gap for their dogs simply by taking them 'beating' and 'picking up' on the estates in their neighbourhood. On the other hand, there are those who, for one reason or another, just cannot get any shooting and consequently their supply of cold game for the purpose of training a puppy is severely limited. Yours truly, for instance, for many, many years had no shooting to speak of and had to 'use his loaf' in devising various means of getting a steady supply, even to keeping an eye out for 'road casualties' that weren't too badly beaten up. In the distant past I have even purchased a brace of birds from my local game dealer on occasions when I was desperate.

Since the advent of the freezer, this is no longer a problem, for it is simply a matter of building up a 'game bank' of perhaps one or two of each species for use *exclusively* as 'retrieves'. I have utilised a freezer for this purpose for nigh-on twenty years and have yet to encounter a pup that refused to pick one because it had been kept in a freezer. I mention this because the organisers of a field test a number of years ago, in a commendable attempt to make the tests a little more realistic, decided to use birds from a freezer. The correspondent of a shooting publication reporting on this test said that whilst in his opinion this *new approach(?)* held possibilities he was rather concerned to note that some of the dogs were reluctant to pick *half-frozen birds.* Honestly, the mind boggles; when our *self-styled experts* drop clangers like that, it is no small wonder that the novice to the sport gets confused.

Therefore, I feel sure that you will not feel that I am being condescending, or that I am insulting, when I implore you to make sure that the bird, rabbit, or what-have-you, is *thoroughly thawed* before use. You may use the same bird over and over again, *provided that it is frozen* again in between to dispel the scent of the previous dog that picked it up; *never, never* use the same bird on different dogs without freezing it in between. It goes without saying that these 'retrieves' kept in your freezer should be *clearly labelled,* for I do not want anyone contracting *Salmonella* because of my writings.

Nevertheless, freezer 'retrieves' are only, at best, a substitute, a means to an end – they can in no way compare with the bird or rabbit shot the day before; however, apart from the scent or lack of aspect, they are, as far as I can determine, *fair game* as far as the dogs are concerned.

If it is a rabbit or bird shot the preceding day, so much the better; however, it is imperative that it is not badly shot up. Never use a 'bloody' rabbit for a retrieve with a young dog, for this is a common cause of inducing 'hard-mouth'. The approach to and the procedure in introducing your pup to them is the same, whether they are fresh or freezer game.

You will remember the procedure you used in weaning the pup from the canvas on to the fur and feather dummies; the approach and procedure in this instance is exactly the same. Remember also that, with the retrieving aspect of training it is always given at the beginning of a training session, especially with a hunter, for he is keen and fresh – whereas at the end of a session he is more liable to be tiring and lack interest.

If it is a cold 'fur' retrieve, then you would obviously throw the fur dummy first and, on his retrieving it, give him his reward in kind – praise, then quickly chuck out the rabbit (don't use a hare at this stage, they are too heavy; plenty of time once he is experienced on cold game for these; we do not want any more problems than are necessary). As soon as he gets to the rabbit, get him back to you as quickly as possible, before he starts sniffing or licking at it, even if you have to get up and run away to encourage him to you. On occasions, you may find that the pup will leave it and come running after you without it; this is not a good sign, but do not get excited. Drop him, go back and pick it up yourself, forget this lesson for the day. The next time, try him with a smallish hen pheasant; I have found that in the initial stages, dogs that showed wariness and suspicion to a rabbit very often got over the cold game hurdle with birds; basically, I think that there is a very strong smell from the anal glands of the rabbit which tends to be a bit off-putting to some pups.

Do not use snipe, woodcock or pigeon in the early stages; the first two have an unpleasant odour and the third is notoriously loose feathered and can put a pup off retrieving for a very long time indeed. Hen-pheasant, grouse and partridge are the species that I use, plus a proliferation of rabbits, of which I have an inexhaustible supply.

I have, on many occasions when dealing with a reluctant puppy, found that if he didn't pick the rabbit, by calling it a day and armed with the foreknowledge, I could get over the problem the next time by *securing the skin off the dummy that he was used to picking firmly around another cold rabbit; he usually picked it without hesitation – once again, a little thought gets you there.*

Once you have surmounted the initial hurdle and he will pick cold game without hesitation, it is a simple matter to integrate the occasional cold game retrieve into the general training format and it is desirable that, as time goes on, before you proceed onto the warm, fresh game, you give him as wide a variety as possible; in this way, if you are going to have a problem, then it will be within the training environment, not the shooting field where you are more liable not to bother to solve it.

Laying a line

It is essential that your dog can 'take a line'; after all, a dog that has to retrieve cannot be considered trained if he cannot follow and collect a 'runner'. On the other hand, a dog which is ultimately to be used as a 'bird dog', such as the setter, would not be desirably taught to follow a line because, obviously, this would teach him to dwell on footscents, which would be detrimental to his prime function, which is to hunt to the air scent and draw up on point to the body scent.

There are various ways to go about this, *viz:* my own personal approach to this is the one which I consider the simplest. Taking a rabbit or bird – I prefer a rabbit, for this, because of the stronger scent – I attach a strong cord, approximately thirty feet long, around its waist. I then walk *down wind* away from the rabbit, paying out the cord as I go. Once I have arrived at the end of it, I then complete a semi-circle, keeping the cord taut until I am *upwind* of the rabbit (see Fig. 16).

It is then simply a case of pulling the rabbit up to me and untying it. This provides the dog with a 'drag line'. The object of this procedure is to *avoid leaving your own footscent* for the pup to follow, for he will recognise your scent and follow it to the rabbit; consequently, if you are careless in this respect, you will achieve nothing, for you have defeated your purpose which is to teach the pup to recognise and follow the scent of the rabbit. The scent of the rabbit alone is not enough, however, for the dog would not learn to differentiate between the *wounded game* scent and the normal game scents that abound on the shoot; consequently, especially with the hunter, he would tend to follow willy-nilly every game scent he came across, thus destroying his hunting pattern, which, as I have explained, is known as lining – a most undesirable habit.

To teach the dog to recognise the wounded game scent, it is common practice with most trainers to cut the rabbit's legs and/or throat, so that it will leave a blood scent. This, obviously, is successful, for the dogs ultimately learn to recognise the wounded game scent, follow it, ignoring all others, and collect the runners. I say ultimately for, in my view, the fact that the dog trained by these means learns *eventually* to differentiate between the scents, does not necessarily indicate that the reasoning behind this regime is correct.

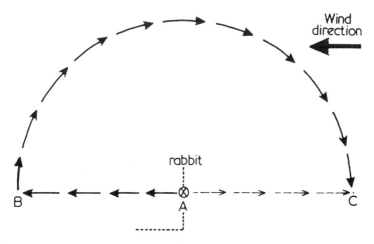

Fig. 16. Laying a line.

If we are to learn and thereby improve, it is necessary that we question and apply reasoning. I have never subscribed to the belief that because so-and-so has been doing such-and-such for so many years, he or she is necessarily correct. Where would we be if we followed blindly behind our elders, believing, as no doubt many would like us to believe, that because they have been engaged in something or other for thirty years as opposed to our ten, they are necessarily better at it? A dead-end doctrine if ever there was one. Experience is not necessarily a pre-requisite to the acquisition of skill. Indeed, I would not be in the slightest bit surprised if you, the reader, learning to train your first dog with the aid of this book, by applying a little thought and questioning, in the due passage of time improved upon it. Far from being disappointed, I would be flattered if you did for that is, surely, progress.

Having given a great deal of consideration to this question of 'blood scent' within the context of training, various drawbacks make themselves all too obviously apparent. Firstly, the question of the wisdom of encouraging a young dog to collect game with gaping wounds in its carcase. To my mind, this is most definitely not a *natural* progression at this stage of a young dog's education; in fact, it is a blatant contradiction of the methods outlined in every gundog training book that I have ever read. The novice is repeatedly entreated throughout the training and *well into his first season's actual shooting* over his dog, not to send it for badly shot game; yet at this stage he is being sent for a decidedly gory carcase – it just doesn't add up.

Secondly, why take the risk of inducing hard-mouth? Is there a valid reason for doing so? It would appear that the idea is to give the dog a blood scent to follow, but why should he? He hasn't, or shouldn't have, encountered blood scent in his training up until now; why should he instantly recognise this unfamiliar scent as the scent to follow? Ask yourself, also, where is the connection between this blood scent and the scent of a wounded bird or ground game in the future working situation? Naturally, your first thought is – the game that has been hit gives off a blood scent. Does it? Consider this: a pheasant is 'wing-tipped', he probably has two or three pellets in his wing; on plucking this bird, is there any blood? How much blood scent emanates from these few minute puncture wounds? On the other hand, if he has been hit so severely as to give off a blood scent, is he going to be a runner? I rather think he is going to be stone dead from such devastating wounds.

I have arrived at the conclusion, therefore, that your dog derives very little benefit from the practice of cutting the rabbit's legs and throat, but that the trainer probably acquires some psychological satisfaction from doing so.

Indisputably, however, there is a scent that enables the dog to distinguish the line left by a runner from all other scents and it must be a most distinctive scent, for even in the worst scenting conditions imaginable, a dog can be seen to be unerring on a line, very often across ground which abounds in myriad footscents of unwounded game.

In my opinion, the only scent sufficiently distinctive to mask all others to the extent that it is instantly recognisable to the dog is 'powder scent' from the hot pellets.

The proof, if proof be needed for this theory, is there for all to see on a day when the ground is damp; if you take a shot at ground game, you will see a cloud of steam or smoke rise from the ground as the pellets strike the game and its immediate surroundings. Should you take the trouble to investigate this area soon after, you will smell the powder scent left by the pellets without even having to bend down. How much more distinctive must this be to a dog whose scenting powers are vastly more acute than ours?

In the general context of training, your dog has become familiar with this scent, from the dummies launched for him, the powder scent on your hands and clothes from the starter pistol and, so, in the laying of a line for your pup, far from deviating from the natural progression, it is fortuitous in that it illustrates to the dog at the very outset that this is the scent to follow. My advice, therefore, is not to cut the legs, *etc.*, but to fire two or three shots holding the pistol along the side of the rabbit or bird lying on the ground, before commencing laying the 'line'.

As soon as you have completed the laying of the 'line', go and get your dog, taking a circuitous route once again to avoid leaving your footscent within the area of scent.

If it is the no-slip retriever that you are training, then you simply approach the area of 'fall', *i.e.*, the area where you started the line; fire one shot with your starter pistol, to which your dog should drop – pause, then send him with the command 'dead, get out', accompanied by the appropriate hand signal as you have been doing in the go-back exercises. If you are not too ambitious at the first few times with this exercise, and send him from approximately six to nine metres (twenty to thirty feet) from the 'fall' area, you should encounter little or no difficulty with this. Thereafter, as he has only thirty feet to go from the 'fall' area *into the wind*, I do not think that it is advisable or necessary that you distract him once he is working out the line. As time goes on, you may increase the length of the line simply by using a longer cord.

In the case of a hunter, you would quarter him up to within six metres or so (twenty feet) from the fall, fire the shot, to which he

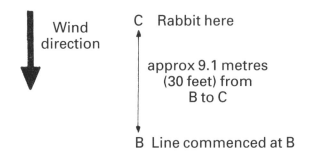

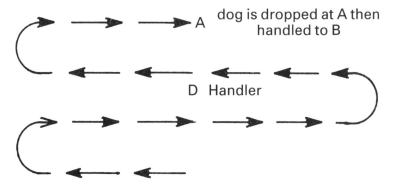

Fig. 17. The dog quarters his ground to A, is dropped by whistle, accompanied by a shot, then handled to B and should then take the line to 'C'.

should drop, *wait until you have his attention*, then send him with the command and a clear hand signal (see Fig. 17).

I am a firm believer in leaving a dog to his own devices once he has acknowledged a line. In the initial stages of *teaching a young dog* to take a line it may, on occasions, be obvious that he is just not making anything of it, in which case I am in favour of your helping him. For it is vitally important that once you have indicated to a pup that there is a retrieve to collect, he must, as often as possible, succeed in collecting it himself, even if you have to help him by slowly moving forward, giving repetitive, indicative signals until you are almost on top of it, for should he fail too often, he will begin to disbelieve you; thus, in the future, whilst working him on to a blind, he may refuse to take your signals, believing that he knows better than you where it is. That's gundog training for you; one problem usually manages to beg another. As I have said, there are other methods of laying a line. One is to enlist the aid of an assistant and, attaching the rabbit in the middle of the cord, you may then stretch the cord out and, keeping pace with one another, you can walk for quite a distance, dragging the rabbit between you.

One rather ingenious young man I discussed this with, informed me that he attached a length of fishing line to an arrow and could then loose it sixty-nine metres (seventy-five yards) with his longbow; it was then simply a case of taking the detour and dragging the rabbit up to him. Great stuff – provided that you are careful where you drop the arrow. I, personally, would be scared stiff to try this approach, for – knowing my luck – I'd be just as likely to pin some courting couple to the ground and inherit the consequences.

A little imagination is a commendable thing, though, if it makes life a little easier.

Introduction to and retrieving from water

I have purposely left this aspect of training until now in an attempt to play safe, for there are a great number of puppies put off entering water simply by their owners' eagerness, curiosity and ham-fisted methods in introducing them to it, either at too early an age, the wrong time of the year, or both.

As with the rest of the training, if approached sensibly with tact and understanding, as a rule little trouble is encountered. Surprising though it may seem, I have found that generally it is the retriever fraternity that has given me the most problems in relation to entering water. And it is in the *entering to water*, the initial stages wherein the problems lie and, consequently, where the problems *may be instilled*, for once a puppy is swimming freely, he soon learns the enjoyment of splashing around in the water.

There are a few dogs who are *inherently reluctant* to enter water; thankfully, few – however, they do exist. Sometimes they are just the product of breeders' mistakes, a mating that just didn't pay off. Most breeders will, if they are honest, admit to them and, if possible, will not endanger the breed by repeating the mistake for the sake of making a few pounds.

Indeed, I must plead guilty in that, only a few years ago, thinking that by purchasing the services of a particular sire dog, I could breed back to a good bitch that I had owned some years before, which was in the sire's pedigree. Sound reasoning, as you will learn when you read the Chapter later in the book on 'breeding'. However, 'The best laid schemes o' mice and men gang aft a-gley' and this particular scheme most assuredly went 'a-gley' in no uncertain terms. For the resultant litter were some of the 'softest' pups that I have ever bred; furthermore, I was to learn too late that on the very *sight* of water at six months of age and on throughout their lives, with the exception of *one*, they were *terrified*. A certain indication of inherent water-shyness. Lo and behold, the one exception achieves success in field trials and immediately the owner of the sire wrote to me, *requesting that* I repeat the mating – well, would you? I hope not.

It does not require much imagination to recognise the sire owner's motives; for, surely, if the owner of the dam of this highly successful dog repeats the mating, he is shouting out loud and clear for all the dog-world to hear that *he endorses this sire dog's capabilities*; no finer advertising could a stud dog's owner procure and he could then rub his hands greedily in expectation of the pot of gold to come from sire fees from the unsuspecting public, with no regard to the proliferation of potentially water-shy dogs that would be loosed upon them to breed in this fault for many generations to come. Not my idea of the honest thing to do – nor yours, I hope. No matter how many sire fees such irresponsible practices could produce would justify the end results, and I am a firm believer that 'whatsoever a man soweth, that shall he also reap' and that, consequently, sooner or later, the 'pigeons will come home to roost'.

As with hard-mouth and gun-shyness, water-shyness, on the whole, has been bred out of the various breeds by dedicated, honest breeders who have only the good of the breeds at heart. However, just as hard-mouth and gun-shyness may be instilled by the wrong handling, such is also the case with water-shyness, and there is no need for it if a little patience is employed.

This is one of the few areas where I can honestly agree that running the pup in the company of an older dog is most definitely an advantage, particularly so if the older dog loves water. In the possession of such a dog, the approach to the water education of the pup is simplicity itself; all that it entails is taking them both to the water, preferably on a hot day in summer, because water temperature in the early stages is most important if the pup is to have a pleasurable experience. Simply let the old dog go for a swim and leave the pup to its own devices; curiosity, in nine cases out of ten, will do the job for you.

It helps tremendously if it is a pond with gentle, sloping sides, so that the pup can run around in the shallows, gradually getting deeper until his paws leave the bottom; thus, his confidence will grow and in only a few outings he will enter boldly and really look forward to his excursions, on a hot day, to the waterside. Running water, especially if it has a ripple to it, can be quite off-putting to a pup, for in the pup's view, movement represents life; he is instinctively afraid of the unknown. Remember his limited reasoning powers and act accordingly. Make the extra effort to find a suitable venue for his early water education; it pays dividends in the long run.

Another highly successful method that I employ is to don my fishing waders and go for a wander around unconcernedly in the water; this very often is sufficient inducement for the pup to forget his inhibitions in relation to what, after all, is a new element to him and, in no time at all, he is gambolling around in the shallows, which to my mind is sufficient success for one day. Naturally, it will depend on your individual pup's temperament as to his rate of progress in this aspect, perhaps even more so than in most other exercises. However, I have found that with a sensitive pup who has shown after a few outings that he is just not going to 'take the plunge', a little encouragement can be employed to help him over his initial suspicions with regard to the water, *without frightening him.* This is done simply by taking him out of his depth, *once he has entered the shallows of his own free will,* by taking him by the collar gently and holding his chin above the water level, steering him out into the deeper water for a few strokes of his feet. If you follow this regime in small doses for the next few outings, you will find that he will be swimming like a veteran in no time at all; once again, by the application of a little thought and common sense, we achieve success.

Once your dog is a keen swimmer, the training appertaining to retrieves from water is similar to that on land. A dog that is a good swimmer will retrieve from water. It entails, as always, giving him the simple 'marked' retrieve initially and, on subsequent trips to the water, building on this gradually until you can proceed as on land with the 'marked' and 'blind' retrieve, sending him for them alternately.

Now to the words of warning with regard to water training: it is a common practice to take a pup to the water for the first time and *throw him in;* believe me, this will only cause trouble in the majority of cases; it would be an extremely precocious puppy who could take this kind of treatment in his stride without any after-effects.

Lack of thought is also a prime suspect in causing problems with water training. It is not unknown for an owner of a late summer pup to take the pup to the waterside at perhaps the tender age of seven or eight months, even younger in extreme cases, in the middle of January or February and try to get it to enter. No small wonder that problems ensue; would you go for a swim in January? I think not, not unless you are a member of that brave little band that I used to watch in amazement at Brighton beach as they charged into the cold English Channel on New Year's Day. As an Irish spectator remarked to me at the spaniel championship at Crieff in Perthshire a few years ago, whilst we watched an underkeeper floundering in the water where he had fallen in, as he was trying to break the ice to allow the dogs to get a water retrieve, 'Sure, I'd rather be dead for the rest of me life, than a hero for two minutes in there.' Very droll, and I had to agree; so bear your pup's feelings in mind – a cold douche in January may have long-reaching repercussions. There is no need to worry about his age, as with most training; the dog's education suffers in the majority of cases from its owner's impatience to get on; there is plenty of time to wait for the warmer weather.

As to the dos and don'ts of retrieving from water, the obvious one, of course, is related to trust in that, in the light of what I have said, you would not throw the dog in if it was reluctant, for some reason, to retrieve the dummy; you can always get another dummy – a dog is a different matter.

Watching a psychiatrist a few years ago training a keen young labrador to retrieve from water, prompts me to draw your attention to an extreme lack of thought and consideration for the future. He was throwing stones into the middle of the river, then sending his dog to 'fetch it'. The pup was an extremely bold one and, each time on command, launched himself fearlessly into the river to go swimming out to the ever-widening ripples for the retrieve. Needless to say, there wasn't one. A few months later, I was not surprised to see him bring his dog to me to have a retrieving problem cured. I was even less surprised to hear that, whereas the dog had been a keen retriever, he now refused to – no small wonder, for the dog had been *taught not to believe the trainer* when he told him to 'fetch it'. As I have said before, one problem begs another.

Steadiness to game

This is essential in the fully-trained dog. If you are neglectful regarding the training in this, once you introduce the dog to the shooting field he will quickly degenerate into a wild, uncontrollable pest and not only will all your hard work in training him go down the drain rapidly, but you will be in grave danger of losing your shooting companions.

There is no question about it; if you are fortunate enough to have access to a rabbit pen, it makes the task a great deal easier. However, there are very few of you who will ever have seen one, far less have access to or even own one and, as this book is written for the benefit of the majority, it is incumbent on me to instruct you on how to go about the various alternative methods.

Steadying a dog to game, that is, stopping him from chasing it, is a great deal simpler than at first you may have been led to believe. It is, once again, just a case of all things in their proper order and, as such, is a natural progression on what you have been teaching your dog until now.

By the time you have arrived at this point in your pup's education, providing, as always, that you have been diligent in applying each lesson in his learning chain so that he has thoroughly absorbed it at his own pace, then he should be indoctrinated thoroughly to the drop whistle. If he only sometimes drops to it *when he has no temptation* to encourage him to disobey it, then there is no point in proceeding further until he is one hundred per cent steady to the whistle. For if he may, or may not, drop to the whistle when there is nothing to induce him to disobey it, then he will most certainly *not obey it when there is.* That again is only common sense.

However, should he be efficient to the whistle, then you may proceed without trepidation, for it is perfectly feasible that from now on you could build up a high degree of steadiness to ground game simply by walking him, if he is the no-slip variety, or hunting him if he is of the hunter ilk, on gamey ground and by exercising vigilance you could maintain steadiness by *stealing the initiative* in those *first few vital seconds that he first sights,* or in the case of the hunter, *finds game for the first time.* For it is not the first bunny that he meets that should give you problems, but the third or fourth; by then he has had time to think things out and consider that perhaps it might be fun to 'have a go' and, therefore, he is probably going to take a chance. So be on your guard, for once a dog has known the thrill of the chase, it is doubly difficult to stop him in the future.

Consistency is your greatest ally in this procedure, more so than in any other; remember, as I have said, the stop whistle must be regarded as the final *deterrent* – the dog must learn that if he disobeys this signal then, as sure as night follows day, *he* will reap the benefit of the harvest that he has sown, in that *without fail you* will mete out his just deserts.

Condition yourself at the outset that on no account will you be lax in this respect, for you will only get, at the end of the day, *what you are prepared to accept.*

Should he, in the excitement of the moment, break and chase, a little quick thinking is required; you must consider the situation, mark the *exact spot* that the game sprang from in your mind. There is no point in shouting and blowing whistles at him; you have lost the initiative; for once a dog is in full cry after the game, rarely will he stop. If you cannot stop him with the whistle in the first half-dozen yards, then all that you can do is wait until he comes back, and please do not indicate your displeasure to him *as he is coming back;* remember what I have said about anxiety instilled in relation to coming back and *one problem borrowing another.* It may appear at times as though I am 'waffling on' a bit; 'labouring the point' might be a better way of putting it. But I have learned from bitter experience that these small points are the *most important*, and require to be emphasised over and over again if the message is to be got across to the novice trainer. Far from confusing the issue, I feel that in emphasising, drawing the novice's attention to the small, but all-important detail, it clarifies and prevents the possibilities of problems arising through forgetting or overlooking, in the excitement of the moment, the 'little things that mean a lot'. It is in this attention to detail, *without apparently labouring the point in the dog's eyes*, that differentiates the successful from those less so. However, let us get on. Your young dog has just returned to you after a thrilling chase; naturally, you will say nothing, having made a mental note of the spot that the game was flushed, you take the dog back to that spot by the scruff of the neck and mete out his just reward there.

As I have said, consistency is your greatest ally in this and you must approach this with determination, bearing in mind yet again your individual dog's temperament. If he is liable to take things to heart, then you would gear down the chastisement accordingly; a couple of blasts from a stop whistle in the ear is rather a 'mind blowing' experience in more ways than one. Simply push his nose into the seat and 'hup' – 'there', accompanied by the whistle signal in his ear. Thus, he associates exactly what your meaning is with the action he committed on that spot and, furthermore, he is not going to forget in a hurry the chastisement he is likely to receive, should he throw caution to the wind again.

There are dogs who react like one possessed both to scent and sight of the quarry; very rarely are they of the sensitive type; they may be highly intelligent, but rather highly strung – generally speaking they are of the hard type of temperament; these require a much more salutary lesson – a blitzkreig – the lightning war, would be an apt description. Swift, severe retribution. By now, you should know your dog, you should know what his reactions are liable to be to a given approach.

Should he be of the hard type, then the 'namby-pamby' approach will avail you nothing; make sure with his type that the lesson goes home in no uncertain terms, for if you are too soft with this, by the time that you have realised your mistake, it will be too late; and, if you persist, continually punishing him by degrees getting more severe, you will be in grave danger of 'case-hardening' him; in other words, he will build up such a resistance to chastisement that you could deal out the severest punishment without its having the slightest effect on him. Chastisement, at the best of times, is an unpleasant aspect of training, one that we would all like to avoid; however, it has to be said that there are dogs who have to be shown just who the 'pack leader' is.

In saying this, however, I feel that I must point out that I do not approve of the bestial methods employed by some so-called trainers. If you cannot train a dog without the use of the boot or stick, then I think it would be better for the dog and yourself if you resign yourself to being dogless.

Furthermore, again I must emphasise that there is no secret formula for the training of dogs; you cannot purchase a magic wand. If you cannot control your dog at distance, then *it is your fault*, not the dog's, and *there is no commodity that money can buy that will solve it for you*. Over the past few years, a great deal of helpful aids have been manufactured by reputable companies for the gundog public. These are, as a rule, harmless and, as I have said, 'the tool is only as good as the craftsman who uses it' and so, whilst they are helpful, they cannot cure your problems. However, there is a certain contrivance known as the 'electric collar' that is on the market. This device purports to steady the dog to game by the deliverance of a shock through the collar, via a remote control carried by the trainer. I personally know of no professional trainer who would use or condone the use of it. In my opinion, the person who manufactures this creation is a poor trainer, or he would not have found it necessary to dream up such a device; consequently, his 'blurb' on its advantages can be discounted as so much sales jargon, for he is obviously unaware of the most basic rule in the training of animals: *i.e.*, maintain trust in your dog as long as possible.

I appealed to Parliament regarding the availability of this contrivance and was informed that an investigation was pending. To date I have heard nothing further.

There is no place in dog training for such devices; furthermore, the chances of steadying a dog to game by its use are extremely remote: nine out of every ten unfortunate animals exposed to this treatment would be so frightened as to make them useless for a very long time indeed, if not for the rest of their natural working lives.

The check cord

From the early days this 'aid' has been developed from a nine-metre (thirty-foot) long cord to the present day, when it is now a sophisticated piece of equipment, with a brake in the handle, plus a retraction device built into it to prevent it snagging on every twig and tuft of grass as it used to do. All I can say is, top marks to the manufacturer for their genuine efforts on behalf of their clients.

I, personally, do not like or use them; I consider them more of a nuisance than a help. However, it may be that, due to advancing years, infirmity or physical disability and possessing an extremely hard-going dog, you have difficulty in controlling him. In such cases, if you think it will help you, then so much the better. Certainly it is not cruel; far from it, for it is no more or less than a very long, sophisticated lead. As with any other 'tool', it has its disadvantages and advantages and, as with any other, its misuses as well as uses. I think that before purchasing one you should know why I do not like them.

I have found that those puppies brought in to my kennels for training, that the owner has been trying to train with the aid of a check cord, have invariably been the wildest of the wild.

You do not have to look far to see the apparent reasons for this; for, if you tether up a dog for long enough, the end result will be a nasty, distrustful individualist, owing allegiance to none. The greatest asset you have in your relationship with the dog is the fact that it is you who gives him his freedom; above all else, even food, he loves his freedom. It is this *unrestricted* activity that you *channel with subtlety* to your own ends and the more subtle you are in concealing from the dog that you are training him, the better the results will be.

If you can get the desired response to a particular stimulus in such a way that the dog does it *willingly*, as opposed to his doing it because he is *forced* to, then surely that is better, for there is less chance of him 'kicking over the traces'; that is, again, only common sense. Therefore, by instilling good habits and preventing the dog from acquiring bad habits, as time goes on he will respond and, consequently, perform much more efficiently; for in his memory this is how it has always been, so why should he question it? Thus, by training him in a succession of progressively related lessons, curative methods in gundog training should be as surgery is to medicine – the last, unfortunate resort. And the check cord can only be regarded as a 'curative method' and, so, if you have progressed through the dog's education at a leisurely pace, avoiding the many temptations, there should be no need for the check cord. Granted, the dog has limited reasoning powers, but he is by no means stupid – he knows when he is on the check cord; consequently, once he is released from it, you are drawing his attention to the fact that he is now free. You are also showing him that whilst he is on the cord you are in control, and that once he is off, you are not.

Furthermore, as you will see later on in this book, tethering a dog to a lead is frustrating him, which we make use of in the hunting aspect, for it *excites* him, *it keys him up so* that once he is released he can be so excited; you *have induced* in him such a degree of excitement that the greatest dog trainer ever born would have difficulty in maintaining any semblance of control, far less teach the dog anything.

Therefore you will understand why I have reservations to its use and why I say that only when all else has failed should you contemplate its use and then, only sparingly.

The rabbit pen

I consider that the erection of a rabbit pen for the training of one dog, or perhaps two or even three, is an unnecessary expense. For the professional who has to be able to present game at a moment's notice for the benefit of demonstrating a young dog's prowess to a client, or by virtue of the numbers of dogs that he has to present game to, it is part and parcel of his every-day equipment. It is an essential, for he could not possibly get through the requisite number of dogs to make a living by hunting for game in the open, purely from the time and motion standpoint; commercially, it would be prohibitive.

However, no book on gundog training would be complete if it did not explain the erection of a simple pen, its upkeep and management.

It consists simply of an enclosure which is escape-proof, in which a few rabbits are kept. There are various authorities who advocate keeping tame rabbits in the pen; why, I just do not know, for I have tried this and found them of no practical use whatsoever. Indeed, because they will not 'bolt' like their wild cousins do, and disappear out of sight into the nearest cover – but with more of a hop, skip and a jump, stopping every few yards, in full view of a young, trembling dog – I consider them a darned nuisance. Furthermore, as I have seen dogs which would stop to the tame rabbit every time, yet would chase the wild rabbit around the pen, others would – whilst hunting in the pen – 'blink' the wild rabbit in his 'seat' consistently, yet unerringly find the tame rabbit. I can only conclude that there is a very different body scent between the species. A further disadvantage in keeping the tame rabbit out in the open is that having been bred for generations in hutches, they have naturally become much softer than their brethren born and bred in the wild and, consequently, do not survive the inclement weather to the same extent. Their one advantage would appear to be that they are not as susceptible to the dreaded myxomatosis; to my mind, in this concept, it is their only advantage.

In the situation where you have only one or two dogs to train, it is extremely tempting to be forever hunting them in the pen; this is a practice that should be avoided at all costs if you are training a hunter, for it will lead, eventually, to his hunting with his eyes – sight-hunting– to the exclusion of his nose, which will ultimately lead to his missing game which is tightly tucked in its seat in the future.

Once a dog has learned the basics of steadiness in the pen, I never again take him in, unless it is to manufacture a situation that he has fallen foul of in the shooting field, perhaps the day before. If he has given chase, for instance, then obviously a short refresher is indicated; in such a case there is no harm done – indeed, it is advantageous to utilise the pen for this. Not only is the pen invaluable in teaching the young dog the initial lessons in steadiness, it is also extremely useful if you have a hunting dog which is liable to 'peg' game; in other words, seize the game as opposed to pushing it out. This is a fault that requires to be 'nipped in the bud' before it becomes a bad habit and, so, from the amount of game that can be presented to him in only a few minutes, the pen is of tremendous help in driving this lesson home to him swiftly. This is a fault that is more common in a hard-going dog, for he is on top of the game before it has time to leave its seat. The very first time that your young hunter does this, swiftly command him, in as stern a voice as possible, 'no – leave it'; immediately you see that he is not going to comply, a swift, hard slap with the palm of your hand on his rump is required. If you treat this more of a shock tactic than a punishment, he will associate very quickly just what it is that you require. You would, of course, reinforce this by *praising* him the next time that he flushed the game cleanly and remained steady to it; remember, it is always just as important, if not more so, to praise the dog when he has done the right thing as it is to be continually rebuking him without letting him see that you recognise when he has done the correct thing.

The format for hunting a young dog in the pen is exactly the same as you would use in the open, albeit your area is restricted to the size of the pen. Hunt the dog into the wind as much as possible, giving him time to cover his ground and investigate every clump of grass or cover and, by remaining alert, you will be ready to spit out the stop whistle command the second that he finds the game. His disobedience to the whistle will be met with the appropriate action, just as, whenever he drops to the whistle or flush, you will walk slowly forward, bend down and praise him in an exaggerated manner *on that exact spot*; thus he learns.

Consistency in this will pay dividends; indeed, simply by preparing a pup and bringing him on through the basic training at his own pace, never allowing him to be subjected to temptation, until I was sure that he was ready for it, I have on more occasions than not succeeded in training a dog without his ever chasing a rabbit throughout his entire training and very often over his first season's experience.

Nevertheless, sooner or later, most dogs worth their salt will 'have a go' and usually when you least expect them to; it is a great advantage, however, if you can keep your dog steady for as long as possible so that when he does 'kick over the traces' it will be all the easier for you to show him that nothing has changed and that his actions will get their just rewards.

Therefore, if you have implemented his training properly in relation to the stop whistle, you need not approach the steadiness to ground game with trepidation.

The reason such emphasis is placed on the steadiness to ground game is, quite simply, this: if a dog will stop on finding ground game, he will stop to birds that much more readily, for he knows that he could catch that lovely little furry bundle, whereas he knows, just as surely, that he cannot catch the bird once it has risen off the ground; it's a case of crediting the dog with some sense. I regard a dog which attempts to chase birds as one of, or a combination of, three things: (a) he is immature, (b) he has had little or no training, or, (c) he's a nut-case.

The approach to pen-work in the training of the no-slip retriever is different from that of the hunter and is accomplished much more easily.

It really boils down to a walk in the pen: at first this is done with the dog at heel on the lead and then, after a few rabbits have got up in full view of him and he has shown that he is beginning to cotton on to what is required of him, the walk is continued with him at heel off the lead. Nothing very difficult in it at all, but it entails a little effort and restraint on the part of the trainer in not succumbing to the temptation of trying him off the lead too early.

Remember that it is his natural instinct to chase and, even if he has never seen a rabbit in his life, these instincts' effects are pretty instantaneous the moment that he first sees the bunny; so be ready, and act accordingly.

Walk him back and forth at heel; your movements will disturb the rabbits from their seats, and as each and every rabbit gets up, give him the sharp command 'hup'; then, once the rabbit has disappeared from view, turn and walk in a different direction – the idea being in the early stages to demonstrate *by deed*, as well as voice, that he is not to follow the rabbit. All but the dimmest or highly-strung dogs will quickly grasp what you require and you will find that, very often before you have given the verbal command, he is down, or half-way down. Once you have achieved this standard, you may then risk him off the lead at heel over the next few days. It is helpful to use the stop whistle as well; short and sharp, but not necessarily loud – together with the occasional shot with the starter pistol – a pause, then 'gone away', or/and 'leave it'. In this way you are once again endorsing what has gone before within the general format.

When you are completely sure of his steadiness to heel, you may then introduce a variation; and that is, sit him down in the middle of the pen, as you would when leaving him on the drop, then wander around the pen yourself, putting up the rabbits as you go; these will bolt past him and, providing you are vigilant, watching him out of the corner of your eye, you will be ready to spit out the stop whistle signal at the first indication of his yielding to temptation.

A further variation to pen-work which may be utilised for the training of both the hunter and the no-slip varieties is to give the dog some cold game retrieving in the pen, both 'blind' and 'marked'. This should only be attempted, however, once the dog has proved that he has attained a high standard of steadiness, for it is extremely tempting for a dog, if in the act of picking the 'retrieve', a bunny should get up under his very nose. This exercise can really put the polish on the 'gone away' or 'leave it' aspect, as well as encouraging the dog to develop a 'nose', for a rabbit pen ground is absolutely fouled up with scent, making it extremely difficult for the dog to find what may appear to you to be staring him in the face, under such conditions. Therefore, it is advisable, before going and getting the dog out of the kennel, to fire a couple of shots with the starter pistol along the body of the rabbit just before you place it; the powder scent will help him enormously to differentiate between the fresh and old scents that criss-cross the ground and the 'retrieve'.

I need hardly add, yet again, that every time the dog does the right thing in the pen you will add to his confidence by taking the trouble to walk up to him and give him his reward with exaggerated praise, and that you must always allow a suitable pause after he has flushed the game for things to sink in, before continuing in the opposite direction to that which the rabbit has taken. These are the all-important little details that we are, to a greater or lesser degree, all too guilty of forgetting; but these are the small details that make a great deal of difference as far as the dog is concerned.

The construction of a rabbit pen is very much a do-it-yourself affair. I dare say there are many fencing contractors who will be only too glad to undertake the job for you, but I have wondered what their reaction would be if you were to ask them, especially once you had outlined its purpose, *i.e.* to fence in an area of ground to keep wild rabbits from straying. I have the feeling that, whilst they would probably not show it, they might think that you had lost a few marbles.

I remember, one very hard winter, going to a local farmer and purchasing a few turnips for the inhabitants of my pen. Farmer – 'Turnips? Yes, certainly; how many would you like?'

Me: 'Oh, could you give me two or three sackfuls?'

Farmer: 'I think I could manage that. You must have a few tame rabbits.'

Me: 'Oh, they're not tame, they're wild rabbits.'

Farmer, straightening up, with a queer look: 'I see, you want some turnips to feed the wild rabbits,' he said slowly.

Shouting over his shoulder, 'Are you there, Jim?', he eyed me up and down. A tall, lanky youth came slowly round the side of the barn. 'Aye,' he answered.

Farmer, to Jim, never taking his eyes of me: 'This gentleman's wanting some turnips to feed his rabbits – wild rabbits,' he added slowly.

As both men eyed me warily, I hastened to explain: 'Yes, you see, they're in a large pen about two acres, and at this time of year they've eaten all the grass and need a few turnips to help them through the winter .....'

Farmer, interrupting: 'I see, you've got them penned up and they can't get out, so you feed them; that's quite a good idea,' he said, obviously unconvinced as he glanced at Jim, whose eyes were out like organ stops. By this time, I was getting rather hot under the collar and wishing that I was ten thousand miles away. Hastening to try and explain further, I said, 'I don't think you understand; you see, I'm a dog trainer and I need the rabbits for training gundogs.' Immediately their faces lit up with a mixture of relief and understanding. 'Oh! I see now,' said the farmer; 'Jim, get some turnips for the gentleman.' As Jim disappeared, the farmer turned and said, 'I didn't quite understand there for a minute what you were wanting to be feeding wild rabbits for – so you use them for the dogs to catch?'

Not being content with just escaping from one hot corner, unthinkingly I plunged straight into another. 'Catch them? Oh, no – they're not allowed to catch them; in fact, I train the dogs so that they stop when they find one .....'

Once again, the farmer stopped what he was doing and gave me the once over. 'Oh, yes ... you've got these wild rabbits in this field that they can't get out of, and you feed them, so that you can take the dogs in there, but the dogs can't touch the rabbits?' As he was speaking, Jim had put two sacks of turnips into the back of my car.

Deciding that I would only make matters worse by further explanations, I paid the farmer and left.

That was in 1977 and, to this day, on the few occasions that I have seen the farmer in town, he has touched his forelock respectfully with a strange look and a slight smile. Probably, he thinks, there's that queer man again from the hills that imprisons rabbits so that he can feed them in the winter.

So, my advice to you, if you must have a rabbit pen, to save yourself not only expense but embarrassment and the risk of drawing the attention of the local mental health visitor to your activities, build it yourself.

All that this entails is the muscle to swing a sledge-hammer to drive a few posts into the ground, enclosing a suitable area; the smallest worthwhile is about a quarter of an acre. To these posts is stapled chicken wire, which should be turned in at the top for about forty-six centimetres (eighteen inches) to prevent the rabbits jumping or climbing out and, as a further precaution against them burrowing out, a full width of wire should be laid out flat all the way round the intended pen on the inside, weighted down with large stones until the grass grows up through the mesh. This ground wire must be securely fixed every few inches to the bottom of the upright fence wire; thus you will realise that it is neither a small undertaking, nor an inexpensive one. A gate should be let into the overhang wire so that you can lift it and step over into the pen; this type of gate leaves no chink for the rabbit to squeeze through like a conventional type. When you have considered the work involved, not only in building a pen, but in its upkeep, and your responsibility to its occupants, you must ask yourself: is it really worth it? Especially when, if you think about it and, as I have already said, if you have implemented the train-

An anxious moment for a field trial handler as the young dog approaches with the bird.

ing properly – paying special attention to the stop whistle – a very high degree of steadiness can be achieved simply by introducing the dog to game over a period of time, in natural conditions, exercising vigilance.

During this time it is a good idea to carry a gun, but wise to play safe by leaving the cartridges at home; for it is extremely tempting to 'chance your luck' by taking a shot in the excitement of the moment. A little forethought will greatly enhance the standards your dog will ultimately attain and, providing you are not careless in the future, will maintain these standards. A great deal can be done with a young dog simply by walking him through the chickens; after all, in the dog's eyes there is very little difference, if any, between a chicken and a pheasant.

As the no-slip retriever requires a multitude of birds shot for him so that he may gain sufficient experience in the field, it is of great value if you can procure for him 'picking up' duties on the estates in your area. For at these affairs the dog has your undivided attention; consequently, not only will he reap the benefit but you also; for, by the amount of practice in handling that you will acquire in a relatively short time, your expertise will gain polish apace with his development.

Summary to Chapter Six

1 To maintain confidence and a good working relationship, praise is just as important as rebuke; consistency in both is required.
2 It is vitally important that the progression from the dummy training on to cold game and from there on to freshly shot game is a gradual one.
3 Make sure that 'freezer retrieves' are thoroughly thawed.
4 Never use badly shot game to teach a young dog retrieving, for this encourages 'hard mouth'.
5 Retrieves, especially when training a hunter, should always be given at the beginning of a session, never at the end.
6 It doesn't matter much how you lay a 'line', so long as you do not leave your foot scent for the pup to follow.
7 Before giving a dog a directional hand signal, always stop him first – pause, wait until you have his attention, then make the signal clearly.
8 Never fall into the trap of thinking that by throwing a puppy into the water you will teach him to enter it boldly. All that you are liable to achieve is a pup which will be suspicious of you, and water, for a very long time to come.
9 Do not introduce a pup or young dog to water for the first time during the winter months; wait until the hot days of summer when he will be glad of a cooling dip.

10 As with retrieving on land, it is equally important that the dog succeeds in the early stages of water retrieving, so make the early retrieves from water easy.

11 You should not feel anxious when introducing your dog to game for the first time, providing he is one hundred per cent steady to the stop whistle and you are vigilant and use it to 'steal the initiative'.

CHAPTER SEVEN

THE POINTERS AND SETTERS

Of all the gundog breeds, the pointers and setters can safely be termed the most specialised of all. Those that train and shoot over them, derive their enjoyment from their dog's performance, rather than in the size of the bag at the end of the day.

It has to be said that, whereas you may adapt the retrieving and hunting varieties, such as the labrador or spaniels, for duties outwith those that the breeders intended with a fair degree of success, the same cannot be said of the pointer/setter groups. I hasten to add that, in adapting the other breeds, the least success will be achieved in utilising any one of them for the work that the 'bird-dogs' are bred for.

Much more so than any other, then, the bird-dogs are very much the dog for the purist; not surprisingly, therefore, they are not bred and used in the United Kingdom in any great numbers as compared with the other more popular breeds; this is borne out by the numbers registered at the Kennel Club each year. For instance, the registrations for the year 1996 were as follows, and are fairly typical:

English Springer Spaniel	14099
Cocker Spaniel	14468
Labrador	34844
Golden Retriever	16442
Pointer	704
Setter (English)	899

These figures include those bred for show as well as work; nevertheless they give a reasonably accurate picture of the situation. Added to the English setter group are the Irish setters, sometimes known as the red setters because of their colour, and the much larger black and tans – the Gordon setters – to which I must confess to having a special liking. They are undoubtedly slower than the other setters but, to my mind at any rate, they appear to be of a very kindly disposition and, consequently, very easy to train. Unfortunately, they do not enjoy the same popularity as the others and, consequently, are not seen very often in the shooting field, which I think is a pity.

There are, of course, the 'foreigners', the German shorthaired and wirehaired pointers, which have enjoyed a meteoric rise in popularity

in this country since the end of the Second World War. These pointers have their tails docked, in some cases to a short stump – for the
life of me I cannot think why, for I think it spoils their appearance.
There are some authorities which have labelled these dogs as the
'rough-shooter's dog'. In my opinion, it would be a cold day in Hell
before they could wrest that title from the English springer spaniel,
for the latter, in rough cover, could 'run circles' around them and still
find more game. The pointers and setters come into their own when
used to quarter large tracts of open country, especially where game
tends to be scarce.

Opinions vary from trainer to trainer as to when it is best to start
training a gundog; never more so than when the question is raised
concerning the bird-dogs. The more experienced trainers, in the
main, advocate allowing their puppies to mature and do not commence serious training until the pups are nine months to a year old,
some even waiting until they are much older. I think that it is generally true to say, however, that gundog books are not written for the
education of the experienced, but for the inexperienced, that they
may find within their pages the guidance they require. It is incumbent upon the author, therefore, to try to expound to the novice the
methods that, even allowing for the inevitable mistakes that can and
do present themselves to the inexperienced person training his or
her first dog, will in the final outcome be most likely to succeed.

It is also true to say that, of all the breeds, the bird-dogs are the
easiest to train, simply because in the performance of their duties
and, consequently, in their training, these dogs are confronted with
fewer contradictions to their natural instincts than any other. The
trainer, for the most part, is, therefore, acting in the capacity of advisory assistant to the dog's natural aptitudes, in that he is fostering and
guiding rather than training *per se*. That is not to say that a bird-dog
will not chase game; of course he will, if you let him. But, apart from
this one aspect, the rest of his training calls for the 'trainer' to utilise
the dog's base instincts. Unlike the hunters, you do not require him
to find *and flush* the game, ultimately to *retrieve* it to hand, or pursue
it, should it be a runner; these are unarguably contradictory 'refinements' to the dog's natural instincts and, as a result, require to be
instilled or curbed by his trainer. For the bird-dogs are utilised purely
as *locators* of game. In other words, they quarter their ground in a
wide, sweeping action until they wind the game; they then 'home in'
on it to 'freeze' in their tracks in a characteristic pose, which is the
'point'. This point, or 'set', is instinctive and unmistakable, even to
the uninitiated; the best way to describe it would be a catatonic
posture, for the dog ceases all movement, save for a slight trembling,
eyes transfixed on a given spot, and will remain so for an indefinite

period. Various breeds adopt different postures the classic stance being the pointer standing erect, one foot raised, his whole body with a slight forward-leaning pose. Many well bred dogs display the tendency to point scent holding cover from as early as six months old. In this country, the bird-dogs are not, generally speaking, required to retrieve, whereas in other countries they are. There are many trainers who do not ask a bird-dog to flush the game, being content if he makes good all his ground, locates and remains staunch to the point, allowing the 'gun' himself to walk up and flush the game to be shot, whilst the dog remains steady to the flush and fall of the game. Other than this, the trainer only requires that his dog ignore fur; that is, he does not waste time pointing out rabbits and hares in their seats and, understandably, does not chase them if they do get up and bolt whilst he is beating his ground.

Undoubtedly there are many who will require more of their dog and will want it not only to point, but flush on command; even to retrieve the game once it is shot. Nevertheless, in my view, the novice should know at the outset that there are very good, commonsense reasons for not asking the dog to perform these duties. When it is taken into account that, because the bird-dog is above all a *locator* of game, and his prime duties are to quarter his ground, covering a much larger tract of country than any other breed of dog, one thing should immediately become clear to you, and it is this – he is working at a much farther distance from his handler and, therefore, once he finds the quarry, above all he must *remain* staunch on point; for if he is not, you will *never* get a shot at it. It is an abomination trying to shoot over an unsteady spaniel but if he is working within shot, you do have the occasional chance, albeit, very often, at extreme range. Not so with the pointer; and so the most important facet of his work must be that he does not flush the game prematurely – he must allow the 'gun' to walk up to within shot, at the very least. If you train him to be staunch on point, then add the refinement that he should flush on command, are you not, then, undermining, albeit only to a degree, the standards he has attained in pointing? There is, I feel sure you will agree, a very real danger of his beginning to *anticipate* the flush and moving in prematurely. Remember his thinking processes; he learns by repetitive example and weakening his point by continually asking him subsequently to flush the game can be likened to the retriever or spaniel who runs into shot, misunderstanding it as a command to retrieve, because in the initial shooting stages the handler has been sending him for everything that has been shot.

There are those who achieve a high standard in both pointing and flushing thereafter from their dogs. However, in my opinion, it is better for the *novice* not to take the risk and, after all, if the dog has been staunch to point, he has allowed his handler to get up to his side, has he not? What difference, then, does it make if it is the handler who flushes the game? And by doing so, is he not endorsing in the dog's mind that to remain staunch to the point is his master's desire?

I must confess, however, that I have experienced difficulty in this situation, where a young dog has developed the habit of creeping forward as I progressed past him in order to flush the birds. This is one of the many situations in the shooting field when, the handler's attention being diverted, the dog has the opportunity to drive in the thin edge of the wedge. You are then faced with the task of either foregoing the chance of a shot by returning to him and dragging him back to his original position, or ignoring it, flushing the birds, proceeding with your shot, simultaneously dropping him by whistle. I have found that, again, as is so often the case in gundog training, the middle road is the best, and have surmounted this problem by means whereby once I have reached the dog on point, pausing for a suitable interval beside him, then softly stalking forward with the dog at my side to make good his point and flush the birds by our presence, dropping him by a low verbal command as they rise.

If you ask the pointer to retrieve, you are then incurring the risk that he may begin running into fall. Not only this but, in my view, you will also orientate him to footscents, which in turn may encourage him, whilst hunting, to dwell upon them – resulting in his becoming a potterer, with the additional bad habit of pointing empty seats; all very irritating and time wasting. Then again, is it not fair comment that if you are going to train a pointer to hunt, find, point, flush, remain steady to both the flush and fall, then to retrieve to hand, would you not be better to purchase a spaniel? For you will encounter far less problems in adding the one refinement of pointing to the spaniel's curriculum than you will in adding a multitude to that of a pointer's.

Sufficiently forewarned of these dangers, the choice of procedure is for the individual's preference.

There are, obviously, subtleties singular to the pointer's or setter's training which set it apart from the other breeds: but these are only subtleties. The following are the methods that I have employed with satisfactory results in training my clients' dogs, which I humbly offer for my readers' guidance.

In first procuring one of the bird-dog breeds, it would be well for the novice to realise and, therefore, act accordingly, that of all the gundog breeds these are the least likely to respond to the 'breakers, big stick' methods, for they tend to be of a highly strung, sensitive disposition. Patience, a firm, but tactful, understanding attitude should be employed judiciously if any degree of rapport and subsequent success in training is to be achieved.

Again, as with training the other breeds, the trainer must set out with a clear understanding of what ultimately he requires the dog to do, so that the initial approach to the fundamental training is correct; for it is in the basic training that the novice implants the embryo of the problems which tend to manifest themselves in the shooting field. The basics are either underdone or overdone, but rarely done to a turn.

As opposed to the training of the rough-shooter's dog, in which you ultimately expect the dog to hunt within shot and, therefore, instil the boundaries early that he becomes orientated to working within them, the pointer or setter is required to range much farther; therefore, such rigid boundaries are not placed upon them. From the beginning, in the early 'games' situation, you must always bear this in mind and, as a result, will not be too pedantic and restrict his liberty over-much, conditioning the puppy to sit to the raised hand, initially at meal times, progressing on through the little games whilst out at exercise, with the exception of the fetching and carrying of dummies, so that he becomes orientated to coming back to whistle and voice, on to sitting at distance; habit-training him in the embryonic stages of ground treatment, in that you school him not to go ranging straight out, by attracting his attention as you turn first this way and that, in conjunction with the single peep on the whistle; training him to drop to the whistle and shot – all are implemented as you would with any other breed.

There are those who advocate the use of the check cord, in order to peg the dog down whilst teaching him to sit and stay at distance and, whilst I would unreservedly concede that it is within the training of the pointers that the check cord really justifies its existence, I would not advocate its use for this purpose. Indeed, I can see no valid reason for doing so; granted, these dogs do tend to be rather puppyish for longer than the other breeds and, as such, make greater demands on the trainer's patience; nevertheless, providing patience and kindly understanding is used, little difficulty should be experienced.

Again, as with any other breed, the stop whistle must be regarded as the ultimate deterrent; you must school him in dropping to the whistle and raised hand until it becomes second nature to him. Remember this: these dogs have scenting powers like nobody's business; they can take an air-borne scent of even a small bird, quite a long way off – at least twenty yards – and, should you be dilatory in bedding in the stop whistle, it will not be unusual for him, whilst you are trying to put some pattern into his ground treatment, to 'wind' a small bird out in front, break off his 'quartering' and go boring on ahead. You will recall what I have said earlier; in such circumstances it is imperative that you drop the dog first, thus arresting and commanding his attention; then, after the mandatory pause, call him back and swing him into his pattern.

Facilities available to the trainer very often determine the ultimate standards he may achieve with his pupils. You would be grossly mistaken if you were to believe that the man who had access to the gamey ground had the greatest advantage, for on innumerable occasions I have encountered those who had ideal facilities whose dogs were as wild as hawks, simply because it was too easy to succumb to temptation and introduce the pup to game too early. Then again, if you have game all around, you cannot be on your guard twenty-four hours a day and it is not unusual to let Bonzo out for a call of nature, only to find that he has gone off into the darkness after a rabbit. Consequently, whilst we may envy the man with unlimited facilities, there are advantages in not having access to such ground too readily; for, by not being so blessed, the novice trainer is more likely to dwell a little longer on the all-important basic training and thus achieve a far higher standard of performance in the dog's control when he first gets the opportunity to introduce him to the real thing.

I would say, however, that whilst one can adapt, by using one's initiative, most terrain to good purpose with the other breeds, it is much more difficult when training the pointer/setter variety, simply because you must have unlimited space; for to hunt them in restricted areas defeats the purpose for which they are bred.

As with any of the hunter variety, I am not a great believer in being too severe and expecting a high degree of performance in walking to heel *off* the lead. Sufficient for my purposes is if he does not pull whilst on the lead, for I believe that to be too demanding in this respect is to court problems with the dog's hunting.

The check cord

As I have already said, these can be purchased from the gundog requisite manufacturers and over the past few years have been developed to quite a sophisticated standard, with a built-in braking device in the handle; I can assure you that this is a boon. Anyone who has tried to stop a headstrong pointer with the home-made type will tell you that quite nasty rope burns can be acquired; therefore, the use of a pair of stout gloves with a check cord is a wise precaution. A piece of stout cord, five-and-a-half to six metres (eighteen to twenty feet) long, is sufficient for the purpose. It is not a good idea to use a slip knot, as I have seen, neither would I advise a choke collar for obvious reasons. You may attach the cord to the dog's leather collar or make a *no-slip* loop in one end large enough to slip over the dog's head, but not large enough that he can manoeuvre himself out of it. At the handler's end, I have found it useful to tie a few knots at intervals, thus affording a grip.

Early check cord lessons

It is advisable to allow the dog to become used to this encumbrance by letting him run around, trailing it about with him; this can be done indoors as well as out-of-doors; again, as with any other aspect of training, in short doses – fifteen minutes is ample time, otherwise he is likely to become irritated by it.

'Stay' or 'to-ho'

I feel that it is not important which commands you use in the training of a dog but that it is more important that the commands chosen should be such that they are not likely to be confused with another 'sound'. For instance, it would be foolish to teach a dog to drop to the command 'sit' if its name was 'Kit' for, at distance, especially on a windy, blustery day, the human voice distorts. At the same time, I dislike double word commands such as 'to-ho', preferring the one word command, 'stay'. In my view, the less verbal commands the better. Whether you prefer the word 'stay' or 'to-ho' is entirely a matter of personal choice; the main thing is to choose your word of command, then stick by it.

The idea behind the 'stay' or 'to-ho' command is simply to associate it in the dog's mind that he must pull up short and refrain from going on until commanded to. In other words, this is the dog's introduction to staying on point.

Bribery in the shape of tit-bits can achieve the desired end in this. Normally, apart from the very exceptional case of a problem in training the other breeds, I have little use for the reward system, relying on encouragement and praise to bring about a satisfactory result. However, it is not quite the same in this respect, for in using the tit-bit regime together with the 'stay' training of the pointer ilk, it is not so much the reward but the *scent* of the morsel used that is valuable. To that end, I do not propose that you use biscuits for, although there may be a faint smell – the object is to make the finding of it easy –

success is essential, so use something with a distinctive smell and, just as important, a delicacy that the dog likes to eat. I have found the use of two-inch square pieces of corned beef, or unwashed tripe, infallible for this purpose.

Taking the dog out onto your lawn, attach the check cord to him, let him trail it around for a few minutes, then call him up to you, praise him and, if he hasn't tasted corned beef before (which wouldn't be surprising at the current price of it these days), give him a piece to eat. Chuck another piece out in full view of him, restraining him with the other hand, holding the check cord gently, then tell him to 'get-on'. He should bound out to it without a second telling and make short work of it; let him do this the next two or three times until he is obviously expecting to rush out on command for his little snack. Around the fourth or fifth time, throw it a little further so that you will have a little more leeway in which to pull him up short of it. Now send him – as he approaches it, pull him up as gently as possible with a jerk on the cord, accompanied by steady pressure and the command of your choice, 'stay' or 'to-ho'. It is not unusual for a headstrong dog not to take too kindly at being thwarted thus, and to act like one demented, straining this way and that trying to reach the meat. Do not relent on this; you must show him that you are boss, but in as pleasant a way as possible. Simply maintain a steady restraint as you approach, slowly gathering up the check cord hand over hand until you reach him; thereupon, soothe him and stroke him until he is quiet. As soon as he has settled down, tell him to 'get-on' and allow him the reward. Cheese, tripe, or anything else that the dog shows a preference for, as long as it has a distinctive smell, may be used for this exercise, for the next step in his learning chain also helps him to develop his sense of smell in savouring the wind-borne scent of the tit-bit in order to find it. Which is, after all, a natural progression again.

Go out into a large open field, devoid of livestock *and their droppings*, throw out pieces of your chosen tit-bits at suitable intervals; not too many, for you will have difficulty in remembering where you have placed them all; furthermore, it is most undesirable that you should be forever pulling the dog up – he must be allowed a fair proportion of 'hunting' to each 'point'. Returning to the kennel, or car, whichever the case may be, fetch the dog into the field, attach the check cord and quarter him *into the wind*. You will note the difference in his performance as he begins to indicate that he is getting the by-now familiar scent. Try not, inadvertently, to let him reach the 'bait', but pull him up short in the prescribed manner, together with the command.

As with all other aspects of training, a satisfactory standard will not be achieved overnight, but by regular, repetitive lessons over a period of time. Most pointers are not too difficult in getting the idea across to; as in all things, though, it varies from dog to dog, depending on their individual aptitudes. Once you have reached a standard whereby it is obvious to you that he is coming up on point without the added restraint of the check cord, then you may dispense with it and carry on without it. Needless to say, should he disobey the command at any time in the future training, a short refresher on the cord should be implemented.

As the ultimate duty of the dog entails his remaining on point whilst there are people moving around beside and behind him, I have found it useful to walk around the dog in the basic training stages so that he becomes used to this and does not misinterpret my movements as an excuse to break off from his point.

I suspect that it has been negligence of this procedure in the past that has ultimately led to my problems with the dogs creeping forward whilst on point as I proceeded past them It is by our mistakes that we learn.

Bearing in mind, as always, the future purposes for which you are training him, whilst giving him his quartering lessons you may note that he will stop to investigate an interesting scent; you must be on your guard against this and quickly 'gee him up' by telling him, 'gone away', or 'get-on'; for the last thing you want a bird-dog to do is run around with his nose on the ground – he must cover the ground at speed with his *head held high* to savour the air-borne body scent of game; therefore, if you are dilatory and allow him to develop the habit at this stage, you will live to repent it at leisure.

In the basic ground treatment exercises and, indeed, as much as possible throughout his first season's experience, you must hunt him into the wind, as you would with a spaniel. For it is only by repetitive unvarying guidance that he will become conditioned .

Quartering

As I have said, the bird-dog must cover a much wider beat than the rough-shooter's dog and therefore his scope is not so limited. For the initial quartering lessons, it is a good plan to seek out a largish, flat field or ground with boundary fences or, better still, dykes approximately 91.4 metres (100 yards) apart.

The format for quartering a pointer is similar to that of the spaniel, the only difference being that you desire, and thus will encourage the pointer to range much farther out and turn at the fence or wall, whichever the case may be.

The 'Schoolmaster' dog

It is whilst giving a young dog his first lesson on ground treatment that I believe the use of an older, more experienced dog can be utilised, simply to encourage him to range and turn on the whistle. Again, however, if you have implemented his development for training properly, there should be no need for this. But it is as well that you should know, as you go along, the variations to the theme. Apart from this instance, the only other circumstances where I might consider the use of the 'Schoolmaster' of any value would be in the, thankfully, isolated cases where a rough-shooting dog being trained to hunt, due to having been dealt with too severely in relation to heel-keeping before he came into my hands for training, has been reluctant to 'get up and go'. Nevertheless, might I draw your attention yet again to the way that a dog thinks; he learns by example; consequently, should your 'schoolmaster' have some fault or other, that fault will be visited upon the pup, for he will copy it. So be warned.

The format is simply to cast the pup off with the older dog with the customary 'get-on' and, once the older dog has reached the limit of his beat, give the 'turn' whistle command, accompanied by the exaggerated hand signal. In nine cases out of every ten, the pup will follow his 'teacher' and it is truly astonishing just how quickly, in these circumstances, the 'penny' can drop.

Initially, then, you will begin by having him sitting in front of you; then, with a wide, sweeping, exaggerated signal to one side or the other, you command him to 'get-on', proceeding in the same direction yourself. All being well, he will outstrip you and proceed towards the wall; if and when he reaches it, with a single 'peep' on your whistle you would thus attract his attention; immediately on his looking in your direction, indicate to him by giving another exaggerated hand signal and, commencing to proceed in the direction of the opposite wall. That is about all there is to it. Sounds easy, but, depending on how well you have instilled the basic obedience, coupled with his temperament, will determine the degree of success or problems (I hesitate to say failure, for this is most unlikely) that you may or may not encounter. Now, when he reaches the limit of his beat he will tend to turn and run along the wall, hedge or fence; you must not allow him to proceed too far along it, for by doing so, when you do manage to turn him, he will have taken up too much ground which, in the shooting situation, would result in large areas of ground being missed, which could hold tightly tucked in game.

Before he has had the opportunity to progress along the boundary any more than 2.4 to 3 metres (8 to 10 feet), turn him with the whistle. Immediately that you see he is not going to pay attention to it, drop him on the stop whistle, command his attention, then indicate once again with the hand signal and whistle that you wish him to cross in front of you. If you are lazy regarding this and allow him too much leeway along the boundary habitually, then in turning him he will be inclined to progress back towards you before turning and progressing on past in front of you which, if allowed to develop, very often results in the dog becoming what is termed a 'down wind turner', an instilled fault fairly common in spaniels, but through no inherent fault of their own.

As with the training of any hunting dog, when first trying to instil a methodical pattern of ground treatment, it is wise to walk over the ground yourself first, in an effort to clear off any game. If you possess another dog this simplifies matters; nevertheless, there are times that, even after doing this, your young dog will encounter game. This need not be all that drastic, however, for if you are vigilant you will note a marked change in his behaviour as he indicates that he is 'winding' it; this affords you the opportunity to 'drop' him with the whistle and he should do so, for if he will not obey the stop whistle when he is faced only by scent, what earthly chance have you to stop him in the much more exciting situation when game suddenly bursts out in front of him? Failure to drop to your command can only make it abundantly clear to you that, if you are to enjoy even a modicum of success ultimately, you must abandon further progress in training meantime, and give him a refresher on dropping to the whistle.

First things first, however; should he drop to your command walk slowly up to him and praise him for doing the right thing. Leave him on the drop and, with the occasional backward glance to see that he is 'staying put', proceed forward and flush the game yourself. It is a wise precaution as soon as the game takes flight, to turn to the dog and quickly give him the appropriate hand signal endorsed with the drop whistle again, simply to emphasise to him that he must remain where he is; it is also a good idea to fire a blank shot at the same time, for this is simulating the situation that he will encounter in the future. On scenting game whilst quartering their ground, there are many young dogs who will come up on point; should he do this, then you would be pleased and there would be no need to drop him at all. Simply walk forward cautiously – do not, for goodness sake, go rushing up to him, for nothing will encourage him to break off the point faster than being startled thus. Once you have reached him, stroke him gently, whispering in a soothing tone: 'stay' – 'good boy' – 'stay' – 'stay'. Then, leaving him on the point, *slowly* go forward and flush the game yourself, firing a blank shot and dropping him by hand signal and whistle simultaneously.

There are some who say that it is a wise precaution to run the dog initially trailing his check cord, that you may then have the advantage of being able to run forward and stamp on the trailing end, should a 'hot' situation develop. The theory seems sound enough to me; however, in practice I have not found this so successful. I think you would have to be very fleet of foot, or lucky, in that the situation developed whilst the dog was close at hand. However, if it makes you feel more secure, then I can see no harm in doing so. Again, there are some who say that in giving the pup his initial lesson on ground treatment, you should use a sixty-nine metres (seventy-five yard) check cord; but, let's face it, if you cannot turn the dog to your single 'peep' on the whistle, then you haven't devoted enough time to the early little games and his subsequent exercise periods. I feel that if you have to rely on mechanical means to encourage a dog to turn to a whistle, a perfectly simple and the least demanding of all the commands, then your whole preparatory regime is out of synchronisation and you have little hope of attaining a good standard from your dog in the final outcome. Furthermore, anyone who has worked with a check cord of such length will tell you that it is extremely cumbersome and will try your patience to the limit. In saying this, however, I would stress that it can be a positive boon to use a *short* check cord trailing for holding a young dog on point during his early introduction to game – more anon, however, for I am rushing on too fast.

In the initial stages of giving the dog guidance in ground treatment, just as with the rough-shooter's dog, you are progressing upwind in a zig-zag fashion; the ground treatment regarding the 'cheek wind' and 'downwind' are dealt with in Chapter Four, and with each subsequent lesson, as the dog (hopefully) gets more proficient and learns what you require of him, your progress forward will become more and more direct, until you are proceeding forward in a straight line with the dog galloping from side to side, working his beat in a methodical manner. This may take many weeks to accomplish, depending on the dog; however, you must work at it and not be tempted prematurely to introduce the dog to game before he is ready for it. You must be on your guard not to make these lessons too long in an effort to make progress, for by doing so you will be in danger of boring the dog, to the extent that he may lose a great deal of his style and drive.

Training to fur

Many trainers do not like their dogs to point 'fur', for they consider a dog that does is a time-waster; consequently, the majority train their bird-dogs to ignore it completely whilst quartering their beat, but to drop to it should it rise in front of them.

Steadiness to fur

Again, as with any other facet of advanced training, success or failure in this is determined by the degree of attention that has been paid to the basics; in this instance, the make or break regime is the stop whistle – if he has reached a high degree of obedience to it, then you need not approach the idea of steadying him to ground game with any trepidation.

As with the steadying of the rough-shooter's dog, you are doing little more than stealing the initiative from the dog at the crucial moment when he finds game. That is about the long and the short of it.

Some trainers employ the good old standby – the check cord – for this but, again, I reiterate, there should be no need for this if you are alert to him and he has achieved a satisfactory standard in the basics; and if he has not, then it begs the question – what are you doing intro-ducing him to ground game at this stage?

It is advisable to try to find ground that does not have too much ground game in residence, for simply by being continually con-fronted with it, the dog's excitement gets little chance to diminish in between 'finds', resulting in his finally succumbing to temptation. If you can procure a venue that could provide, say, eight to ten 'finds' for the dog in a two-hour hunt, that to my mind would be ideal. For whilst you do not want too much game, too little, on the other hand, and a young dog quickly becomes discouraged.

Hunt the dog as you would normally in a quartering lesson, into the wind, and hope that he gets a few minutes to settle down into his beat before he encounters game; for I maintain that even with an experienced dog, especially with a spaniel in a field trial, it is within the first couple of minutes' hunting that you are at the most risk. For they are liable to riot much more readily in those first few minutes, before they have settled down, than at any other time.

Be attentive to his every move; be on your guard at the slightest deviation in style or speed, for he will indicate by his demeanour when he is getting scent, and be ready with your stop whistle. It is better to be too quick with the whistle than to be too slow for, with the latter, you are too late – in all probability all you will see of your dog is his tail-end disappearing over the horizon.

At this juncture I would like to make it plain that whilst the other breeds may be trained, for the greater part, by artificial means –

indeed, those bred and trained purely with field tests in mind are a prime example – it is not so with the bird-dogs, for it is essential that once these dogs have been thoroughly schooled in the basics, they are introduced to and worked on live game.

On first introducing the rough-shooter's dog to fur, a great deal can be done in the rabbit pen, if used with some circumspection. Again, however, there are not many who own or have access to a rabbit pen, least of all the chap perhaps training his first dog. Those that do have the chance to work their dog in a rabbit pen would do well to take into account the fact that, due to both the proliferation of game and footscents in the pen, together with the restricted space, it is not the ideal venue in which to train a bird-dog. Over-indulgence will almost certainly curb his range of ground treatment; then again, due to repeatedly being dropped by whistle as game gets up in front of him, or his coming up on point, very often to vacant seats, he may become sticky. Furthermore, if you are too severe with a young dog regarding his pointing, whether it is recently vacated seats or not, this may lead to his 'blinking' game altogether. So you must be careful. Consequently, again I must advise you to play safe and, unless you are privileged to have access to a pen of expansive proportions, where the dog can be allowed freedom to range (I would say at least five acres), then forego the chance and train him in more natural conditions.

As with the training of any other breed and even allowing for the fact that when training a bird-dog live game is necessary, a little initiative and ingenuity can go a long way in 'manufacturing' what appears through the dog's eyes to be natural conditions.

The procedure known as 'dizzying pigeons' has, I have found, helped me whenever either I have not had ready access to suitable ground or I was giving a bird-dog advanced training at the wrong time of year (Spring, when the birds have paired, is best), to surmount the problem of giving the young dog sufficient practice in finding game and coming on point. Granted this entails extra work, but it is well worth it and I will deal with this in detail presently. There are dogs which, on first being cast off on a piece of good game-holding country with its added scent, react like one demented, high-tailing it all over the parish with little or no heed to the whistle or the handler. Should you be so unfortunate as to encounter this on your first outing, there are various avenues of remedy open to you.

First of all, immediately he bolts or illustrates that he is paying little heed to you, drop him on the whistle; if he ignores it, there is little you can do for, believe me, you have no chance of catching him in the act. Ignoring the stop whistle when only faced with the temptation of scent must be regarded as the most heinous of crimes, indicative that he has not the slightest respect for his handler. On noting this, stand still, forego blowing the whistle any more and do not give him the return whistle command either, for when he does return – and he must, sooner or later – we do not want him to be confused regarding the treatment he receives and why he is being reprimanded.

When he does return, put his lead on and, without a word to him, walk him to the spot where he was when you gave him the stop whistle command. Flap his ear back and give him two or three short, sharp blasts, at the same time a couple of good, hard whacks with the lead on the rump whilst grasping him with the other hand by the scruff of the neck will not go amiss. Command him to sit, then walk off and sit on the nearest boulder or wall for five minutes in full view of him, leaving him to think on the errors of his ways.

It is by no means unusual when casting the dog off after having had a little 'talk', to note a marked improvement in his attention to his handler. As soon as you note that he is beginning to go astray again, blast the stop whistle and repeat the operation. Nonetheless, even if he is reacting like a paragon of virtue, it is a good plan a few moments after such an altercation to drop him on the whistle, slowly walk out to him and, providing he has not moved, of course, make a great fuss of him. The benefits of this are two-fold. You are restoring any lost confidence he may have experienced and, at the same time, pressing home your point.

To return to the theme: once you have dropped him, allow, as always, the mandatory pause; then, with a patting motion in the air at your side, give him the recall whistle command and, as he approaches, cast him off to either side of you. The more consistent you are with this, the sooner he will realise what is required of him. It follows that if your motive for steadying him to fur is so that you can shoot it, then you must limit the area in which he hunts so that the game flushed is within shot, a regime which again is detrimental to the pointer's normal duties. The method whereby you steady him to fur is, therefore, in this instance, more or less exactly the same as that employed in steadying the rough-shooter's dog.

Ignoring fur

As I have indicated, this is, in my opinion, a much more natural progression in the training of the bird-dog; furthermore, far from undermining his achievements within the normal scope of the duties required of him, it is a definite advantage. For, by training him to ignore fur, he is less likely to become orientated to footscents and waste time pointing recently vacated 'seats'.

A hill or moor that abounds in ground game is ideal for the purpose. Hunt him as usual; obviously, if it is ground that contains ample stocks of game then it will not be very long before he encounters it. If it gets up whilst he is hunting and is sighted by him, blow your stop whistle and give him the verbal command to sit or, if he is out of earshot, the hand signal. Walk slowly up to him, endorsing the verbal command softly, then, as soon as the game is out of view and you have his attention, give a clear hand signal in the opposite direction from where the game has gone and tell him, 'gone away' – 'get-on'. Very often you will note that he is pointing a rabbit or hare in its seat, in which case you simply tell him 'no' – 'gone-away' and encourage him to hunt on.

The check cord, in this instance, can be a positive boon, especially if the dog insists on pointing fur and some dogs will insist for the rest of their lives even. There is little that can be done about this, for under no circumstances would I punish a pointer for pointing, any more than I would punish a retriever for retrieving. Letting him hunt whilst trailing the check cord gives you the opportunity (not always, I grant you) to get forward and pick it up whenever you notice that it is ground game that he has come up on point at. Grasping it, you would give him a firm jerk away from the squatting game, accompanied by the verbal 'no, gone away – get-on'. Whilst, as I have said, some dogs cannot be cured of pointing ground game, there are others who become really efficient in this respect and will ignore the ground game completely, yet be unerring on birds.

Introduction to birds

Without a shadow of a doubt, it is quite impossible to finish the training of a pointer without live birds and, just as surely, wild birds are best – grouse preferably, for they seem to sit better and give off a stronger scent than either pheasant or partridge.

There are many men and women, however, who like to train dogs purely for a hobby, enjoying the challenge, who may never shoot game; such people are normally to be found training a retriever or spaniel, for these can reach a very high standard of hand training, sufficient for them to be successful in field tests.

I feel sure that the pointer variety might enjoy a little more popularity if those who had not the access to game-holding ground knew that where there's a will, there's always a way, and the fact that you may not have ideal facilities, nor the inclination to shoot even if you had, need not dissuade you from training one of these fascinating dogs.

Fig. 18.   Make a 'nest' in the grass for him

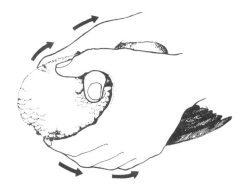

Fig. 19.   Dizzying the pigeon

In days gone by when, perhaps through lack of good ground or not having permission at a particular time of year to work a dog on the moors, especially in the middle of a shooting season, the dog trainer will not be made welcome; I have 'made do' by planting pigeon to afford a young dog practice at hunting and pointing.

To that end, it unfortunately entails keeping a few tame pigeon in a coop, with all the added responsibilities that this entails.

The procedure is quite simple though. Once you have your birds used to being handled, take one out of the coop at a time and carry it gently to your chosen site. Once there, tuck his head under a wing, then rock him gently around and around with a circling motion of your hands for approximately two minutes. Make a 'nest' in the grass with your foot and gently place the pigeon into it, arranging the grass around and over him as much as possible to give him added concealment (see Fig. 19), then go and get your dog. The pigeon will remain in this 'seat' for some considerable time, if he is not disturbed, for he will be 'dizzy' so there is no need for hurry. Returning with your young bird-dog, with or without the check cord – whichever you prefer – cast him off into the wind some distance from your 'plant'. The procedure as he comes up to point is as you would in normal circumstances. Encourage him to 'stay' as you make your way up to him slowly, then, after a pause, either proceed on past him by yourself and 'flush' the bird, or take the dog with you to make good his point. The pigeon will rise and fly back to the coop, quite unharmed by his experience. In this way you can provide a dog with a multitude of 'points' over a protracted period of time, together with the additional practice of dropping to the shot whistle and flush as the bird rises. In the dog's eyes, which is, after all, the only thing that matters, this seems quite natural. I have used this method on many occasions and can find no fault in it other than the extra work, in the training of not only bird dogs, but have also utilised it within the training of a spaniel. Where you have livestock you must also, on occasions, have deadstock and, whilst I never shoot my 'home-grown' pigeons, on their inevitable demise I have used them for a 'cold' retrieve as, unlike the woodpigeon, which is useless for this purpose because of its loose feathers, the domestic pigeon is quite tight feathered and the dogs will retrieve them with alacrity. As I have said, the gundog trainer has to be an opportunist and, if he is to be a success, must use a fair bit of initiative and inventiveness.

To return to the more natural environment, however, should you be fortunate enough to have the necessary facilities whereby you can introduce your dog to birds in their natural habitat, then of course the whole procedure is that much more simplified. The months of March and April are best for this, for the birds are paired off and sit better than at any other time of year. Casting him off in the prescribed manner, you would be vigilant, as always, to his behaviour. Should he indulge in 'false pointing' (this is usually because of the strong scent left by the birds recently having vacated the area), get him going again as soon as you are sure that he has made a mistake; young dogs are prone to do this because they haven't got sufficient experience in differentiating between body scent, that given off by a squatting bird, and strong air scent left at the site after they have departed. You may note, also, that on occasions he does not seem to be holding to his point very well, but is slowly moving forward; more often than not, this would appear to be caused by birds slipping away ahead of him without rising. Do not scold him on this; simply drop him on the whistle, walk forward and make sure that the birds have gone; then, after returning to him, cast him off with a 'gone away – get-on' in the opposite direction to that which you think the birds have taken.

Whilst remaining staunch on point, there are many dogs who will indicate that birds are restless by a tail-wagging action; you will, in time, notice that whereas a young dog will come on point quite close to birds, as he gets older, and therefore more experienced, he will indicate and draw up on point much farther back than before.

For the first few introductory excursions among the birds, the object is purely to give the dog practice in his ground treatment finding and pointing the quarry. You must not succumb to temptation and carry a gun, for in doing so you will be courting disaster. The shooting situation must remain for a little while longer a simulated one, utilising your starter pistol; in this way you can put the finishing touches to all that he has learned so far, without your attention being diverted from him.

Backing

Once you have reached a degree of efficiency with your dog, you may then introduce him to working in the company of another dog for the purpose of teaching him to 'back'. The 'partner' dog should be a very reliable, experienced dog; in other words, a dog more interested in his work than other dogs. You should be on the look-out for your younger dog, in the initial stages, tending to follow the other dog, for this is not the object of the exercise at all. He must be encouraged to work independently of the other dog *until he sees that other dog on point*; then he must stop. Again, may I remind you of the dog's foreshortened horizons so that you may make due allowance for it – for there will be many instances when dog (A) comes on point, but the younger dog hunts on, because he cannot see the older dog on point due to undulating ground. Obviously, there is not much point in dropping him in such circumstances, for he will not know why; therefore is not going to learn anything to his advantage. So, whenever you see the older dog pointing, take note of where your young dog is and the lie of the intervening ground.

In the normal course of events, as soon as the older dog 'points', attract the younger dog's attention, then drop him with your stop whistle and raised hand. Again, it should be obvious that, if you have been diligent in teaching him in the preparatory training as regards one hundred per cent obedience to the drop whistle, then you should experience little difficulty in this *the first few times*. But do not be lulled by this into a false sense of security for, just as with the rough-shooter's dog on first being confronted with the rabbit in a state of surprise will drop to the whistle on the first few; until he begins to get the idea of what it is all about, then may very often 'kick over the traces'. The young pointer is likely to obey the whistle until he begins to 'get the picture', thereupon to be spurred on by jealousy into disobeying and rushing in to 'steal the point' from the other dog. This can be an absolute pest for this reason: in first introducing him to 'backing', you would be wise to work him trailing the check cord. Whilst I don't think you are likely to be able to get a hold of it in the majority of cases, I think it is as well that you enlist its aid, for there will be times when you will get hold of it and thus prevent him from committing the crime. However, in the majority of cases he will beat you to it; you would do as you normally do, grab him by the scruff of the neck and drag him back to the spot where he should have dropped and point out to him the error of his ways in the prescribed manner.

Some dogs are natural 'backers', others are not and these therefore need a little more work to bring about the desired end. Then again, there are those that spend most of their time looking for the other dog to 'back'; these are virtually useless for working in conjunction with other dogs and, therefore, must be worked alone. In time they may sort themselves out, for I have more than a suspicion that initially this is due to lack of drive and experience, which encourages them to depend on the other dog. However, to persevere in working such a dog with others will only exacerbate the problem and he will become increasingly more dependent and lazy. You must work him alone until he indicates that he is becoming a very keen hunter, then try him in the company of other dogs once more. Once you have reached the stage where the young dog will stop at distance when he sees the other dog on point, you are almost 'home and dry'; on seeing him stop, quietly walk out to him, stroke him gently and speak to him in a soothing tone, telling him to 'stay'.

Any tendency in the young dog to move forward as the birds are flushed must be discouraged by dragging him back to his original position and a mild reprimand given.

When your pupil has accomplished a satisfactory standard in 'backing', all that remains to put the polish on his performance is to take him shooting, continuing his education, of course, throughout his first season.

Shooting over the 'bird-dog'

The time has come for you to assess your dog's performance so far and if there is a doubt in your mind at all regarding any aspect, it is now that you would do well to give a short refresher, before taking him shooting. Ask yourself the following questions:

160

Does he work a good beat with a range of approximately 137 metres (150 yards)?

Is he staunch on point?

Steady to flush, shot and fall?

Does he back on command or, better still, automatically?

If you are satisfied that he meets the necessary standard on these four points, then you may take him shooting and, providing you set out in a frame of mind which is to resolve that you are not so much going shooting, but enlarging upon the dog's education by giving him experience, you should have few problems.

It is wise that, as with the introduction into the shooting field of any dog, you take the precaution of not carrying a gun yourself for the first few outings, and enlist the aid of a reliable dog-less friend to do the shooting for you. In this way, you will not be distracted at some crucial moment and will, therefore, be able to devote all of your attention to the all-important details regarding the dog's work.

A 'good gun' is extremely beneficial; furthermore, the less excitable and noisy he is, the better. If he has not shot over a pointer before, you must explain beforehand what you require of him. Above all, before and after the 'flush', especially when the dog is on point, he must be quiet. Furthermore, collection of shot birds must be carried out in a casual, matter-of-fact manner and, should he have a 'runner' down, he must know that it is desirable to put another shot into it rather than run forward excitedly, as some 'guns' are wont to do, for nothing will unsteady a young pointer to the 'fall' more than a lot of noise or activity in the area.

When he comes up on point, proceed as you have been doing within the training regime; on reaching his side, speak to him soothingly; pause, slowly make your way forward to flush the game, either accompanied by the dog or commanding him to 'stay', proceeding forward yourself with the occasional glance to see that all is well with him. As the birds rise, drop him with your raised hand and whistle signal and keep him there as the birds fall. After a suitable interval of pause, the gun may go forward and collect the game. Once this is done and the gun is back in position, you may commence hunting again. Cast him off in the opposite direction from that where the game fell with a 'gone away – get-on'. Many young dogs will want to go and investigate the 'fall' area; as soon as you see that he has disobeyed your signal, drop him on the whistle, pause, hold his attention, then cast him off again and insist on it, even if it means dropping him again and, this time, showing him that you mean what you say by endorsing your verbal command with physical exertion, in that you grab him by the scruff and heave him in the desired direction with a firm 'no, gone away'.

Providing you have devoted enough attention to the training that has gone before, you should experience few problems in shooting over your bird-dog; time will put the polish on him for, as I have said, these are probably the easiest dogs of all the gundog breeds to train; furthermore, they are working within their natural environment, the most aesthetically pleasing to watch.

Flying hawks over pointers

This is a practice that has come back into vogue over the past two decades and it may be that sometime in the future, as more falconers realise the advantages, this may encourage a more prolific use of pointers.

I must confess that I have only had the opportunity on two occasions to work a pointer to a hawk, but I enjoyed the day thoroughly and found the trilling of the bells on the hawk's 'jessies', which are the long, trailing leather thongs attached to its legs, as he swooped and stooped overhead, most exciting.

My friend, who is a keen falconer, had a spaniel which was utilised to flush the birds; to my mind he would have been better left at home for, as soon as he was off the lead and after he had flushed the birds, he careered all over the parish. Enquiring as to why he was not unsteady to the fall and thwart the hawk, I was informed that initially he had been, but a Large Goshawk had taught him the error of his ways, and I don't doubt it. I certainly would not like to tangle with those talons. Apart from the problems entailed with the pointer being tempted by the spaniel's wild cavortions, I felt that whilst hawking was exciting, there seemed to be frequent, interminable delays caused by the hawk flying off after a failure and sitting on distant outcrops of rock. I am told that this is called 'sulking'. So, if you do get the opportunity to have a go with your pointer for a falconer, you will know what to expect and be able to make up your mind for yourself.

CHAPTER EIGHT

BREEDING

The sire dog

Due to well-intentioned human intervention into the breeding of our pedigree dogs, many survive which, by virtue of unfortunate character weaknesses, would undoubtedly have perished in the natural selection of the pack environment.

Such dogs are very often of a 'bitchy' temperament and, due to their effeminacy, tend to be easier to train than their more masculine and challenging brethren. These are then, in the main, a positive boon to the inexperienced trainer, for they make little or no demands upon his limited expertise; such is their temperament that not only are they easier to train to a very high standard but maintenance of attained standards is much simplified also, for whereas a bolder dog may reach a very high standard of performance, difficulty in maintaining that standard may be experienced by the trainer as the dog gains experience in the field.

The bolder dog will wish to use his initiative and is quite likely to do so, thus demanding more expertise from his handler in curbing his natural aptitudes. It follows, therefore, that due to the ease with which the softer dog can be handled, success in the field trial scene does not elude them and, consequently, it is by no means unusual to see such a dog attain the title 'field trial champion'.

Timidity is an inherent fault, however, and as such is the end product of a double-recessive gene, one from either of parents that have paired. The single recessive gene is subservient and is masked by the dominant gene until such time as it finds a partner to draw strength from, to influence inherent characteristics in the progeny. Therefore the recessive gene may be carried in the dormant state from generation to generation and not manifest its undesirable influence until it is paired with another recessive gene. As a result, the sensitive dog, whilst he may be a pure dream to shoot over and highly intelligent to boot, must not be bred from, for the fault will transmit, and once a fault has been introduced into a family, it is extremely difficult to eradicate.

The author 'under battle conditions'. *(Malcolm Morgan)*

Let us consider the bolder dog: he could be, and very often is, quite a handful; nevertheless, intelligence does not pass them by either. Such dogs have been known to possess many more all-round talents than their softer opponents in the competitive sphere, yet, by their abundance of exuberance, or flair for embellishing their training due, perhaps, to an attitude of 'the devil take the hindmost – for today is a special day', they defeat themselves. This is a well-known syndrome which has been aptly dubbed 'trial-mindedness' and is directly attributable to the dog of superior intelligence in that he has the wherewithal to differentiate between the trial day and the ordinary shooting day and realises that, on the trial day – for some reason beyond his limited powers of comprehension – master seems to let him get away with deeds that would normally incur his wrath and bring about certain retribution. Nevertheless, as such, this could be classed more of a fault in the preparation for field trials, not an inherent fault; it is a great pity that by being 'bloody-minded' on a trial day, such dogs rarely attain the limelight and, so, due to the lack of publicity, few bitches are put to them. Such dogs could well be stallions of the breed – that is, those with the ability to pass favourable traits on to their descendants – therefore, providing, as always, that there is a genetical tie-in to both sire's and dam's pedigree, they could be of great value.

It is most unfortunate that there is an ever-growing tendency for many of the contemporary breeders on the gundog scene to mate their bitches to the 'fashionable' dog each year, irrespective of his relationship to the bitch concerned. This, to my mind, is one of the most common contributory factors to the lack of continuity of inheritance, due to the abundance of outcross matings that go towards making up the preponderance of pedigrees today. Such breeders scoff at genetics, purely through their ignorance of the subject; but, like it or not, by virtue of indulging in any kind of breeding, they are applying genetics. The fault is in their methods, or complete lack of method. The motivation behind their choice of sire would appear to be two-fold: (a) in their inability to judge a dog for themselves – they require the judge's decisions to guide them – and, (b) if the sire is a field trial champion his title will sell the puppies. Without rhyme or reason, however, the inevitable result can only be a 'lucky chance' if the puppies turn out to be a success, their favourable aptitudes to be fragmented in their progeny by their being mated in turn to yet another famous, but unrelated, sire. The fact that their father is, or is not, a field trial champion, has no effect in itself upon the puppies' future capabilities. At best, awards obtained are no more than a guideline as to the sire's capabilities.

If you breed dogs you are involved in genetics and, no matter how well versed you become, you will always be subservient to nature and her laws; to flout them is to court disaster. You must ask yourself, 'Why was it that Mother Nature decreed that the law of natural selection was to be the taproot of evolution? That the weak, the abnormal should perish and only the strong survive?' Obviously, for the improvement of the species. Prudence decrees, therefore, that you do not ignore those laws and that you apply them, even if only as guidelines when contemplating a possible sire for your bitch. Field studies in the pack society leave little doubt that the submissive, sensitive dog would have occupied his place in the pack at a level so low that he would never have the opportunity to perpetuate his abnormalities, that is if he survived at all; in all probability he would have been cast out to fend for himself, inevitably to perish. At the other end of the social scale would be the dominant males, headed by the pack leader – the current champion, if you like – for he won and retained his position against all-comers and earned his rewards, *i.e.*, the pick of the females, so long as he remained the strongest. It was from these few dominant males that nature bred her pack for the future – the survivors of the fittest.

It is reasonable to assume that not only would the pack leader and his immediate subordinates be the fittest; to maintain their high rank and provide for the pack they would also require to be intelligent and enterprising.

So, whilst femininity is perfectly acceptable – indeed, desirable – in the bitch, it is completely unacceptable in the dog.

Naturally enough, in looking around for a possible sire, you would examine the 'goods' on display in the field trial 'shop window'; this in itself is no bad thing: on the contrary, it is the sensible thing to do. For, should a dog be able to advertise his capabilities by means of his success in these affairs, by so doing he provides the breeder with a yardstick by which the future breeding policies may be founded.

Here again, I must reiterate to emphasise the point: *providing that there is a genetical linkage* in his pedigree to that of your bitch. Allow me to explain this further, albeit for the sake of space, simplistically.

If a breeder, by virtue of possessing a bitch in which he cannot see a fault, seeks to reproduce her ilk, he tends to look for a sire of comparable excellence. This is more or less what the contemporary breeders are wont to do. Such matings can, and very often do, result in the birth of puppies of a very high quality. However, the difficulty arises in maintaining that quality in the *next generation* – the grandchildren, if you like, from the original mating pair. For, whilst the first generation were of a high quality, they are no more than the product of *chance*; such unrelated matings on occasion may bring together good, inherent qualities; what they cannot do is carry them on in sufficient numbers to dominate the genetical characteristics in the next generation, without being endorsed by line-breeding, *i.e.*, grand-daughter back to grand-father, grand-son back to grand-mother, or in-breeding (whether we like the prospect or not) by at least mating first-cousins.

Due credit must be apportioned to the show breeder in the application of sound breeding principles; for, even allowing that most breeders of the working dogs do not adhere to the principle that 'beauty is in the eye of the beholder', we must admit that as regards breeding for a specific, meritorious standard, albeit from their point of view, the show breeder can and does acquire and, just as importantly, *retains* the standards by which he may gain success in his chosen field.

It is, unfortunately, a fact and therefore has to be said, that we of the working dog fraternity fall rather short when it comes to breeding for the *continuity* of the qualities that we are desirous of acquiring in our dogs. For, simply by being too pre-occupied with mating what might be considered 'quality' to 'quality', using the results of the field trials together with no more than an 'eye for a dog', a talent which only a few possess anyway, we relegate our breeding regimes to that of a lottery. There is little, if any, method behind them, resulting in the majority of pedigrees being no more than a conglomeration of random matings – a hotch-potch. A system of trial and error, whereby pure chance produces at regular intervals a good dog whose qualities are promptly lost again in the subsequent welter of 'hit or miss' matings.

This, of course, is no doubt the reason why there would appear to be many more sensitive dogs appearing on the gundog scene over the past decade or so, for by such random selection there is little to halt or prevent a deterioration once the rot sets in.

Not only is there an ever-growing number whose only criterion for choosing their sire is the idea that if he is a field trial champion – or, better still, a Kennel Club champion – he must be the best dog for the job. There are those who still adhere to the Victorian theme called *Telegony*, *i.e.*, the theory that characteristics may be transmitted from a former sire to the puppies from a later sire to the same mother. Laughable though it may be to credit the humble spermatozoa with such mystical powers, it is akin to adhering to the ancient belief that if a pregnant woman is frightened by an animal, her unborn child will inherit some physical feature of that particular animal which, if universally subscribed to, would place genetics at the level of witchcraft. Nevertheless, as I had this theory expounded to me as late as 1980 by one of the United Kingdom's most well-known trainers, a chap who is most vociferous in his opinions, I cannot help but wonder how many believe it and, as a result, apply such ridiculous theories to their breeding programme.

Genetics is a very complicated science, certainly far too lengthy and involved to go into in any detail within the space of this Chapter; indeed, a weighty tome could be devoted in its entirety to the subject and still be incomplete. But there is nothing mystical about it; there is much that is not, as yet, fully understood; that is not to say that there is any likelihood of some magic formula coming to light as our knowledge progresses.

Nevertheless, if progress is to be made and maintained within the gundog groups, the newcomer to breeding must have, at the very least, a fundamental working knowledge of what he is doing, sufficient to enable him to form his own conclusions in a sound, sensible manner, that he may be independent of the high-blown theories. In any event, I hold firm to the conviction that even a little knowledge can only add to the satisfaction that the breeder will derive from the results of a successful mating based on informed judgement.

The following is no more than the 'nuts and bolts' of genetics and is included so that the novice breeder of serious intent may derive a basic understanding of the laws of genetical inheritance. By outlining the fundamentals, I hope to illustrate just how 'chancy' the majority of breeding methods are, that in time, with *further reading*, the newcomer may not only avoid 'the journey into the unknown' approach to breeding but that, by using a little insight and planning ahead, he may improve and maintain the qualities of the breed or breeds that he is interested in.

The Cell

This is the organism from which all living matter is formed. The animal cell consists of a nucleus wherein are housed the chromosomes and attendant genes. The nucleus is surrounded by protoplasm, the foodstore of the cell, which is encased in a thin, membraneous, elasticated wall. Each cell is capable of splitting into two, a process that is known as mitosis, thus forming two other cells which in turn divide into two to form four, and so on. This fission is rapid and goes on constantly and, as each cell divides from its parent cell, the chromosomes contained split longitudinally, dividing into two equal halves, one half being retained by the parent cell and the other uniting with the other half of the other chromosome in the infant cell.

Chromosomes

These are rather rod-like in appearance and arranged along their structure are rows of genes arranged in pairs; it is these genes that transmit the physical and intellectual characteristics from parent to puppy.

The Reproductive Process

The cell division that occurs when the male and female cells unite and fertilise each other is slightly different in that the two cells divide, each half containing equal numbers of chromosomes and genes but, in this instance, only fifty per cent of the number contained in the original cell. One new cell from each parent, male and female, then unite to form the egg-cell, the ovum, which thus contains the same number of chromosomes and genes as each parent, but to a different pattern and combination.

It is generally believed that for every characteristic there is a gene to influence it; furthermore, that these genes may be dominant or recessive. That is to say, if you had mated a black dog to a yellow bitch and the resultant litter were all black, then it would be fair to assume that the genes influencing the black were dominant and that the genes affecting the yellow were recessive. However, the pups – whilst black – may still carry the recessive gene for yellow; and so it is that, due to our ignorance of the recessive genes' presence, which may be carried in the dormant state from generation to generation, it is not unusual to mate two blacks and produce a litter of blacks and yellows. For the sake of illustrating the point, I have used the physical characteristic of colours.

We of the working dog fraternity, however, are more concerned with the less visual characteristics, such as nose, intelligence, temperament, mouth, *etc.* Nevertheless, the same genetic rules apply. Consequently, a trait may lie dormant for one or more generations, only coming to the surface when that particular gene affecting the specific characteristic is united with a similar gene.

To put it in as plain language as possible: if you had a bitch which, as far as you could determine, had no fault and neither her father nor mother had apparent faults, you could in all good conscience breed from her and expect quality puppies from a sire of comparable virtue. For hypothesis, let us assume that, unbeknown to you, farther back on the prospective sire's pedigree there is a dog or bitch that had a reputation for 'yipping'. The fact that his or her descendants had not displayed this tendency in no way signifies that it has been bred out, for should your bitch also possess the recessive gene then there is every likelihood that the gene from the male line could combine with the gene from the female line to form what is termed a double recessive gene, thus reinforcing the tendency to 'yip' in some, not necessarily all of the, puppies. The puppies which belonged to the same litter, however, even though they may never give tongue in their entire working lives, still carry the gene for yipping; consequently, if they in turn are bred to another dog that also possesses the recessive gene, the inherent fault is thus carried forward down through the family tree.

This example again only deals with the result of one set of genes, but in each living thing born there is a complexity of instructions passed on to the progeny from both parents and, due to nature's way of random genetic pairings, no two individuals are ever duplicated.

First generation puppies derive fifty per cent of their genetic heritage from each parent, the gene pairings varying from puppy to puppy, so that whilst closely resembling one another, no two are completely alike either in appearance, intelligence or character.

The second generation therefore inherit twenty-five per cent from each grandparent and a correspondingly greater permutation of genetic pairings has taken place. Thus, within the confines of two generations in one family group, genetical inheritance can be seen to manifest itself in a wide and complex variety of ways; nevertheless, the similarity of the genes contained within one family can be seen in the strong family traits that emerge. This alone is indicative that the genes that owe their origin to one common source in pairing with one another, tend to hold true to a pattern. Intelligent observation also shows that on introducing foreign genes, *i.e.*, those from an unrelated source, the pattern begins to fragment and, should the progeny in turn be mated to unrelated animals, the genetic inheritance factor will fragment further and will not breed true to type.

It does not require a genius, therefore, to realise that even in dealing with closely related animals, dabbling in genetics can be likened to dipping one's hand into Pandora's box; for what may come out is never certain – the only certainty is that by 'dabbling', you have set in motion an irreversible chain of genetical inheritance which will alter all that which comes after. An arresting thought, and one that should indicate that, if dabble you must, then you should at least apply some thought to your responsibility to the breed, if not your customers.

In mating related animals, the chances of similar genes (*Homozygous*) pairing together and therefore endorsing one another's influence on the progeny's inheritance are greater. This is a process that is by no means selective in that whilst meritorious traits may be inherited, undesirable traits may also be acquired or perpetuated, indeed exacerbated, should there be a genetic fault apparent or dormant in one or other of the parents. Therein, perhaps, is the reason as to why so many breeders fight shy of in-breeding methods. But it is not the method that is at fault; in my opinion, it is in the breeders' ineptitudes or lack of application regarding genetics and their manipulation of the laws governing breeding, wherein lies the fault. Undoubtedly, by its whimsical nature, genetics is not the 'magic formula' for success, but it does provide methods whereby the breeder may set his or her sights on a particular goal, which is preferable to the indiscriminate use of random, unrelated sires, to be content if occasionally a good dog or litter should result. For this, by any stretch of the imagination, cannot be construed as success.

On the other hand, if you had a bitch which proved herself your ideal in every respect, but perhaps left a little to be desired as far as style was concerned, on deciding to take a litter from her, you would look for a sire which was renowned for his exceptional style; if he were a field trial champion, then well and good, for it is unlikely that he would have manifested a serious fault, setting aside for the moment that he could be a carrier of undesirable genetical inheritance. If this dog had a genetic link to your bitch's pedigree – in other words, he was related to her – then there is a good chance that he would carry homologous genes to those of your bitch, thus increasing the percentages of two combining; and if his genes for his characteristic – style – were dominant, the puppies might well display a degree of style superior to that of their mother. The danger being, of course, that if he also carried the recessive genes for a (by our standards) fault, and your bitch also carried the same recessive genes, there would, in all possibility, be one or two, or even more, puppies born who would manifest that particular fault. A risk, albeit a calculated one, in any line or in-bred mating. Such progeny would be unsuitable for future breeding; that is, every member of that litter – for they are carriers of the inherent fault. It is all too easy to decry the stud dog in such instances; however, blame cannot be apportioned in such a way, for without embarking on back-cross matings, there is no way of determining whether it comes from one or both parents.

Let us assume, however, that the mating was successful in that none of the puppies showed undesirable traits and, indeed, a few showed that they had inherited an aptitude for style, it would be one of the latter that you would retain for future breeding purposes – and let us say that it is a bitch. Again, in seeking a possible mate for this bitch, you would seek a sire with an abundance of style and, again, with a genetic tie-in to your bitch's pedigree, preferably within the first three generations. If the resultant litter again did not manifest any undesirable traits, yet again there was an increase in their style, you might consider that by methodical means you had acquired what you set out for. That is, success – for you have not only improved upon what you started out with, you have maintained it.

Choosing the best of that litter, again a bitch, you could then mate her to a dog that was unrelated, *i.e.*, the out-cross mating. However, in the choice of this particular sire you may introduce a recessive gene into your strain which, in the genetical re-shuffling, could find another of its ilk from your bitch which until then had been masked by being singular to the stronger, dominant genes; however, in the double recessive state, it now has the power to make itself felt and, so, choosing a sire is a matter for much dipping into the think tank together with a great deal of research into his background, if any hope of overall progress is to be entertained. A very good guide can be taken from the puppies that he is leaving behind, for if pups from two or three different bitches of unrelated pedigree showed a tendency for a particular fault, then the odds are on that fault coming from the dog. This, of course, could be construed as the cowardly approach, for it necessitates that some other poor souls take the plunge before you do; I prefer to call it the prudent approach, for it is always better to be safe than sorry.

You would be wise to cast a speculative glance at the progeny from a prospective sire's brothers and sisters also, should you have the opportunity, for obviously if a particular fault persists in cropping up in the puppies from different bitches that had hitherto never manifested itself, that, then, would be a sure indication as to its source. The fact that the fault had as yet not shown itself in the puppies from the dog that you are contemplating using in no way indicates that he does not possess it; indeed, it is very likely that, even should it not come out in the litter from your bitch, it will appear in their puppies, for he is very likely to be a 'carrier'. So circumspection is always the order of the day, especially when considering a 'stranger' to your bitch's pedigree, for chances are you will be much more versed in her ancestry than you are in his.

Neither should you ever lose sight of the fact that, in advertising a dog's merits for the purpose of stud, the sire owner's motive is stud fees; experience has taught me that very rarely will the owner of a dog at stud tell the bitch owner that his dog has a fault. There are very few dogs which attain the distinctive title 'Field Trial Champion', who do not get advertised as available at stud almost immediately. Would it not be rather naive of us to believe that *all* those dogs are faultless? Attainments in field trials are, at best, only *indicative* of quality; it must never be taken for granted that simply because a dog has had the good fortune to win a couple of trials, he is necessarily quality – for to do so would be to credit the system of field trials as foolproof, and these affairs are anything but.

I must confess that in my early days I adhered, as most seem to do, to the belief that in using a field trial champion or, at the least, a field trial winner, at stud, I was going to the best available; experience has taught me otherwise. For in a highly competitive and mercenary world, the lure of extra money can prove decisive for some. Consequently, unfortunate though it is, there are people who, purely through a sequence of fortunate circumstances all coming together on a trial day, promptly take advantage of their good fortune by cashing in on the stud fees, with little or no regard being paid as to whether or not the dog has an inherent fault. Such people can only be described as rapacious opportunists. As I have said, there is good and bad in all things, so be it.

From what I have said, I hope to convey to you that the maintenance of any given trait in your dogs is tenuous enough when dealing with animals that have a genetic link and that, by a process of random selection of sires, the percentages against acquiring success and then maintaining the qualities are very much more increased.

In searching for a suitable sire you are primarily interested in the instinctive talents that he is liable to pass on to his progeny.

Therefore, in considering a dog that has never competed in public, you are pretty much on your own; you are left to trust your own judgement, for you have no other guideline. At least, in employing a field trial dog, his merits, or lack of them, are displayed for you in his achievements; it is for your discernment as to whether you are prepared to accept them at face value or not. I prefer to see a dog and judge for myself. It is only courteous, on deciding to view a particular dog, to make an appointment and, when doing so, you should make it quite clear that your bitch is not due yet and that the purpose of your visit is that you may see the dog and, if possible, have a short demonstration. Such a request will not meet with universal approval and it would be remiss of me to give the impression that it would. Indeed, there are some who will be, to say the least, uncivil in their refusal. Nevertheless, providing your intentions are genuine then, as a prospective client you are entitled to the request; needless to say, if for any reason you are fobbed off, you would look elsewhere.

It is also advisable to prevent urgency influencing your judgement; to view all possible sires well in advance of when your bitch will be due to come into season.

On first seeing the dog, it should strike you immediately that he *looks like a dog*; he should look *masculine*, not a weedy-looking individual. Look for a good eye, one that has a kindly look about it. He should come out of his kennel with an air of get-up-and-go about him – a merry, perky attitude. A dull, lethargic, washed-out sort of gait is decidedly off-putting. If he pays little or no heed to you, then fair enough – why should he? – for a good stud dog is 'king of the walk', he should be haughty. Take special heed, however, if he should show signs of unwaryness and don't be placated by the time-worn cliche that 'he doesn't like strangers'. The fact that you are a stranger is of little concern to a good dog; if anything, he should be, and I would prefer that he were, disdainful.

When observing him going through his paces, it is desirable that he goes about his duties as though he enjoyed them; if he is one of the retriever breeds, he should be attentive to his handler, get out smartly, use his nose to find the 'retrieve' and, if it is lying in a difficult piece of ground, perhaps a 'blind' retrieve, watch for him to look for assistance from his handler and as to how he reacts to his instructions. Now quality of execution may be highly desirable; indeed, if you are viewing a field trial contender of any worth, you would expect a degree of slickness; nevertheless, a dog should not be condemned out of hand simply because he falls short on the performance aspect. Indeed, there are many dogs which, due to trainer or handler inefficiency, or complete lack of training – with the correct pedigree background – are excellent potential sires. Inefficiency is not necessarily *inherent*. What you must do is determine the quality of the dog's nose, mouth, temperament, style and courage during your short demonstration. If, for instance, you were watching a hunter, you would pay special attention to his attitude to cover, reluctance or failure to enter would naturally influence your judgement of him as a sire quite severely. On the other hand, if he entered at speed, yet *looked as though he was searching for game*, then you would be pleased with that aspect of his performance. You would look for signs of hard-mouth, naturally, also his reaction to shot; observe him as he delivers – did he slow his pace and perhaps show signs of reluctance to deliver? On seeing a dog hunt, you would prefer to see him quarter his ground within shot; however, should he show signs of uncontrollability, that neither is necessarily an inherent trait, it may just be that his handler does not measure up to the dog.

In short, let your eye be the judge: if you like what you see and there is a genetic reason for your interest in him and he has not shown you a failing in the inherent department, then there is every probability that, notwithstanding his attainments, or lack of them, he will be beneficial to the puppies.

The brood bitch

As I have said, within the gundog breeds there are groups that have suffered by the human's intervention. It is a sad fact that, should a particular breed become fashionable, it is generally to the overall detriment of its kind. This is simply due to the haphazard breeding of puppies by the general public who do not have the knowledge required, and the puppy farmers who cash in until the breed's popularity wanes, by which time they are onto another 'good thing'. I hasten to add that if the breeding of puppies is carried out in a judicious manner, the bitch and her puppies are given the proper care and attention, there is no profit in rearing puppies simply to supply a demand. The puppy farmer or dog dealer makes his profit by breeding from a bitch *every time she comes in season*, which is normally twice a year. They are very often kept in squalid surroundings, little care or interest being devoted to time-consuming hygiene. Generally, the bitch is served sub-standard food and only lip service is paid by the breeder to any kind of weaning programme; his only interest being to get the puppies sold at as early an age as possible, for as much as he can get for them. Like the dog dealer who buys in and sells out, such people are a blight, not only on the poor unfortunate animals in their

174

care, but to the breed as a whole; they are not only to be despised, but avoided like the plague, for you will rarely get satisfaction from dealing with them. Without adequate legislation it is left to the individual conscience of those of you who wish to breed puppies as to how you treat them. Personally, I feel that if you are instrumental in bringing life into this world, you inherit the responsibility of ensuring that, within your capabilities, that life gets its entitlement. It is no excuse to dismiss neglect because it is 'just an animal'; as with each of us, they did not ask to be born, and if you are not prepared to allow the progeny their rights, then you have no right to bring them into the world in the first place. As with any activity, you will only get out of dog breeding, rewards in relation to the amount of thought and effort that you are prepared to devote to it. Undoubtedly, it is a time-consuming and very often expensive hobby; nevertheless, providing you are inquisitive enough and prepared to study the subject, you will discover its fascination and derive a great deal of pleasure from it.

You must breed for quality, otherwise there is no reason for getting involved for, as I have said, the rearing of puppies is just not cost-effective.

You may well ask, what is quality? How are you the novice, to recognise what is or is not class? Quality is a gem beyond price and just as rare. It is the quality that a few dogs possess that others do not – that extra *something*; it is an intangible, for you cannot point to it and say – that is quality. Out of literally hundreds of dogs that I have put through their training, I have only seen it three times. That is not to say that a dog that is not quality is a poor dog; not in the least; for there are multitudes of good dogs – whether they reach their peak performance or not, or whether they ever get the chance, is another matter. Indeed, I firmly believe that there are dogs which spend their lives on the hearthrug in front of the fire which, given the proper training, could show some of the 'quality' owned and trained by the narcissistic, the way home.

If you have a bitch, or dog, which has the requisite capabilities regarding their work and they perform to the same high standard consistently, show no faults – added to which is displayed a degree of unusual panâche and initiative – then you could safely assume that that is quality. It goes without saying that, should a dog have a fault, no matter what – by the widest stretch of the most optimistic imagination it cannot be mistaken for quality.

It is a well-established fact that the strength of your kennels lies within the qualities of your bitches. The dogs are of secondary importance to any breeding programme, for if you do not own a quality sire you have the choice of the sire dogs nation-wide. Not so with bitches; you must possess quality; for to persevere in taking inferior bitches to quality sires will almost certainly only result in the perpetuation of faults. It is possible, by judicious selection of quality sires and a ruthless culling regime of sub-standard puppies over a protracted period of time, employing all the policies of line, outcross and the occasional inbred mating, to improve the quality of the bitch line. But when it is considered that, even when using top quality mating pairs, there is always the likelihood of an unexpected, undesirable genetic effect coming to light, even after a generation or two, the folly of using sub-standard animals at any time should be more than apparent.

In short, you can always employ the services of the best available stud dog for your particular bitch's breeding and, providing she is quality, your successful matings will far exceed the failures. '*One fault is one fault too many*'. If you note that your bitch has an *inherent* fault then you cannot, you must not, breed from her.

I know it is difficult not to succumb to sentiment when looking at the apple of your eye but woe betide you if you do, for in so doing, should you perpetuate and spread the fault, you will have grave difficulty in living it down, if ever and, in the future, when perhaps you are selling quality, you may well regret ever having bred that litter so long ago. There are the 'fly-by-night' types, but they rarely enjoy any success and, if they do, it is usually short lived.

Nothing worthwhile is easy, or it would soon lose its interest; so if you know that your bitch has a fault – if you cannot bring it upon yourself to get rid of her, well that's understandable: you can console yourself in her company as a shooting bitch. If you still intend to indulge in the breeding side, then you will have to procure another bitch, preferably from another blood-line, and start again.

As with a sire dog, the brood bitch should not only be a good example of her breed, she should be kept in tip-top physical condition – not too fat or flabby, nor too thin; her muscles should be kept well-toned. Such standards can only be achieved and maintained by good food, regular exercise – in short, a happy and active life. To breed with a bitch in poor body condition will certainly make the birth that much more difficult and, not uncommonly, can cause the death of the bitch.

At a reasonable interval before mating it is wise to ensure that your bitch's inoculations are up to date; if a 'booster' is required, it is essential that it is attended to at this time. It is at this time, also, that treatment for worms should be undertaken; to leave these treatments until after mating can be very dangerous and it is not unknown for abortion to result.

176

The bitch in 'season'

Most female pups come into season anytime after the age of six months old and usually, with most breeds, it is easily recognisable; cockers, however, tend to be a little less obvious, showing little or no signs of having their first 'heat'. However, should you own a dog, or there are dogs in your neighbourhood, they will be most obliging in letting you know that they find her more interesting than usual.

The 'season', or oestrum, lasts approximately 21 days, the most fertile period falling between the ninth and fourteenth day; therefore the most propitious moment for mating is the eleventh day. Nevertheless, it is possible for a bitch to conceive at any time during these six days and it is truly amazing how far the scent from a bitch can travel during this time; therefore you are well advised to take precautions against the unwelcome attentions of the roving dog population in your area. The best plan is to keep her confined to the kennel or house, except for restricted and supervised exercise and, if you are having trouble from the local 'strays', spray the entrances to the garden, house, *etc.*, with one of the proprietary anti-mate deodorant sprays. These are readily available from pet stores, are extremely potent and have a similar effect to tear-gas on any dog who ventures too close. Naturally, should you not intend having her mated during that particular season, you would spray her, also, with this at the base of her spine, tail, between her hind legs and underneath. Take care not to get the spray on your hands or clothes, as it is rather an unpleasant smell and clings for some time, as it is designed to do.

Apart from the cockers, many people have difficulty in recognising when their bitch is coming on heat and tend to start counting the days from perhaps the third day. Indeed, sometimes they are completely unaware that she is in season until she is actually 'standing'. For those of you who do have difficulty, here are a few guidelines. As their season approaches, many bitches become progressively more affectionate. On the other hand, they may react by becoming rather naughty, whereas normally they are very obedient; in other words, downright bloody-minded, hence the term 'bitchy'. So be on the lookout for any dramatic personality change at or around the time that you would expect her to come 'on'.

As I have said, the physical signs can vary in degree from breed to breed, also between individual bitches. However, as a rule, there is a slight swelling of the vulva, accompanied by a minute discharge of pinkish coloured fluid. At or around the fourth day, you should have your suspicions confirmed by a marked increase in the swelling; you may then, with confidence, count from the first day. Should your arithmetic be correct, the bitch should be ready for the dog on the tenth, eleventh or twelfth day from when you first noted the tell-tale signs.

Mating

What should be a perfectly normal and problem-free act is, very often due once again to our meddlings, not at all the case. For instance, a maiden bitch put to an inexperienced dog, whilst displaying every sign of being quite keen, may react in a hostile manner as soon as any attempt is made by the dog, which is discouraging to the extent that he may lose interest altogether, especially if he is not a forceful type of character. On the other hand, a dog skilled in the art of male prostitution may persevere until his sexual excitement reaches its crescendo and he ejaculates prematurely, whereupon, as far as he is concerned, the bitch holds no further attraction.

There are occasions when, purely through having an audience of gawking humans, both dogs refuse to comply – which is not all that surprising either, if the trouble is taken to give it a thought. Surprising though it may seem, dogs like a period of courtship; animal lust plays very little part in the proceedings – a bitch likes to be wooed and, understandably, is not too keen on being raped by a strange dog.

It is feasible, also, that a maiden bitch taken from the nest environment at eight weeks of age, brought up in the family home, for the larger part segregated from her kind, *may not regard herself as a dog* – remember her limited powers of reasoning. If so, pitched in with this strange creature, she's going to wonder just what is going on; in which case, conflicting emotions and instincts are hardly surprising.

Not all the problems arise from the bitch and her owner, though, non-matings have been known to stem from the sire owner's ignorance and mismanagement also. A classic case comes to mind readily: the sire and his owner had been away trialling for four days, which meant that the dog had to reside in the car and subsist on meagre rations (for the purposes of travelling). Returning home after an overnight journey of 500 miles, the dog serves a bitch that very day. The next day, both owner and dog are *out shooting all day*, then on the following day the dog, who is in poor physical condition anyway, is expected to mate *another* bitch. When he shows no interest, his owner then blames the bitch. Takes all kinds, I suppose.

At the very least, a dog at stud should have a restful period *before and after* mating and he should be fed on the best; after all, it is not unusual for a busy stud dog to earn more than his master per week, so it could be argued that he has paid for his food.

Anxiety from the owner can transfer to the dogs and this alone can

178

be the prime factor in discouraging them from mating. Very often, if things don't go according to plan, the bitch either has to be held, or bound and gagged in extreme cases, to assist the dog in mating; such a course of action is always a last resort and, although generally a success, it is by no means unusual to find that this procedure turns the dog off also.

It is always more satisfactory for nature to take its course in as natural a way as circumstances will permit. To this end, if the dog and bitch can be introduced to one another within an enclosed and secure space, such as a large concrete square exercise area, and left alone, that they may gambol around and get to know one another though, unbeknown to them, under surveillance for a period of time; in nine cases out of ten, human interference will not be required.

After mating there is usually a period of time when the two dogs will remain connected, standing rump to rump; this is known as the 'tie' and is due to a swelling unique to the canine, which takes place in the dog's penis. Whilst failure to tie does not necessarily mean that the mating is unsuccessful, generally speaking the longer the tie the better the chances are that the bitch will conceive. Under no circumstances should a dog and bitch be forcibly separated during the tie, for internal damage to the bitch and injury to the dog is most likely. To be reasonably certain that the mating has been a success it is a good plan to put the dog and bitch together again the next day; however, due to the vast distances that have to be covered these days to reach a suitable stud dog, this is not always practicable. Nevertheless, should your bitch not conceive from the union, then it behoves the sire owner at some suitable, pre-arranged time in the future, to furnish your bitch with another mating from the same sire, free of any further charge, or return the stud fee to you. Unfortunately there is increasing evidence to suggest that this is another practice that is steadily falling into disuse.

Not only is it important for a sire to have a period of rest after mating, it is doubly important that the bitch be allowed a quiet time for a few hours also; again, due to distances involved, such practice may be inconvenient, if not quite impossible and, therefore, if you must travel immediately after she has been mated, it is essential that she has as smooth a journey as possible; for it is not unknown for a bitch to expel the majority of the sperm if thrown about in the back of a speeding car.

Gestation

Pregnancy, or gestation, lasts for sixty-three days; the birth of the puppies may occur a few days before or a few days after the sixty-third day and, whilst I do not worry overmuch about a premature birth, other than the extra supervision and care of the pups that this may entail, I do tend to have a feeling of disquiet if the bitch 'goes over her time', and it is my contention that as soon as the sixty-third day has been and gone with no puppies born, a visit from the vet is necessary. Very often all that is required is an injection of Pitacin; but then again, it can and very often is something much more serious – play safe at this time; twenty-four hours can make all the difference between saving and losing your bitch.

Due to the prevalence of the syndrome known, for want of a suitable medical term as 'fading pup', which I believe can be the result of the haemolytic streptococci – although recent research has indicated that it can be due to a variety of factors – I think again that it is prudent to take precautions, experience having taught me that to attempt chemotherapy once the symptoms have manifested themselves is very often unsuccessful. Therefore, within three or four days at the latest after having the bitch mated, take her to your vet and ask for a vaginal swab to be taken for a culture and sensitivity test, explaining why you wish it; for it is by no means unusual for the veterinary profession not to be conversant with all the canine complaints and the 'fading' syndrome, although quite well known, *preventative* methods, as far as I can determine, are not in wide use.

A healthy litter will snuggle up to mum and suckle eagerly.

Should the culture prove positive then it is a simple matter for your vet to inject your bitch with the antibiotic indicated. Again, one week before the puppies are due to be born, a further injection of the antibiotic should be given, or a seven-day course of the appropriate antibiotic tablets may be crushed into her food.

During gestation, normal exercise and diet are the order of the day; do not, for goodness' sake, stuff her full of food – this is not required, and a fat and flabby bitch will have a difficult delivery. Exercise should be modified as soon as signs of pregnancy make themselves apparent, which is usually around the fifth week; from then on, any attempts to jump or squeeze through under fences, *etc.*, should be discouraged.

From the sixth to the ninth week of pregnancy the puppies inside the womb will grow and thus make correspondingly increasing demands on the bitch's resources of food. From this time on her meals should be split into three, or even more, throughout the day, increasing by roughly half her usual amount per day overall. This is to prevent her from added discomfort in loading her stomach with one large meal. It is not necessary to administer vitamin supplements should the bitch be in good condition; nonetheless, a 'fad' of mine is to give extra adexoline, starting three days before the puppies are due; I would not recommend that this is done any earlier, for by so doing the puppies may be so well developed as to present added complications during birth.

Instinctively a bitch will seek out a quiet, secluded area in which to have her pups and, to add to her peace of mind, it is better to have her settled into a routine and sleeping in the whelping box for at least a fortnight before her time is nigh.

The whelping box

This should be of sound construction, preferably tongued and grooved boarding, measuring, for the average sized dog such as a spaniel, 1.2m × 1.2m × 0.6m (4ft × 4ft × 2ft) high on three sides and the front constructed in such a way as to allow the addition of boards as time goes on (see Fig. 20). Depending on the breed will determine the size of the box; a Gordon setter, for example, would require a box of larger dimensions, such as 1.8m × 1.2m × 0.6m (6ft × 4ft × 2ft). In addition to the existing floor of the box, cut a piece of three-ply to dimensions of exactly 1.3cm (½in) smaller around its perimeter, so that it can be dropped easily into the box; the reason for this will become apparent to you later. A moulding 5cm × 5cm × 5cm (2in × 2in × 2in) should be measured and cut exactly to fit around the floor

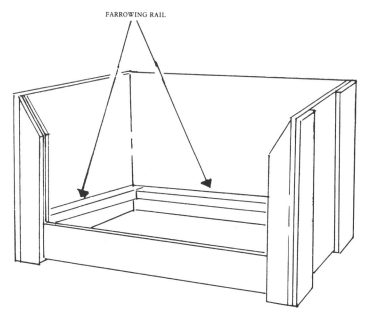

FARROWING RAIL

Fig. 20. The whelping box

and screw holes drilled both in the moulding and correspondingly in the lower walls of the box. The ply and moulding, plus the screws, should then be stored for future use in a convenient place.

There are those who, no doubt in an effort to cut costs, will attempt to utilize any old cardboard box or tea chest for the purpose; believe me, these are completely inadequate and will almost surely present problems at a time when you can well do without any more.

Should your bitch be a kennel dog then all the better; simply put the box into her kennel in sufficient time for her to get used to it. The house dog is quite another matter for, amidst the noise and goings-on in the average household, she is less likely to settle down and get on with the job than she would if she were in a more secluded and private place.

A heat bulb of the infra-red variety is essential, as hypothermia in newly-born puppies is very common and can kill. It is preferable to procure the red-coloured bulb for this is kinder to the puppies' eyes once they are open, than the white or clear type of bulb. Position this heat-lamp approximately three to four feet from the floor of the box, the object being that the floor should have the chill off it, but that neither the bitch nor the puppies should experience any discomfort from over-heating. A few days before the puppies are due, give the bitch a tablespoonful of liquid paraffin to open her bowels and to prevent constipation; this will assist in an easier delivery.

The bitch in whelp

Instinctively, the bitch will want to build a nest, so as soon as she begins to scratch around in the box, provide her with a few newspapers; she will tear these into pieces and strew them around in the box. She will indicate the pending arrival of the puppies, sometimes as much as twenty-four hours beforehand, by her restlessness and bouts of stertorous breathing. Do not under any circumstances, put straw into the box. This is almost certain to result in puppies becoming lost and smothered by the bitch lying on them. Straw is a material that I have no use for at any time. It becomes soiled and wet in no time at all, encourages a dog to wet in its bed and is a natural breeding place for all kinds of vermin.

Birth is a natural process and so there is no need for undue anxiety or interference; in fact, far more harm than good will come of fussing around her. Left alone, the bitch will get on with the job, but it is wise to pop in quietly every now and again to keep an eye on things.

At this stage, be on the alert and keep an eye open for signs of a dark green discharge; if this is present *before* the first pup is born, call in the vet immediately, for almost surely things are not what they should be. However, a green discharge after the first pup is born, or during the birth of later puppies, is by no means unusual and, consequently, in the majority of cases nothing to worry about.

Plenty of cool drinking water should be placed within easy access; give her food if she will take it – most bitches refuse food and this is normal, so when in doubt, don't bother. She will eat the placentas and, nauseating though it may seem to you, this again is nature's way; these 'afterbirths' have the nutrients *i.e.,* high protein, to give her the stamina to see things through. Without getting into a panic, as soon as the first puppy is born remove the soiled wet newspapers, replacing them with a flat wad of clean newspapers; this should be done slowly and calmly – very often a bitch will not want you to touch her puppy, so do not be alarmed if she picks the puppy up in her mouth; let her and, as you are clearing up, speak to her in a soft, reassuring manner. After taking away the soiled newspapers (and these must be removed out of her reach or smell, or she will be distracted by the scent, to the extent of her delaying the rest of her deliveries), leave her alone. Puppies should arrive at regular intervals of between one half-hour to two-hourly intervals, providing that she is left alone and there are no unusual noises to worry her. However, should there be a delay of more than two hours and she begins to show signs of distress, get your vet to have a look at her, for there could be a dead pup or a puppy inside lying across the neck of the womb. That is not to say that you should go poking around yourself; this is very much a job for your vet, and it may even mean a caesarian section.

In the vast majority of cases, everything will go off smoothly with the minimum of assistance from you.

A healthy litter will snuggle up to mum and suckle eagerly; they will have a shell-pink colour on their muzzles and paws, blueness denotes hypothermia and is a pretty sure sign of a poor 'doer'. Prolonged squeaking is also a very bad sign; this usually accompanies fading pup, which I have mentioned earlier; on the other hand, it could be a sign of hunger – whatever, if it continues you are better to call in the vet.

I am a firm believer that if the litter survives the first twenty-four hours then, except for the one in a hundred incident, I am over the worst. But it is during this time that you should keep a look-out for any untoward signs, such as distress in the bitch, or the onset of *Eclampsia*, which is a condition which tends to be inherent and the root cause is low calcium in the blood. It may occur any time between a few days before the birth and up to two weeks after – rarely after this time, although there is always the isolated incidence. The onset is indicated by the bitch becoming restless, excitable, whining and stertorous breathing. This is followed by an increasing unsteadiness when she is on her feet. The body temperature is likely to be high. She will probably fall over and lie there panting, salivating, and will commence a 'galloping' motion with her legs; at this stage she is nearing the end and will die of exhaustion if the vet is not called in. Treatment is by intravenous injection of calcium. Whilst the bitch is still busy delivering the pups, you can prepare the piece of three-ply mentioned earlier for its purpose. Cut a piece of clean, stout sacking so that it overlaps the board by approximately 5cm (2in.) all the way round; stretch it taut and pin it with drawing pins on the underside of the board, making sure that there are no folds or wrinkles on the upper side.

You are now ready to put into operation the next phase of your plan, which is as soon as you can be reasonably certain that the last puppy has arrived (which is indicated by the bitch lying quietly with her pups snuggling in a heap, probably asleep, close to her body); the person she identifies as her master should then quietly take her from the kennel for a short walk on a lead. The assistant should slip into the kennel, unseen by the bitch, remove the puppies and place them in a cardboard box on the bottom of which should be a warm hot-water bottle wrapped in a towel. The soiled newspapers are then removed from the whelping box and taken away; the bottom of the box is wiped with disinfectant and the piece of sacking-covered three-ply dropped into position and secured by screwing the 5cm (2in.) moulding into position. The puppies should then be gently removed from their cardboard box and placed in a heap in the corner of the box from whence they came. The whole exercise should not take more than three to four minutes and it is important that this operation should be executed calmly, efficiently and in the minimum possible time, for the bitch will be reluctant to go out and leave her puppies and will be most anxious to return to them.

From this point on, your duties are simply to supply the bitch with adequate nourishment which she, in turn, will convert rapidly into liquid sustenance for her puppies. Again, it has to be realised that a large litter of growing puppies places a tremendous strain on the bitch's resources. Adequate, good quality, well-balanced nourishment is essential and it is no use giving it in the form of all-in-one food, or tinned meat; these are only a stand-by: milk and raw egg, baby foods, fish, meat, and all-in-one meals given in small, but adequate and frequent, amounts will compensate for the added demands from her puppies. The cleaning-up jobs in the box will be attended to by the bitch herself and it is important for you to know that it is necessary for her to lick the puppies' rear-ends; this stimulates bowel and bladder evacuation – a puppy cannot do this on its own for the first few days of its life, so remember this if you are hand-rearing, for you will have to stimulate the puppies' motions by simulating the mother's licking action with a swab of cotton wool.

Tails

At approximately four days old, puppies from breeds such as the spaniel or German short-haired pointer, require their tails docked. This is a bone of contention much gnawed at for the past few years by the veterinary profession.

By and large it is their opinion which, of course, as such, they are entitled to, that this constitutes a mutilation of the dog purely for the aesthetic pleasure of the owners. In the case of breed standards as laid down by the Kennel Club, show judges for the use of, I would agree wholeheartedly; that it is an unnecessary mutilation; and when I see these self-same vets performing the operation which very often, by their methods, results in something closely akin to a blood-bath, then stitching the resultant wound, I could even go as far as to say – a cruel mutilation. In my opinion, which I am just as entitled to, where the working spaniel is concerned this is a must; aesthetics do not enter into it; the working spaniel with an un-docked tail, especially if he is enthusiastic in facing cover can, and in more cases than not, does, inflict on himself the bloodiest wounds by the thrashing of the tail as he hunts through heavy cover. Furthermore, when dog-trainers begin to instruct the veterinary profession as to how to go about surgical procedures then, and only then, will I concede that they have any entitlement to interfere with the working dogs. Unfortunately, as is very often the case with such hobby horses, the most ardent supporters and, consequently the most vociferous in their protests, are those who have little insight or, indeed, interest in making themselves conversant with the full facts. As with most do-gooders, their motives are of the highest, though unfortunately, in the main, misguided.

I have always maintained that if one elects to criticise, one should be able to furnish a more efficient alternative and, so, having criticised the methods employed by the veterinary profession, allow me to provide you with what, I am sure, once you have tried it, is by far a less painful and messy business.

For this a 'docking' tool is required; these cannot be purchased and, therefore, you must make one yourself. You will require a piece of mild steel 0.3cm (⅛in.) thick by 5cm (2in.) long and 2.5cm (1in.) broad, sharpen one end with a reaper file until an edge is obtained. This is then honed on an oilstone to a razor-sharp edge. A rod 1.3cm (½in.) round bar is ideal is then slotted over the blunt end of the blade and welded into position; a wooden handle is then attached to the other end to provide a 'grip'. The whole tool when assembled should be approximately 0.3m (1ft.) long from the handle to the cutting edge (see Fig. 21).

Since first using this implement, I have never had a puppy's tail bleed nor require stitches, consequently have never lost a puppy through docking its tail; yet I once had an entire litter annihilated by a vet's docking, stitching, then, when called out again because of the excessive bleeding, resorting to dabbing the tails with permanganate of potash – all to no avail, for the last pup died twenty-four hours later. Yet with this tool I have docked a pup's tail on more than one occasion whilst it was asleep and it was still asleep when returned to the box, so not much cruelty or risk apparent there, is there?

As the tail and its main blood vessel get thicker each day, it is advisable not to delay this operation, but get it over and done with on the fourth day. Take the docking tool and lay it flat on your cooker hot-plate, with the cutting edge on the element, until it is hot enough to 'brown' a piece of newspaper when laid flat on it. As soon as this degree of heat has been reached, and it must not be overheated, dock the tail and lay the tool back on the element in preparation for the next puppy. This not only slices through the tail with ease, but cauterises the blood vessels and numbs the nerve endings at the same time; thus, little pain, if any, is experienced by the puppy and there should be no bleeding as a result. Should a spot of blood appear, simply lay the flat of the blade on the tip of the tail for a split second; this will complete the job.

For the actual operation it is better to enlist the aid of an assistant to hold each puppy, as you will require one hand to hold the pup's tail in position whilst the other hand manipulates the tool. Place the pup's tail on a block of wood about 5cm (2in.) thick. Holding the docking tool rather like a dagger, lay it in line with the site where you wish to make the cut, touching the block of wood with one corner of the blade so that by a swift, forward motion it will slice through the tail with one stroke. In a working spaniel puppy it is desirable to leave approximately two-thirds of the tail on, for nothing looks more

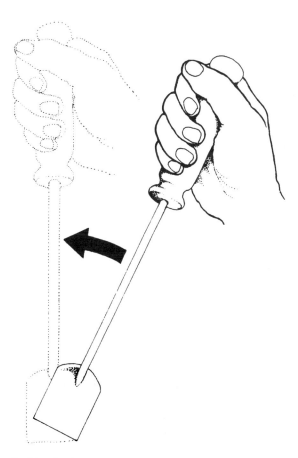

Fig. 21.   The docking tool

187

ridiculous than a spaniel with a stump for a tail. The likes of the German short-haired pointers should have approximately one-third left on. If you are slightly high on the tail, or the blade has cooled, occasionally a spot of blood will appear; however, by cauterising with the re-heated blade this is soon remedied. Heat the blade after each puppy and do not use it before testing it on the newspaper each time. You will find that this is the most humane method of docking tails that you are ever likely to encounter and certainly there is no need to feel squeamish about it. After you have done the operation for the first time, you will find it simplicity itself; however, if you are not sure of the instructions, it will help to have a 'mock' run.

When removing the pups from the nest it helps to get the bitch out of the way for a few moments while you take half the litter and, again, when you are returning them to the nest after docking. If they are in an outside kennel then it is advisable to have a cardboard box containing a hot-water bottle wrapped in a towel, with another towel to cover the top of the box to protect the puppies against a sudden change in temperature or draughts.

Dew claws

I rarely remove dew claws unless they are abnormal to the extent of being a deformity and, as yet, have never encountered, for all the dogs that I have trained, a single one that tore his dew claw off, or had a claw that grew round into his leg. I do not doubt that it can happen, only that it is not as common as some authorities make it out to be. Therefore, my advice is, if they are not abnormal, leave them alone. However, should you decide to have them removed, it is a job for the vet for, strange though it may seem, there are more puppies lost through cutting dew claws than docking tails.

Worming and claw trimming

Puppies are born with intestinal parasites from their mother's blood-stream and at or around the four-week stage of their development these worms are reaching maturity. They will now absorb the nutrients from the puppies' food, with the result that the condition of the puppies will degenerate. Worming puppies at such an early age has always been a bit of a problem, due to the debilitating effect that the majority of vermifuges have. Nowadays, this is not such a problem, due to the advent of a product known as Shaw's earliworm, which is available at any good pet store. Earliworm may be used with complete safety on the pup from as early as three weeks old, thus catching the worms before they can do too much damage, though with any other product it is better to wait until the pups are six weeks old, unless otherwise stated. Administration is simplicity itself. Place the thumb and forefinger over the pup's muzzle, gently squeezing the jaws open, while at the same time tilting his head back. Pour the prescribed dose off the spoon, letting it trickle over his gullet; as it has a chocolate flavour, the puppies take it quite readily. Results, even in puppies who have shown no outward sign of infestation, can be quite dramatic.

At this stage of their development, the puppies' claws will have grown considerably and, as they can be as sharp as needles, can cause the bitch a great deal of discomfort; therefore it is advisable to trim them with an ordinary pair of nail scissors.

Hand rearing

It is not unusual, for a variety of reasons, to be faced with the choice between hand rearing one or even more puppies or euthanasia; distasteful though the latter may be, in a great number of cases it is by far the best solution.

Hand rearing puppies is a five-week, round-the-clock pursuit; it is time-consuming in that for the first two weeks, at least, the puppies have to be fed two-hourly. Therefore it is not to be undertaken lightly, for if euthanasia is to be employed, the sooner the better.

I have known of cases where, motivated by sentiment, the breeder has attempted to hand rear a poor doer, one that the bitch had discarded – and the bitch will do this, it is nature's way. She knows instinctively that it is a waste of her resources to feed that particular puppy. In such cases no good will come of interfering; there are the isolated cases of successful hand rearing a runt, but by and large, in one way or another, it is inadvisable – nature knows best and so, in my opinion, except in the case of orphan puppies, hand rearing is just not worth it.

Should you decide to hand rear puppies, there is much that you should know. As I have indicated, you must be prepared to feed the puppy at two-hourly intervals, around the clock, for the first two weeks.

Cow's milk is useless; I have found that this causes diarrhoea and consequently dehydration and, eventually, death. Apart from this, it resembles bitch's milk not one bit, for it doesn't have the fat content and it contains far too much milk sugar, which I suspect is what causes the diarrhoea. There are proprietary brands of bitch milk substitutes in abundance on the commercial market. Any vet will advise you;

however, I am a firm devotee of Lactol. I have used it many times and, as yet, it has never let me down; it is readily available at any pet store.

Directions on how to prepare bitch's milk substitutes should be adhered to scrupulously and, just as with the preparation of your baby's food, sterility is of prime importance; furthermore, it should be fed at body temperature. Tiny puppies can be fed with an eye dropper; however, I have found that with this method it is very easy to choke the puppy by inadvertently dropping too much down the gullet at one time. I much prefer the use of a 10ml injection syringe (without needle, of course); using this, I have better control and can administer the feed drop by drop; a 20ml syringe can be used for a larger puppy and with this method an accurate assessment of the quantity received by the pup can be kept. As the puppy gets older, the feeds are enlarged correspondingly; it is not practical to outline a feeding guide for puppies as regards quantity, for it differs from puppy to puppy. But if the puppy is crying, then in all probability it is hungry and, naturally, if it is quiet and contentedly asleep, then it is not. There are puppy feeding bottles readily available for the growing pup at most good pet stores as well; these should be scrupulously cleaned and sterilised between feeds. A point to pay special attention to is to avoid allowing the pup to suck air whilst feeding.

Don't make a 'big thing' out of the delivery, especially with a sensitive dog like this one – time will tell.

Puppies lose body heat rapidly and therefore require to be kept cosy at a constant temperature of between 24°C and 26.7°C (75° and 80°F); a cardboard box lined with newspapers, covered with cellular blanket for the pups to lie on and the top and outsides of the box covered with another cellular blanket will insulate their surroundings. An infra-red lamp, of course, is invaluable.

There is a school of thought which believes that orphan puppies should be isolated from one another; I have never ascertained their reasons for believing in this – however, it would seem to be based on the 'problem' of the puppies sucking one another. I cannot see what harm there is in that; to me it would indicate that they are hungry and that a little extra food would alleviate it. Furthermore, whilst it is a moot point as to whether puppies are consciously aware of their brothers and sisters before their eyes open on the tenth or eleventh day, I feel pretty certain that a puppy brought up in isolation must lose out psychologically, so I would not advocate the isolationist approach; again, nature knows best.

After every feed, stimulate the puppies' bowel and bladder movements by massaging the lower abdomen and rectum area with a damp cotton wool swab; if you neglect this, death is certain, due to colic. This stimulation must be done firmly but gently, as would the bitch's tongue, and you must continue each time until an evacuation has been effected.

CHAPTER NINE

PICKING UP AND BEATING

It is an unarguable fact that there is nothing quite like a day picking up at a formal shoot for giving a young dog experience in the field. When training a retriever it is particularly advantageous in that the dog will procure a tremendous amount of experience in a very short time. Indeed, I would go as far as to say that in one outing day at the local estate's 'big day', a novice dog and, indeed, his handler also, is likely to see more birds falling than he normally would in a whole season out walking up game on the rough shoot. Nevertheless, as in all things, there are the inevitable drawbacks, for the young dog will also witness other dogs at – for want of a better word – work which, unfortunately, in the majority of cases, may not be of benefit to his education.

Neither is it easy to procure a day picking up if you are not known; for, surprising though it may seem to the novice trainer, the local gamekeeper is not falling over backwards to enlist your aid and it is advisable that you do not approach him and give him the impression that you may be doing him a favour. There is an abundance of dogs in every area throughout the country who, mostly through lack of training – a few because of doubtful genetical inheritance – are nothing short of the 'wildest of the wild', possessing every fault imaginable, such as running in to fall, shot and moving game, hard-mouth, giving tongue, whose owners are also looking for a day picking up or beating. Consequently, the keeper is not short of offers of help; what he is short of is good dogs and handlers. Nevertheless, most owners will tell him that their particular dog is a paragon of virtue. As a result, he has learned through experience not to accept you at face value; therefore, understandably, if he does not know you personally, he will be reluctant to give you a chance unless you can get some mutual acquaintance to vouch for you and your dog. Remember this, whilst you are indulging in your hobby he, on the other hand, is pursuing his daily business, which is to present the maximum birds over the guns, then see to it that, once they have been shot and gathered, they are delivered to the game cart in a saleable condition.

Should you be lucky enough to acquire a day for your dog, you will be on trial; therefore, do as you are told as quietly as possible, go

Make sure that there are no other dogs 'down' on a bird before sending a young dog.

where you are told as quickly as possible and, once there, remain as motionless as possible. Noise and unnecessary movement will most definitely not encourage the keeper to invite you back another day.

If a gun is having an 'off' day and is shooting badly, that is none of your affair – you are not there to voice your opinion. Neither will it be appreciated if by word or deed you distract him. Should he have a bird or birds 'down' after a drive that due to some circumstances or other you yourself were unable to 'mark', ask the 'gun' for directions as to where he thought it came down; this can save you and your dog a great deal of unnecessary leg-work and can make all the difference between 'picking' the bird or not. It is only good manners to let the 'gun' know when you have successfully collected his bird.

It is essential for the performance of your duties as 'picker-up' that you station yourself as advantageously as possible behind your 'gun'. You are of little use standing beside him, as is often the case, nor is it of any advantage either to him or you to stand within a few yards of him. Get well back, approximately forty yards is ideal. Station your-self, if possible, on some rising ground so that you may get a good all-round view of the terrain and thus mark the game falling.

The collection of dead birds can be left to the end of the drive, whereas a bird down and running has to be collected straight away. And it is truly amazing that by being in an advantageously positioned spot, your dog can not only mark game down well, but many dogs have better memories than their handlers and can memorise a number of birds and their positions, to go straight to the spot at the end of the drive, some time after.

On taking up your position, always let your 'gun' know you are there. Await the commencement of proceedings quietly. Do not move from your stand at any time, especially whilst the drive is nearing its conclusion and the birds are breaking from the covert. It will be frowned upon if, by moving, you alarm the game and turn it back away from the gun. Remember, whilst wildlife does not appear to react to a motionless figure, perhaps regarding it as part of the surrounding terrain, a movement catches their eye much more readily, as any pigeon shot or wildfowler will testify.

It is a good idea, as these birds thump into the ground all around you, to note your pup's reaction to them; he will soon become quite attentive and in every probability 'hot-up', *i.e.*, become quite keen; a quiet but reassuring 'no – leave it' is usually sufficient to calm him somewhat. Whilst this is going on, it is invaluable to a young dog, for not only is he learning or furthering his experience in 'marking', he is also learning that, just because the other dogs are allowed to go running in to all that falls, he is not – and do play safe – no matter how steady you may think he is to the fall, keep his lead on; remember, prevention is always better than cure.

If it is a retriever that you are training, you will note very often that he seems to take to this like the proverbial duck to water; and so he should, for this is his forte – this is what he has been bred for, for countless generations. On the other hand, if you are giving a young hunter, such as a cocker or springer, 'picking-up' experience, and they *do* require it every bit as much as their retriever brethren, you may note that he gets rather fidgety, perhaps begins to set up an excitable squeaking; now this is the thin edge of the wedge – you must 'nip this in the bud'. Straight away, the moment that you first notice it, give him a sharp crack with the flat of your hand or the lead across the rump and sharply command him to 'be quiet'. It is important that you are not too lenient in this, for tomorrow, in all probability, will be too late, for by then it is quite likely that it will be beyond cure.

The bird to which to pay careful attention, if you think the gun has connected, is the high flying cock. Watch it until it is out of sight; if after quite a long flight it suddenly rockets skywards, then falls, mark it – for it is a dead bird. If, on the other hand, a bird should slowly lose height and plane down, probably landing at the perimeter of the field, it is quite likely to be a very strong runner. If it is one of the vanguard of birds to break from the covert, then you are in a difficult position – between the devil and the deep blue sea, so to speak. For, if you move, you may turn back the birds that may be breaking from

194

cover at that moment. At the same time, should you not pursue it post haste, it may very speedily become an unpickable bird. This is one of those situations where you must use your initiative and await the opportune moment to make your way after him. Obviously, if there isn't much noise coming from the beaters, then it is a safe bet to get after it, keeping a weather-eye open for any birds breaking from the covert; should a bird emerge, then it is simply a matter of freezing in your tracks until the gun has his or her shot, then carry on as before in your pursuit of the runner. Try to choose a gun who is dogless, for there isn't much point in standing behind a gun who possesses a business-like looking retriever if there are guns who are dogless. Never, ever, lose sight of the fact that today more and more formal days are let out to syndicate guns, therefore most guns are there in the capacity of 'paying guests' and, as such, will regard giving their dog the retrieves as part of their day out. Such guns would rather you asked first if they required your services.

At the end of each drive, make yourself available to the keeper, after having deposited the birds that you have collected in the 'game-cart'. He may still have birds down that he will require you to pick. The end of the drive is not an excuse for coffee-housing, and it will be noted as to whether you appear eager to help or are just there for a spot of dog-training.

Beating for the rough-shooter's dog

Before seeking a day at beating, you are well advised to give your dog's training standards serious thought, for, though very tempting to get into battle conditions in earnest for the first time with your dog, there is little doubt that at the 'big day' on the local shoot, your pup will be subjected not only to a great deal of temptation but, for the first time in his life, he will see dogs committing the most heinous of crimes, all of which – to his juvenile point of view – may look as though they are having all the fun. Whilst the shooting etiquette may be exemplary, the standards regarding dog work at such affairs, unfortunately, are probably about the lowest you will ever encounter, and so premature introduction to the beating scene can, in one half-hour, undo the greater part of a summer's training.

Just as surely, though, the benefits far outweigh the disadvantages; for not only will a day beating illustrate to the young dog just what it is all about and 'oil the wheels', so to speak, in the dog inclined to be rather sticky, it can really work wonders for the dog with crowd-shy tendencies. And, above all, should you really be attentive to the steadiness aspect of his work, simply due to the proliferation of game that he will meet in a comparatively short period, you can really 'put the icing on the cake' regarding his steadiness to the flush.

The first thing that will probably strike you on entering a beater's line is that the beaters themselves appear to pay little or no heed to their dogs. You will be surprised, no doubt, to note that their dogs may chase game all over the place, yet they will not so much as give the dog a 'toot' on the whistle; in other words, dog-handling is almost non-existent. This is for a very good reason, and it is this: the majority of dogs have had no more than lip service paid to any form of training, therefore the 'handler' gives no commands for the simple reason that he knows that the dog will not obey them anyway. These are the lads who will tell you that your dog is working too tight and that you should 'let him go a bit more' – woe betide you if you do, for in less time than it takes to tell your pup, he will illustrate that he has a terrific capacity for learning that to be naughty is great fun and, what is more, what he learns he will never, ever forget. On attending a formal day with a young retriever there are occasions when, due to a shortage of beaters, you may be asked to join the line. By all means do so but, take my tip, *you* do the beating, not the dog; keep him on the lead – remember, he is a retriever, not a hunter. Should you succumb to temptation and hunt him, you may regret it for the rest of your life. After all, no-one can fault you if you keep him on the lead; you are fulfilling your function in doing your share of the beating, for your dog was brought along to do the picking-up – no more.

Whilst beating with a hunting dog it is important that you keep in touch with your neighbour on either side of you, for the line will progress forward at a varying pace, as and how the keeper will regulate it; this is to ensure not only that the maximum birds are flushed over the 'guns', but that they flush so as not to fly back over the beaters, away from the guns. Try to keep in touch with your dog – and this is not as easy as it sounds, either, for in thick undergrowth and cover, where the density may prohibit your forward progress in an upright position, you may be compelled to move forward on all fours; not the ideal position from which to handle and control an exuberant spaniel.

A young dog can see game running forward, whereas you may not, and is liable to pull out ahead; the noise and bustle around him, the cries of the beaters and multitudinous whistle signals are all very confusing to the novice dog and contribute to his excitement, all of which may cause him to be, at the very least, more difficult to control than usual.

As the drive nears completion, birds with ever-increasing frequency will break cover to be greeted by a fusillade of shots, and it is very difficult to be forever dropping your pup to the whistle as the shots ring out; for it seems so unnecessary, even silly – but drop him, you must, if he is to remain steady to shot in the future.

Very often, as you emerge from the cover after a drive, you may be hailed by one of the guns to be told he has a bird down 'over there', accompanied by a wave of the hand in the general direction of a distant horizon. First of all, it is wise to enquire if there is another dog down after it for, for some strange reason, guns seem to be under the general impression that the more dogs sent after a bird, the better. Such is not the case; in fact, plural dogs down after one bird are a positive nuisance, especially if it is a wounded bird, for by fouling each others' footscents, they will mask the scent of the bird and thus aid his eluding collection. Furthermore, ask yourself what will happen if, in this general 'finder's keepers' situation, your pup, in his inexperience, should be lucky – or unlucky – enough, depending on your point of view, to find the bird first and have it snatched from his hitherto tender mouth on his way back? So it is wise to ascertain whether or not the gun has knowledge of another dog having been sent for it. And it is also worth making enquiries as you go along as to whether or not a bird has been picked in the vicinity, for it is not unusual to waste time searching for a bird that has been picked a few minutes before.

Should you acquit yourself well and the keeper is pleased with your work, you will be asked back; furthermore, there is no advertising to compare with 'word of mouth' and, should you possess a good dog, be eager to please and show willing, then the word will travel and it will not be long before you will be getting invitations to 'pick-up' and 'beat' from a number of estates in your neighbourhood.

Scent and its influence

As I have mentioned earlier, as a rough rule of thumb guide generally speaking, any extremes of weather conditions will result in poor scenting conditions.

It is also true to say that we humans can never fully appreciate or understand scent. Dogs react to the sensitivity of their individual scenting aptitudes; therefore a dog with, as we term it, a good nose will react much more markedly than a dog whose scenting aptitudes are duller.

Other than the huntsman, dog trainer and police dog handler, generally the aspect of scent does not interest most people, and the man in the street would know little or nothing at all about it, other than to make some intelligent sounds about something known as 'fear-scent'. Something that, somewhere, he has probably heard mentioned in some discussion or other – but it does not really interest him, for it is

197

many thousands of years since man had to depend on scent to aid his survival. It is a sense that has fallen into misuse. Where the question of 'fear-scent' is concerned, I doubt if it exists other than in our imaginings; another instance of our crediting the animal world with attributes that suit our purposes of explanation.

The behaviour of game in the stress situation is motivated by their instinct for self preservation and has a direct bearing upon the amount of scent given off. An understanding of wild-life behaviour quickly illustrates that, basically, it survives through relying on its camouflage and ability to remain immobile for long periods of time, until the immediate surroundings are completely devoid of its scent. It is usually only when last-minute flight is induced by the closest proximity of impending danger that they will betray their presence by bursting from their concealment.

To assist the animal or bird to flee, there is an upsurge of glandular activity; there is a sudden injection of adrenaline into the system. I suspect that this has a direct bearing on the secretions, thus there is a marked out-put of scent which, together with the disturbance of air currents by the animal's or bird's sudden activity, pervades the surrounding atmosphere, to hang or be dispersed depending on the prevailing conditions.

The degree to which scent is retained on the ground may vary from place to place; furthermore, retention is directly influenced by the stage of growth or decay of the surrounding vegetation and prevalent humidity. Any pollenating plant in full bloom, especially on a hot day, will mask and decrease the dog's ability to scent game; at such times an experienced dog will come into his own, for his tenacity of purpose will carry him through, whereas the younger, inexperienced dog, will quickly become discouraged.

Potency of scent may vary from day to day, even to the extent that whilst it may be very poor in the morning, depending on the weather, it may be very good within a matter of an hour or so. Wet, boggy ground tends to have poor scenting properties because of the fumes set up by the dog's passage over it from the marsh gases, and yet wet ground that is not of a boggy nature may hold scent very well, especially on a mild day. Dry, arid conditions are virtually scentless and the scent of ground game is swiftly evaporated even within minutes of the quarry passing over it. A point well worth remembering, should you 'leg' ground game and attempt to send a pup for his first runner, is that if he is slow at picking up the commencement of the line, by the time he has progressed only a few yards the scent will have dissipated to the extent of the 'line' no longer existing at all. Therefore, if a successful collection is to be brought about, for the sake of the novice dog's experience it is wise to give him assistance by following him up, giving encouragement; however, it is always much better to bear the scenting conditions in mind whilst shooting over a 'first-season' dog and, in such conditions, forego the opportunity of giving him experience on taking a line by putting another shot into the game.

A bird tumbling out of the sky, head over heels by the passage of air currents through its feathers, will leave much more scent than a bird killed stone dead in the sky; for the latter will tend to fall with wings closed. On a mild day with little wind to dissipate the scent, the former will leave a pillar of scent gently wafting away for some time after; whereas, on a windy day, by the time the dog has reached the fall there will be little or no scent to give him guidance.

There is undoubtedly a 'body' scent to some degree; however, it is my opinion that the most pungent scent emanates from the anal glands and, in the furbearing animals, those glands on the pads of their feet. As I have said, the glandular activity is exacerbated by increased activity; generally speaking, therefore, the more movement, the more secretions – and consequently the more scent will be given off. And so it is that, as the rabbit hops around cropping the grass, he will leave more scent and, as a result, be easier for the dog to detect than his brother who tucked in tightly to his seat and remained there for some considerable time; it is this rabbit that the hard-hunting dog is liable to run right over, especially in a downhill or downwind cast. Likewise, the pheasant, on approaching her nest, will take a straight line to it, thus minimising the scent she leaves behind, to settle down on her eggs, facing into the wind so that her feathers are not ruffled by it so that, in a very short time indeed, there is little or no scent given off in her proximity. In fact, I believe that there are many more nests found by Charlie Fox that would go otherwise undetected but for the curious human who walks straight up to it to inspect the size of her clutch.

It is most important to be wind and scent conscious for, later on, in the shooting field, it is very easy in the excitement of the moment to forget all about the wind aspect and its effect on scent. As I have already outlined, wind carries scent before it rather like smoke from a chimney; therefore, in a stiffish breeze, the scent can be wafted down the wind in a very short time. On shooting a bird there is a tendency in the majority of handlers to send their dog immediately, with little thought as to the 'lie' or 'fall' in relation to the prevalent wind direction. This usually results in the classic case of the more haste, the less speed. There are many situations where, because of the terrain and/or obstacles in conjunction with the wind, a dog cannot, or is likely not to, get out into an area 'downwind' of the 'retrieve'. To illustrate the point, allow me to give you a hypothetical instance. You have just dropped a bird or a rabbit and it is lying on the gravel below a bank beside a stream. Upon telling a dog to get out, in the majority

Fig. 22. Scent.
Rabbit gets up at A, is shot at B and falls over bank of stream at C. The dog is sent downwind to D, dropped, then redirected to E and dropped again. He is then handled into the wind, back across the stream.

of cases he will run straight out along the bank of the stream. If the wind is blowing the scent across the stream, then there is little chance of the dog 'winding' it and, should it be a runner, even less chance of its successful collection. To shout and indulge in wild hand signals will only exacerbate an already deteriorating situation by increasing the dog's anxieties. Bearing in mind that the dog depends much more on his nose than his eyes, in this particular instance it would have been better if the handler had sent the dog over the stream, dropped him to command his attention then, with a clear hand signal, sent him up the far bank, dropping him once more opposite the 'fall', giving the dog sufficient pause. Usually he will pick up the scent coming to him from the other side of the stream; however, upon directing him back across the stream, whether he has scented it or not, you will be virtually dropping him on top of it. Should it be a runner the chances are he will pick up the 'line' by this method much more sharply, and so aid his speedy collection of it. Needless to say, once a dog has his nose down and is obviously working out a 'line', to start shouting at him will only distract him. In this situation it is much better to trust your dog and leave him to it (see Fig. 22). As the wind will waft the scent in the air currents, you will realise that when sending your dog out to the 'fall' of a runner, he may take the 'line' a few feet 'downwind' of the actual 'footscent' (see Fig. 23).

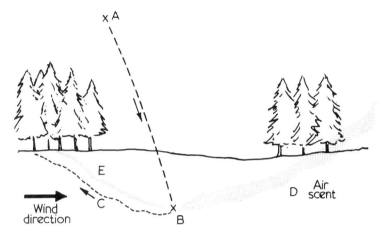

Fig. 23.   Scent.
Bird is shot at A, drops to B, takes route C. In a stiff breeze, scent may be quickly
wafted away (D) and the dog may be seen to take a 'line' a few feet down wind of
the route taken by the bird E.

Similarly, again directly indicative that the dog tends to trust his
nose rather than his eyes, it is quite common to see the dog, on being
sent for a retrieve lying out on open, windswept terrain, overshoot
the 'retrieve' for some yards, then pull up and turn into the wind as
he catches the windborne scent.

Heavy, fresh falls of snow, or severe frost early in the morning
before the sun melts it, are virtually scentless. Torrential rain will
dilute the scent droplets to render them almost undetectable. Gale
force winds will drive the scent away so rapidly, at the same time
drying the atmosphere, to render the surroundings scentless also. In
frosty conditions, scent can vary markedly in only a few yards; that
strip along the bottom of a wall that the sun has not touched will
remain for the better part of the day scentless, or, at best, very poor
scent-holding ground, whilst only a few feet away, where the sun has
shone and melted the frost, scent could be fair to good. Undulating
country on a windy day can produce quite dramatic changes between
the lee and the windward sides of the slopes. So you will see that there
is no hard and fast rule appertaining to scent and a great deal of
scope for debate.

Shooting over your dog

No matter for what purpose you have trained your dog, there are a
few 'make or break' little tips that you should be aware of.

201

Firstly, to take a young, inexperienced dog onto the shoot for the first time, knowing that there are unruly dogs and/or fellow handlers who are wont to beat their dogs in full view of yours, is just begging to undo all your good work in training him. An irate handler lashing out at his dog, observed by a young dog, can have an extremely dramatic, detrimental effect upon him, especially if he is of a sensitive disposition. Should such an incident occur, cover your pup's eyes for, if he sees it, he will take it personally; much better, though, if you know that such is liable to crop up – play safe, don't take the risk, avoid this particular chap's company until such time as your dog has got a fair mileage on his working clock.

For the first few outings, I advocate that you leave your gun at home, letting a friend do the shooting for you. In this way you will not be distracted to the same extent and will be able to devote your full attention to your dog. In training the no-slip retriever you are fortunate if you have a friend with a good hunting, *steady* dog, for he can hunt his dog and shoot, thus providing your young dog experience in dropping to shot, marking, getting out and retrieving. If you 'ring the changes' by alternatively using each dog to retrieve whilst the other watches the proceedings, this adds a further polish on the dog's experience in that it illustrates to him that everything down is not necessarily his to retrieve. Again, when after having discharged the gun you pause, eject your cartridges, then hold the dog by hand signal, on the drop before sending him, this will prevent him from developing the habit of running in to shot. Should your friend's dog run in to shot, fall or flush, keep your dog on the drop, repeating in a soft voice 'no! – gone away – hup'. This will go a long way to prevent him from succumbing to an extremely tempting situation.

This is even more important whilst integrating a young dog of the hunter variety into his particular sphere of shooting, for the temptations as opposed to the retrievers are much enhanced, simply due to his being out in front of you. Many is the young dog which, after reaching a high standard of training, has fallen by the wayside in his first season, simply because his handler didn't pay enough attention to him at a crucial moment. Remember, you can always get another bird – a dog is another matter.

Game sense

This is the final stage in a dog's development. It is an awareness of what his role is in the shooting field. We have seen that, when he is still a puppy, on taking him out he would charge around with unbridled enthusiasm; for there were no restrictions placed upon his behavioural boundaries. Then, as we progressively made more demands upon him during the next few months in his training, he slowed down as the training began to bite, undermining his confidence, albeit temporarily, then to speed up again as he became familiar with each new exercise. This, of course, varies from dog to dog in degree, to the extent that in some of the more extrovert it is barely noticeable.

It is worth remembering that each time the dog is faced with a new situation, momentarily there is a period of uncertainty and contingent loss of confidence; for the learning chain does not come to an end when the training is finished. He will learn, and continue to do so, throughout his active life, as we do.

On first entering the shooting field, depending on his temperament, the degree to which his training has been undergone, he will again for some time be uncertain; on the other hand, should you have rushed the training and taken him shooting too soon, then the whole learning chain will progressively break down.

Assuming, however, that you have bedded in his training properly, you can expect him to build upon it with the correct attention being paid to his performance over the first season, of course.

It is directly in relation to (a) the amount of training he has undergone, (b) his temperament, (c) your attention to him and, (d) the situations that may or may not arise in his initial introduction into the shooting field, that will determine what ultimate standard of performance you will obtain from him. As his experience grows in the shooting situation, so will his confidence and expertise.

He will begin to anticipate and act accordingly whenever he encounters 'hot' scent, for he will remember what has left that scent from times before. This is why an experienced dog will 'flog on' all day on a scentless, hot August day at the grouse, whereas a young dog will quickly give up; for the latter requires the added incentive of scent, whereas the former does not – he has his memories of days gone by to spur him on. It is also for this reason that, *providing* your young dog has *never chased game*, and you have attained a high degree of obedience to the stop whistle, you should have no difficulty in stopping him when he flushes his *first* rabbit, yet may have more difficulty on his fourth or fifth. In finding his first rabbit, he is surprised and, in his momentary dismay, you are afforded the opportunity to *steal the initiative* by interrupting his thoughts with the stop whistle in those few vital moments of his indecision. By the time he has complied with the command and collected his thoughts, the rabbit is gone and the temptation with it. He will remember, though, and as time goes on and he meets a variety of game, he will store the different scents in his memory and learn to differentiate between them.

He will learn also the killing power of the gun; from then on to work *to* the gun, providing all has gone according to plan until then. When you have attained this degree of performance you will experience the thrill of shooting over a good dog. A good shot and a good dog make a first-class 'bag-filling' team; a good shot and a wild, unruly dog do not.

The moment that a young dog realises the killing power of the gun can be termed his 'dawn of realisation' for, from that moment on, he will never be slow or sticky again. The effect upon a hitherto slow or sticky dog is quite dramatic; almost immediately he realises what it is all about. Many years ago, whilst trying to get a spaniel 'going', having trained it – with hindsight, probably over-trained it would be nearer the truth – I decided to take him rabbit shooting in the hope that perhaps this would encourage him to get up a 'head of steam'. The upshot was that after quite a few outings and having shot rabbits into double figures over him, he still had no inclination to get going. I was at my wits' end and was contemplating giving him away. However, driving home after another abortive attempt at speeding him up, it came to me in a flash – my 'dawn of realisation', if you like.

I had been hunting in tall, green bracken on July evenings; he had flushed many rabbits, had them shot for him, subsequently to retrieve them for me, yet had not speeded up to any great degree. Yet this dog, *before I* commenced his training, whilst still a pup, had shown me that he could 'go like the proverbial bomb' – so something, somewhere, was wrong. My flash of inspiration was this: he was hunting in tall bracken; whenever he found a rabbit, what would he see? A fleeting glimpse of brown fur to which he dropped as I blasted the stop whistle and/or fired a shot. Then a short wait, to go and retrieve when told to. He would find a dead rabbit; as far as he was concerned, nothing remarkable in that for, many times in the past, whilst hunting, he had heard the shot and had learned to expect a rabbit to pick up somewhere – albeit a cold rabbit, whereas this one was warm and had a more interesting smell about it. The 'missing link' in his learning chain was – *he had never seen a rabbit toppled*, therefore he had never connected the flush, bolting rabbit, the shot and the retrieve. He did not realise what he was out there for. The very next evening I purposely sought out the few smaller clumps of bracken so that when he pushed a rabbit he would have the opportunity of seeing it break out into the open and, more importantly, *see it toppled*. Within fifteen minutes a rabbit obliged and no sooner had he retrieved it than he showed me in no uncertain terms that he had not lost the speed that he had had whilst he was a puppy. So, thinking like a dog, trying to see through his eyes, pays off.

Dogs can, and invariably do, develop their game sense to a very high degree; whether or not you channel it to your own ends depends on the amount of application you give to his first season's experience.

An indication of a dog's game sense can be seen if you pick up a gun in the house; we've all known the old campaigner who will jump up from the fireside and bound expectantly to the door.

In the shooting field you will see a dog who has been hunting, on hearing the shot and not marking, look at the man with the *smoking gun*, probably hoping to get some idea as to where the game has fallen.

If you are observant whilst hunting an experienced dog, as time goes on you will realise that in thick, somewhat impenetrable cover, he no longer uses his nose as he did when younger, to the exclusion of his other senses, but is now pausing with head on one side every now and then; he has learned to use his ears and eyes as well. I have seen dogs who, whilst coming upon two tightly tucked in rabbits would flush one and drop; then on seeing that the rabbit had toppled, without getting up – flush the other; that is gun and game sense, the result of many hours out shooting being accorded the correct experience by his trainer.

There have been occasions whilst training a retriever, on his first excursion to a flight pond, after waiting some time he has curled up

A young 'springer' fetches a rabbit.

at my feet and gone to sleep, yet after only a few outings to the pond, I could watch him in the gathering dusk and he would indicate by turning his head the direction that the duck would appear from. Again, how many times have we taken a shot and thought that we had missed; yet the dog, by a display of impatience has shown us that we did not; furthermore, on being sent, has proven his point by fetching back his duck.

A good dog is a gem beyond price – to attain that standard is surely worth a little effort and patience. You may even find such satisfaction and enjoyment in the training of him, that dog training may supersede your love of shooting – as I found many years ago. If, by writing this book, I have helped you along the road to understanding your dog's learning chain and thereby training him to a far higher standard than hitherto, then my weary hours walking behind a multitude of dogs and the midnight oil expended in the writing of it will have been well spent. – Happy dogging.

INDEX